MEMPHIS IN FLATBOAT DAYS

THE BIOGRAPHY OF A RIVER TOWN

Memphis: *Its Heroic Age*

By

GERALD M. CAPERS, Jr.

Published by Gerald M. Capers, Jr.
Tulane University
1966

This edition reprinted in 2003
by
Lightning Source

for

Burke's Book Store
1719 Poplar Avenue
Memphis TN 38104
901-278-7484

Second edition, with an epilogue,
"Satrapy of a Benevolent Despot"
from Robert S. Allen's "Our Fair City."

ISBN 0-937130-00-1

To

THE LUCKY ABDULLAHS

They say the Lion and the Lizard keep
The Courts where Jamshyd gloried and drank deep:
   And Bahrám, that great Hunter—the Wild Ass
Stamps o'er his Head, but cannot break his Sleep.

—Omar Khayyám

PREFACE TO THE SECOND EDITION

In response to public demand, I have decided to reprint my book on Memphis, first published by the University of North Carolina Press in 1939. For years it has been out of print, copies are hard to find, and the price is excessive. Moreover, in the last twenty-five years a lot of Yankees who occasionally read local history have moved to Memphis.

In order to bring the study down to the present, I have included as an epilogue my chapter on Boss Crump from Robert S. Allen's, *Our Fair City.* Those desiring more recent information can find it in my article on Memphis in the latest edition of the *Encyclopedia Britannica.*

A note on recent bibliography is pertinent. Professor William D. Miller has done a study on Memphis in the Progressive Era and a biography of Mr. Crump. Professor John H. Davis has recorded the history of St. Mary's Cathedral and Rabbi James A. Wax that of the Jews in Memphis. In the 1940's Shields McIlwaine wrote a superficial book which he called *Memphis Down in Dixie.* Professor Joseph Parks has an excellent article on contraband trade in the city during the Civil War, *Journal of Southern History,* VII (1941), 289-314.

All of the Lucky Abdullahs to whom I dedicated the first edition are still alive, and more or less kicking. Again, I salute them.

FOREWORD

THE cardinal sin of American historians is their neglect of local history. Turner in his later years placed as much emphasis upon the section as upon the frontier; and it is hardly necessary to observe that in a country as large as ours distinct sections, different in their economic and social characteristics, have inevitably arisen. These sections may, in a sense, be considered sub-nations, possessing peculiar physical features and economic interests as well as a definite consciousness of themselves as a distinct social and political entity.

Now that social and economic history has been accorded a recognition equal to that of purely political history, a new approach becomes increasingly necessary. The history of the United States has been written from the top down; now it must be written from the bottom up. Some rough geographical division must be agreed upon, as, perhaps, the upper seaboard, the lower seaboard, the upper valley, the lower valley, the great plains, and the Pacific coast. Each of these must be studied as a complete entity, with due regard for its diverse elements and its relations to other sections. When that task is completed the results must finally be synthesized into a New American History.

The South and the North, vague as such terms are, have long been regarded as distinct sections; but the emphasis upon the Civil War as a focal point in our national story has obscured the existence of an even more significant sectional division, that caused by the Appalachians, which separate the older seaboard from the "Valley of Democracy."

The West had flirted with Spain and had moved along the road to secession before Whitney invented his gin; and the lower as well as the upper valley joined with determination in the Populist revolt a century later. Since both the Appalachians and the Mason and Dixon Line have been sectional demarcations, we must recognize that fact by some such nomenclature as the upper and the lower seaboard, the upper and the lower valley.

The history of cities has been largely ignored as an approach to the study of sections; yet cities, because of their frequently interstate character, are often more representative of fundamental economic interests than artificial political divisions like the state. No metropolis, not even New Orleans, typifies more clearly the character of the lower West than does Memphis. Bound to the upper valley by the Mississippi and by trade, and allied with the lower seaboard because of cotton and the Negro, this city on the middle Mississippi has always been both South and West. Born in 1819 of the westward movement and of cotton, it displays traits of both its progenitors; and when it ultimately favored secession in 1861, its decision was dictated more by emotion than by reason. Socially and economically it has resembled Chicago far more closely than it has resembled any southern town. Figuratively and literally, the South met the West in Memphis.

This study was begun in the graduate school of Yale University under the direction of Professor Ralph H. Gabriel and was submitted to that University in 1936 in partial fulfillment of the requirements for the degree of doctor of philosophy. When it was begun I had no premises on local history and felt somewhat apologetic for selecting so base a subject. After a year's study, however, I became convinced that an adequate biography of any of our key cities—New York, Chicago, New Orleans, San Francisco, Kansas City, and a dozen more—would be more significant to the national epic than the biography of even so prominent a figure as Theodore Roosevelt. A large proportion of our citizens live in cities; yet how much do we actually know about the natural history or the institutional development of that political and social amoeba, the American City? This all-important task, though it interests the sociologist, the economist, the genealogist, and the literatus, is primarily and fundamentally the job of the historian—a job that he has so far neglected.

On the assumption that a scholarly work need not necessarily be a dull one, I have tried to portray the evolution of this river town for both the layman and the professional historian. While I have constantly sought to achieve objectivity, I am quite aware that no work is ever free from personal bias. At least I have been unhampered by any obligation to a chamber of commerce, nor have I been subsidized by any vested interest; and in all that I have written I have been unmoved by the possible clamor arising from the hypersensitivity of local patriots.

This book pretends to be no more than a comprehensive outline of the history of Memphis before 1900, and I shall coöperate to the fullest with anyone who seeks to give more intensive treatment to a certain period or a certain phase of the subject. Memphis possesses a colorful past; many times I was tempted to tarry and expand on points of human interest, but usually I turned my back upon Satan and kept to the more essential economic story. One axiom I have placed uppermost: local history, without perspective and without some correlation between the local and the national scene, may be good antiquarianism—but historically it is almost worthless.

No man lives to himself and no man writes to himself. I am particularly indebted to the late Ulrich B. Phillips, who introduced me to southern history; to Professor Ralph H. Gabriel of Yale, who directed my dissertation; to Professor Leonard Labaree of Yale, who made valuable suggestions as to stylistic revision; to Professor David Potter of the University of Mississippi, upon whom I have called for assistance and advice more than on anyone else; to my brother Claude, who drew the maps and had to listen to me daily during the eight months in which the first draft was composed; to Director Jesse Cunningham, Mr. Albert Johnson, and Miss Mary Davant of the Cossitt Library in Memphis, whose kindness and assistance were unfailing; and to Mr. Albert Rickey of the Yale Law School for generous help in the reading of proofs.

Since I have no wife, both author and reader are spared the hackneyed observation that all this would have been impossible without the help of the little woman. As it seems obligatory, however, to acknowledge either feminine or divine inspiration, I hasten to admit that in critical moments when I had to fall back on foreign aid I turned, not to Venus, but to Bacchus and Diana.

Gerald M. Capers, Jr.

Saybrook College
Yale University
May, 1938

CONTENTS

TABLES

ILLUSTRATIONS

MAPS AND CHARTS

THE BIOGRAPHY OF A RIVER TOWN

CHAPTER I

CHICKASAW BLUFFS

IN 1776 THIRTEEN of the English colonies on the continent of North America declared their independence; in 1783 that independence was tentatively accepted by the European world; but until 1815 the existence of the United States was precarious and its destiny in the New World uncertain. To that destiny the possession of the Mississippi Valley was indispensable; yet in regard to the security of the valley the Washington and Adams administrations were strangely lukewarm. Indeed, attention to this vital problem came only when an incipient movement for secession in the West, dictated by the complete dependence of the frontiersmen upon the Mississippi as an outlet for trade, forced the federal government to make an attempt through diplomatic channels to secure the river for them. "There is on the globe," wrote Thomas Jefferson in 1802, "one single spot the possessor of which is our natural and habitual enemy. It is New Orleans, through which the produce of three-eighths of our country must pass to market. . . . The day that France takes possession of New Orleans . . . we must marry ourselves to the British fleet and nation. We must turn all our attentions to a maritime force."[1]

The struggle for the valley was old in 1802. Spain in the sixteenth and seventeenth centuries had claimed sovereignty over this vast area by virtue of various explorations, but she had failed to establish a single permanent settlement in the valley to support her claim. In 1682 La Salle, arriving at the Gulf of Mexico by canoe from Canada, had taken possession of the same territory in the name of Louis XIV, and in the following century attempts were made, both from the St. Lawrence and the Gulf, to establish garrisons in the intervening area along the Mississippi and its tributaries. England's strenuous opposition to this French conquest had culminated in the Seven Years' War, and at its close in 1763 France had been expelled from the continent, England retaining the land east of the Mississippi and Spain that west of it. During the revolutionary era Spain had entered the war against England as an ally of France, and at the division of the spoils in 1783 had received Florida in reward. Claiming the entire Southwest as far north as the Tennessee River, and actually maintaining forts in the region north of Florida, Spain remained a serious menace to the United States until she evacuated the area north of the thirty-first degree of latitude in accordance with the provisions of Pinckney's Treaty of 1796, and ceded Louisiana to France at San Ildefonso four years later. This was the very territory which Napoleon sold to the United States in 1803 for fifteen million dollars.

The security the United States seemingly achieved by this purchase was superficial, nor did it cease to be so until the close of the Napoleonic wars. A victorious Bonaparte in 1814, had he desired a western empire, would hardly have hesitated to take back from the puny nation what he had sold to it in a moment of duress eleven years before. The grudging assent which Spain gave to Pinckney's Treaty and the leisurely manner in which she carried out its terms indicate that she did not accept that settlement as final. And it was only at Ghent in 1815 that England, faced with a seething Europe and a disturbing domestic situation, definitely gave up ideas of an Indian buffer state in the Northwest. In retrospect it is apparent that the outcome of this drama of the Mississippi was, in the final analysis, determined rather on the battlefields and in the council chambers of the Old World than in the forests of the New. Not until the European nations were at stalemate was the backwoodsman across the Appalachians free to oust the Philistine and take possession of the Land of Canaan on which his fathers for two generations had gazed with covetous eyes.

In this drama the Chickasaw Bluffs, in the southwestern corner of the present state of Tennessee, were the scene of several minor episodes. These bluffs, four in number and located at short intervals within sixty miles along the Mississippi, abut the east bank at a point approximately two-thirds of the distance from the Gulf to the mouth of the Missouri. They were the key not only to the possession of the middle Mississippi but also to the trade with the Chickasaw Indians, who occupied what is today roughly western Tennessee and Kentucky and northern Mississippi.

The strategic location of the Chickasaw Bluffs is readily explained by the topography of the lower valley. The Mississippi proper results from the confluence of the Missouri, the upper Mississippi, and the Ohio rivers, which with their tributaries drain the whole central area of the United States between the Rockies and the Appalachians. Fortunately, each of these rivers, as a rule, releases its spring overflow at a different time, but whenever weather conditions are such that any two of them pour their swollen torrents into the larger river simultaneously, the inevitable spring overflow on the lower Mississippi becomes uncontrollable, even in a day of million-dollar levees.

This condition is aggravated by the fact that south of the mouth of the Ohio the Mississippi flows through the soft soil of a delta from thirty to sixty miles in width. Its course, more meandering than that of any other large river in the world, is now on one side of this delta and now on the other, and rarely for any appreciable distance in the

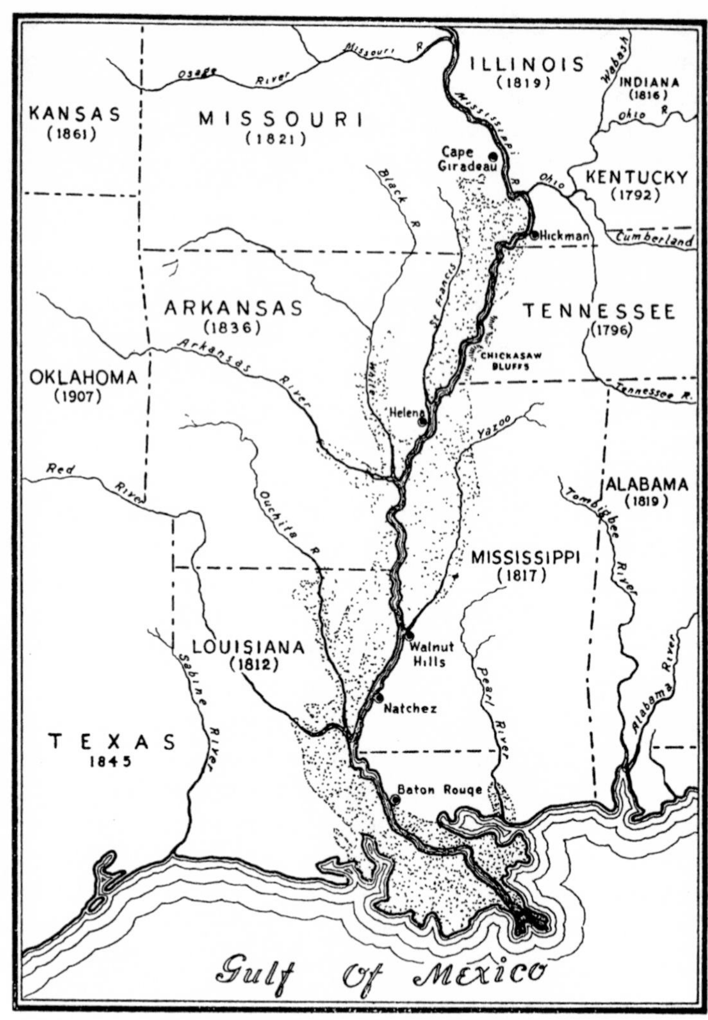

THE LOWER MISSISSIPPI VALLEY

Rivers, bluffs, alluvial region, and states with dates of admission

center. To make matters worse, the course of the stream shifts frequently, and a site on its banks may soon find itself several miles inland, stranded on an old bed.[2]

Along the entire west bank of the lower river, except for a few small hills near the mouth of the St. Francis, there is no ground sufficiently high, were there no levees, to rise above floods. The western slope of the lower valley is drained by two rivers, the Arkansas and the Red, which flow toward the southeast. Along the left bank, however, from the Ohio down into the state of Louisiana extends a low plateau, roughly one hundred miles wide, which runs parallel with the stream, often merely a few miles inland, but which strikes it at only half a dozen points, the most important being Baton Rouge, Natchez, Walnut Hills (Vicksburg), and the Chickasaw Bluffs. The watershed of this plateau is, on one side, toward the Mississippi, and, on the other, toward the Tennessee to the north and the Tombigbee and the Pearl to the south. Because of this barrier no rivers flow directly west from the Appalachians into the Mississippi, and all streams which, like the Tennessee, rise in the mountains are turned aside by it from what would otherwise be their natural course, and empty into the Gulf or the Ohio.[3]

Bluffs, consequently, have always been at premium to the white man on the lower Mississippi. They were so in the century of La Salle and Bienville, when world powers were vying with each other for the possession of a new continent. They retained their value in Mark Twain's day, when the *Robert E. Lee* and the *Natchez* ran their classic race from New Orleans to St. Louis. Even in the twentieth century, as the flood of 1927 proved, their superiority over lower riparian sites remains undiminished. It is significant that the French during the eighteenth century erected forts on the very bluffs where thriving towns were to arise in the early nineteenth.

Sixty-six years before the settlement of Jamestown, an expedition of Spaniards under Hernando de Soto, after fighting its way against wilderness and Indians, crossed the Mississippi somewhere in the vicinity of the Chickasaw Bluffs. Near the river were found villages occupied not by the Chickasaws but by a tribe at the moment actively hostile toward them.[4] Here De Soto halted and within a month's time, in spite of the hostility of the natives, succeeded in building four barges by means of which his force safely crossed the river in June, 1541.

De Soto did not, strictly speaking, discover the Mississippi, although he is the first European who is known to have identified its lower course. The existence of that stream had been known to European cartographers for thirty years, and the famous Spanish explorer himself knew of it when he began his expedition, for in 1539 he had sent a party back to Havana with instructions to rejoin the force at its mouth. Any attempt, furthermore, to determine his exact point of crossing in 1541 is rendered futile by the paucity of detail in the Spanish records and by the changes in the topography of the lower valley resulting from the New Madrid earthquakes of 1811-1812. The most that can be said with any certainty is that De Soto crossed the river at some point within a hundred miles of the Chickasaw Bluffs.[5]

Not until 1673, more than a century later, did white men reappear in the vicinity. In the spring of that year Louis Jolliet, a fur trader from Quebec, and Jacques Marquette, a Jesuit missionary, descended the Mississippi by canoe as far as the mouth of the Arkansas in search of a possible route to the Pacific.[6] On their journey they stopped at an Indian village on the east bank somewhere south of the mouth of the Ohio, probably one of the Chickasaw Bluffs, according to Marquette's map.[7] Here they found a village of the Monsoupeleas, a tribe which the Chickasaws expelled from the region in the next decade.[8]

"They have guns," wrote Marquette in his *Narrative,* "axes, hoes, knives, beads, and double glass bottles in which they keep the powder. . . . They assured us that it was not more than ten days' journey to the sea; that they bought stuffs and other articles of Europeans on the east side [Atlantic Coast]."[9] Already the culture of Europe had begun to penetrate the interior of North America.

Nine years later the bluffs were visited by La Salle, whose chief ambition was to prevent the valuable fur trade of the valley from falling to the English or to his fellow countrymen, the merchants of Montreal. With Tonty of the Iron Hand, his able lieutenant, and a party of half a hundred Frenchmen and savages, La Salle interrupted his exploring expedition down the river at one of the upper Chickasaw Bluffs to spend several days hunting.[10] Here the armorer of the party, Pierre Prudhomme, fancying himself a Nimrod in spite of the fact that he had never hunted, set out into the woods, but failed to return at dusk. For several days the chase was discontinued while the area was scoured for Monsieur Prudhomme, but all in vain. Finding signs of Indians in the vicinity, for the protection of his group La Salle built a rude stockade, which was soon dignified by the name of fort, though it was never afterwards used.

During the search two Chickasaws were captured, and they led La Salle on a wild-goose chase into the interior, ostensibly to their village, which they reported to be at first a two days' and then a five days' journey distant. When he discovered the misrepresentation, La Salle broke off the march and, keeping one Indian as hostage, returned to the bluff, whence he descended the river a few leagues. Finally poor Pierre was found, unharmed except for the discomfort of a ten days' fast, floating like Huck Finn on a raft which he had contrived in hopes of following his party. In keeping with the comedy of the whole episode, the name of the unfortunate Frenchman was given to the bluff and the stockade, which was no more a fort than he a hunter.[11]

Thereafter travel on the river became more frequent, but little information is gleaned from the various journals, which never fail to mention the "Heights of Prudhomme," except that the region abounded in game. Bear, wild pigeon, deer, wild turkey, and bison were plentiful,[12] and the latter were so thick that, as one marksman observed in disgust, "even the most worthless Frenchman can kill one." As late as 1768 buffalo were hunted on the bluffs.[13]

With the eighteenth century the struggle between France and England for control of the valley became intensified—a struggle which began as mere competition between rival fur traders and continued unbroken until Wolfe scaled the heights of Quebec. In spite of the ascendancy of France in the interior, as early as 1698[14] English traders were found across the Mississippi dealing in furs at the mouth of the Arkansas.[15] As a menace to French supremacy they were underestimated neither by Iberville nor by his brother Bienville, who for the first half of the eighteenth century sought to carry out La Salle's policy of holding back the English and of diverting fur to the Gulf settlements rather than to those along the St. Lawrence. Needless to say, constant reports of the activity of English traders in supplying the Chickasaws with firearms did not diminish the apprehension of these Frenchmen.[16]

By the end of the first quarter of the eighteenth century, the prospect of an ultimate French success seemed fair. In spite of the progress of their traders the English were prevented by Indian hostility and the natural barrier of the Appalachians from establishing any settlements in the valley. The Spanish, entrenched near by in Florida and Mexico, were ever a potential threat; but actually, in view of the Bourbon Family Compact and the fact that Spain's real interest lay in South and Central America, there was little interference from that quarter. In addition to the posts in the Illinois country, by 1725 the French had erected forts at Biloxi, Mobile, Natchitoches, Natchez, Arkansas Post, and Toulouse.[17]

That France, in spite of this auspicious beginning, was eventually defeated on the Mississippi is due largely to the Chickasaws, the Iroquois of the Southwest, and, to a lesser extent, to an English trader who lived among them twelve years, James Adair, the William Johnson of the lower valley.[18] Their neighbors, the Choctaws, occasionally wavered in their alliance with the French; the Creeks and the Cherokees to the east were usually unknown quantities, regardless of treaties; but the hatred of the Chickasaws for the French was as constant as it was intense. The presence of English traders among them is a symptom rather than a cause of this hatred, which originated at an earlier date. Undoubtedly the fact that the French were the first persistent white invaders of a soil which the Chickasaws had long ferociously defended against all trespassers, and the traditional alliance of the French with the Choctaws, against whom the Chickasaws were perpetually at war, were pertinent factors.

The Chickasaws, members, like the Creeks and Choctaws, of the Muskhogean family of Indians, had their main villages in the hill country along the upper Tombigbee.[19] Inclined more toward hunting than toward the sedentary pursuit of agriculture, they were the scourge of the Southwest, though the smallest of its more important tribes.[20] By an exceptional tenacity and intrepidity they offset their numerical weakness, and their daring was clearly revealed in the destruction of a party of Iroquois who invaded their territory in 1732.[21] Yet this valor was tempered by discretion, for, with a minor exception during the American

Revolution, they never attacked the English or the Americans.

In the long struggle of the Chickasaws against the French, the Chickasaw Bluffs, though more than one hundred miles distant from the tribal villages, were of utmost importance. Continued control of the bluffs by the Indians would have rendered attack from the Mississippi impossible and would have assured them of safety in the rear in case of an invasion up the Tombigbee from Mobile. Offensively the bluffs long proved valuable, for with the Heights of Prudhomme as bases the Chickasaws carried on such effective guerrilla warfare over a period of forty years that the French were forced to travel on the river in fleets, and even with such protection to hug the right bank.[22]

After several decades of irritating impudence in the early eighteenth century, culminating in the Chickasaws' offer of refuge to the Natchez, who had massacred the French garrison at Fort Rosalie, Bienville's patience was exhausted. "If we cannot gain over this nation," he wrote to his government, "it will be necessary to drive it away from the territory of the colony."[23] In the spring of 1736 he attempted to carry out this policy. While he moved north up the Tombigbee, his colleague, D'Artaguette, led a force south from Fort Chartres in Illinois. With one hundred and fifty Frenchmen and three hundred Indians (Miami, Illinois, and Iroquois), the latter landed at Prudhomme on February 28, where he built a small fort, the second to be erected on that bluff.[24] Proceeding inland, he reached the Chickasaw villages one month later, unfortunately ahead of Bienville, and scarcity of provisions soon forced him into an attack that proved fatal to himself and his cause. Arriving later to find a British flag floating over the Indian stockade,[25] Bienville, too, was decisively defeated and compelled to retreat.

Smarting under this humiliation, Bienville, for the next

few years, burned with an ambition for revenge. After much preparation he managed by the autumn of 1739 to assemble a force of twelve hundred Frenchmen and twice as many Negroes and Indians on the lower bluff,[26] which his engineers had selected as the best base of operations. This expedition of Bienville's is the first historical event that is definitely known to have occurred on the site of the future Memphis. Three quarters of a league south of the Margot (Wolf) River, which skirted the northern extremity of the bluff, Fort Assumption had been erected during the summer.[27] When everything was in readiness for the campaign, however, a strange apathy seems to have overtaken Bienville, in spite of his overwhelming odds. Either because of fear of the Chickasaws or because of the impassability of the wilderness in midwinter, he temporized so long that his Indians, who declared that they "could well perceive . . . he was a squaw," deserted in large numbers and thus further reduced the force already seriously impaired by sickness.[28] Finally, in the spring, a somewhat informal truce was concluded, but its terms were so nebulous as to be meaningless. For a second time Bienville was forced to beat an ignominious retreat.

Despite their success, the Chickasaws suffered severely from their wars with the French. In 1754 the English traders among them sent a memorial to the authorities of Georgia stating that the nation was in danger of extinction.[29] Two years later the chiefs themselves addressed a plea to the "king of Carolina" for the return of the eastern group of Chickasaws living on the Savannah River. "We hope you will think of us in our poverty," they urged, "as we have not had the liberty of hunting for three years. We have enough to do to defend our land and prevent our women and children from becoming slaves of the French."[30] In answer Georgia and South Carolina advised the Indians to leave the Mississippi region and settle farther east, even sending a delegation of Cherokees to escort them on the proposed hegira, but the Chickasaws rejected the offer.

Vaudreuil, Bienville's successor, fell heir to his quarrel with this undaunted tribe. In 1752, disregarding their efforts towards peace, he led the third unsuccessful expedition against them. "By the failure of the expeditions undertaken against the Chickasaws between the years 1735 and 1740," he advised his government, "the Indians have arrived at the conclusion that we cannot conquer or destroy them; and until we erase from our own minds the impression of our inability to subdue them, by giving full retaliation for our unsuccessful operations against them, the honor of our arms will remain tarnished."[31] If the honor of the French arms depended upon the destruction of the Chickasaws, that honor did remain tarnished.

During the Seven Years' War, 1756-1763, the southern frontier was strangely quiet. It is odd that the English failed to take advantage of Chickasaw animosity for the French, since they must have been informed through Adair of its existence. By the Treaty of Paris in 1763, which gave the territory east of the Mississippi to England, the French menace to the Chickasaws was removed, only to be replaced soon by that of the American frontiersmen, who under the guise of friendship were to thrust them from the land which they had defended at such great cost.

In view of their traditional alliance with the English, the American Revolution placed the Chickasaws in a difficult position; yet they seem to have remained neutral until George Rogers Clark, disregarding their remonstrances, erected Fort Jefferson within their country a few miles south of the mouth of the Ohio. They attacked this fort the following year, and only the wounding of James Colbert, their half-breed leader, saved it from capture. The assault proved disastrous to the defenders, however, for the garrison, emaciated by disease and starvation, withdrew a few months later. When the Chickasaws proceeded to attack the infant settlements on the Cumberland,[32] General Nathanael Greene, the commander of the American army in the South, who was aware of the danger of such hostility, appointed a commission to negotiate a treaty of peace. This purpose was finally accomplished in 1783, when commissioners from the state of Virginia, appointed by Governor Benjamin Harrison, drew up a treaty settling the boundaries of Chickasaw territory.[33]

When Spain had entered the struggle against Great Britain as an ally of France, she had set as her price the eastern Mississippi Valley south of the Ohio, and her military efforts during the war were directed largely towards securing that area, and perhaps more.[34] In the North a Spanish force from St. Louis captured the English post of St. Joseph on Lake Michigan;[35] in the South Galvez, captain general of Louisiana and West Florida, seized Pensacola and Natchez, which had been British possessions since 1763. Furthermore, Galvez definitely had his eye on the Chickasaw Bluffs; Miró, his assistant, suggested to him the necessity of a fort "in the ravines of Margot. . . . Your Excellency knows how advantageous it would be to populate the upper part of the river."[36]

The realization of the project suggested by Miró was blocked by the Chickasaws, who easily transferred to the Spanish their former animosity for the French. During the latter part of the war, sallying forth from the bluffs in canoes, they carried on a constant guerrilla warfare which proved lucrative to themselves and costly to the Spanish.[37] Though Spain was technically an ally of the rebelling colonies, General James Robertson of the Cumberland settlements did not hesitate to encourage this looting by sending military supplies to the lower bluff to improve the Indians' proficiency.[38]

By the treaty with England in 1783 the United States gained nominal possession of the Southwest as far as the thirty-first parallel of latitude. That the commissioners expected Spain, then a world power of first rank, to submit without struggle to this high-handed disposal of territory, much of which was actually in the possession of her troops, is absurd. Against this agreement she immediately protested, and soon Floridablanca, Charles III's secretary of state, declared the Mississippi closed to all but Spanish commerce and asserted vigorously his sovereign's claim to the area south of the Ohio and west of the Tennessee, the Hiwassee, and the Flint.[39] In spite of the legal strength of her position, however, the situation in Europe a decade later forced Spain to yield this contention at San Lorenzo.[40]

To the extent that the United States was responsible for this victory, the credit belonged not to the federal government but to the American frontiersman, who did much to earn the reward for which he was so eager. Of the larger struggle, the contest over the lower Chickasaw bluff was fairly typical. In the way of the long-projected erection of a Spanish fort at this strategic point stood two solid obstacles, the Chickasaws and the settlers on the Cumberland. Yet the frontiersmen were as helpless as the authorities at New Orleans, for the remoteness of the bluff and the Spanish Treaty of 1784 at Mobile with the Chickasaws completely tied their hands.[41] Both the Spanish and the Americans were forced to follow an opportunistic policy of cultivating the favor of the Indians and of waiting for an opening. Consequently two factions arose among the Chickasaws, one under Piomingo friendly to the Americans, and another under Wolf's Friend partial to the Spanish.[42]

The latter moved first but only when the course of events made further delay fatal to their interests. Both Carondelet and Gayoso, governors of Louisiana during this period of intense rivalry, were apprehensive of American occupation of the bluff,[43] and their fears were quickened by constant rumors of impending expeditions from the Cumberland or from Kentucky to establish a post on the Mississippi.

Four events in particular spurred Gayoso into action. In accordance with Genêt's plan of sending George Rogers Clark and a party of Carolinians to wrest Louisiana from Spain, the Colonel's brother, William Clark, arrived at the bluff in 1793 with the double purpose to reconnoiter and to win the aid of the Chickasaws.[44] In the fall of the following year, John Overton, who was temporarily Indian agent and titleholder of a tract of land on the bluff which he had recently bought, promised Piomingo to deliver to the Chickasaws a large quantity of ammunition, merchandise, and farm implements.[45] About the same time persistent rumors reached Gayoso's ears of a move by Kentuckians to occupy Muscle Shoals on the Tennessee. Finally, in January, 1795, the Georgia legislature sold huge grants of land in the valley, including the bluffs, to speculators.[46]

Working through Wolf's Friend, Gayoso speeded negotiations with the Chickasaws, and on May 14, 1795, he secured the cession of the riparian section of the lower bluff for thirty thousand dollars.[47] On the last day of that month he proudly raised the Spanish flag over his hastily constructed Fort San Fernando de las Barrancas. Shortly afterwards Panton-Leslie and Company, the trading-house of the Southwest which worked in conjunction with the Spanish, located a post at the fort with John Forbes and Kenneth Ferguson in charge.[48]

Obviously this action would not pass without protest from the United States. "The act of the Spanish in taking possession of Chickasaw Bluffs," President Washington told a delegation of Chickasaws in August, "is an unwarranted aggression."[49] In October General Anthony Wayne at New Madrid demanded of Gayoso by what authority he "had made usurpation in the territory of the United States."[50] But while higher officials were content to indulge in more conventional forms of protest, Robertson with the realism of the frontier sent five hundred stand of arms to Piomingo.[51]

In spite of polite diplomacy and the cruder, though usually more effective, tactics of the frontier, the bluffs remained in Spanish hands until the spring of 1797, eighteen months after Pinckney and Godoy had signed the treaty surrendering all land north of the thirty-first parallel of latitude to the United States. At last in the spring of that year, having burned the stockade, the garrison withdrew across the river and erected Fort Esperanza (Hopefield).[52] Learning of Blount's conspiracy after he had given orders for withdrawal, Carondelet countermanded his earlier instructions, but his second message arrived too late and no attempt at reoccupation was made.[53]

Captain Isaac Guion of the American army stopped at the bluff in July to distribute goods among the Chickasaws, whom he found still divided into bitter factions.[54] Considering the Spanish at Esperanza a serious menace, he obtained through Piomingo a cession of land upon which he erected Fort Adams. Soon its name was changed to Fort Pike, and before 1798 it was supplanted by Fort Pickering, a new structure several miles down the bluff.[55]

While national historians have failed to recognize the role of the Chickasaws in this free-for-all contest for the Mississippi, local historians, on the contrary, have unduly exaggerated its significance. Of all the events in American history which seem inevitable, none is so plain as the ultimate retreat of Spain before the steady and irresistible surge of the pioneers across the Appalachians. Had Spanish intrigue resulted in the secession of the West, such a new nation, whatever its future, would never have remained in Spanish hands. By their hostility to the French and the

Spanish, the Chickasaws unwittingly enabled the young United States to realize sooner its manifest destiny, but to that destiny they were an accidental and not an essential factor.

During the two decades after the acquisition of the Chickasaw Bluffs, problems regarding the Mississippi Valley constantly plagued the nation. The Mississippi question, the Louisiana Purchase, the Burr Conspiracy, the War of 1812, and the Missouri Compromise are striking evidence of the growing importance of the West in national affairs. In spite of these larger events, however, after 1797 the story of the bluffs necessarily becomes the chronicle of local settlement.

From the date of American occupation until the founding of Memphis on the site in 1819, life on the lower bluff was that of an ordinary post on the frontier. Activity centered around the fort and its small garrison, whose chief function seems to have been the rescue of various craft in distress on the river.[56] Near by were the houses of a few white settlers who traded with the Indians and in most cases intermarried with them. These squatters managed to exist by planting a little cotton and corn, breeding pigs and poultry, and supplying passing boats with sundry articles.[57] Around the fort red men were usually found in large numbers, and according to Zachary Taylor, commandant in 1809, there was a large Chickasaw settlement about five miles inland.[58] On the batture at the base of the bluff stood a temporary village where the Indians built a quarter-mile track to test the speed of their ponies.[59] In accordance with Jefferson's expressed policy of encouraging the Indians to run into debt so that they would be forced to cede their land in payment,[60] a trading post was established by the war department in 1802 with Thomas Petertain as factor.

The humdrum existence of the community was on the whole unbroken, except when the arrival of an occasional traveler was used as an excuse for celebration. An English tourist, Thomas Ashe, gives a glowing description of a sumptuous feast in his honor in 1806, consisting of "fish, venison, squirrel, and bear's meat, with a profusion of wine." When the party broke up at one, in view of the necessity of scrambling down the one-hundred-and-fifty-foot declivity to his boat in the dark, Ashe expressed fervent thanks that the dangers and fatigue of his journey had made him "too dull to get drunk."[61]

The names of only a few of these early white settlers have been recorded. First of them, in both point of time and reputation, was Benjamin Foy, a Hollander sent by Gayoso in 1794 as agent to the Indians. Foy cleared a portion of the mud bar at the mouth of the Wolf River and on it planted a crop of corn.[62] When the Spanish withdrew three years later, he followed them across the river, where he maintained a settlement, probably on a Spanish grant, larger for many years than that on the bluff opposite.[63] Here he provided a hospitality which became famous all along the river, and no less a person than the Frenchman Volney spent a winter in his home writing a novel. As judge of the court of common pleas of the District of Arkansas, Foy after 1808 held his court at Arkansas Post. He was such an anathema to the ruffians of the valley that his own settlement was considered the most moral, intelligent, and healthy community between Cape Girardeau and Natchez.[64]

Henry Foy, brother of the Judge, purchased an Indian hut on the lower Chickasaw bluff, where he cultivated a large farm for several years. Guion (1797) mentions as settlers Kenneth Ferguson, the Scotch agent for Panton-Leslie, and William Mizell, a North Carolinian who served as interpreter.[65] Any estimate of the white population can be only approximate. From the four families residing there when the site came into the possession of the United States, the settlement grew in the next decade to at least a dozen, and in 1812 the community probably contained more than fifty inhabitants.[66]

The comments of some of the visitors to the bluff during the early years of the nineteenth century are enlightening. "The land is as rich as possible," wrote Ashe, "and in a garden belonging to the garrison all kinds of fruit and vegetables succeed to a perfection seldom attained elsewhere."[67] "Another of the few situations on the Mississippi," commented Christian Schultz in a prophetic moment, "on which anything like a large and permanent town may be built."[68] John Bradbury, an English scientist who sought shelter on the bluff in 1811 during one of the severest earthquakes in American annals, found a score of people huddled together "almost distracted with fear. . . . They were composed of families who had collected to pray. . . . On entering the house I saw a Bible open on the table."[69] But all comment was not favorable. Reverend Lorenzo Dow, who changed boats near Fort Pickering in 1815, displayed an unusual knowledge of geography when he predicted that "the upper bluff [not the lower] will probably be fixed upon one day as a proper site to convene a portage up and down the river."[70]

Meanwhile certain men on the Cumberland and others far away in North Carolina were slowly perfecting plans which would eventually prove Dow's prediction incorrect, but not until it had almost come true.

CHAPTER II

THE WOES OF A PROPRIETOR

In the American epic, which necessarily emphasizes as its central theme the physical conquest of a continent and the expansion of a people over wilderness and desert, the role of the "noble pioneer" has completely overshadowed that of the "land-jobber" behind the scene. While John Smith and Daniel Boone lead the cast as national heroes, one looks in vain for any mention of Sir Ferdinando Gorges or Reverend Manasseh Cutler in the list of characters. It is generally forgotten that but for the brain of some speculator back of the mountains the pioneer might never have had the opportunity to use his stout heart and steady hand in the "dark and bloody ground"; yet in all fairness it must be admitted that Cutler and his numerous successors, many of them long since forgotten, not only initiated westward movements, but finding them under way also speeded them up or diverted them from their natural courses.

In 1819, half a century after the settlement of Watauga in the present state of Tennessee, Andrew Jackson and James Winchester, generals of the American army in the War of 1812, and John Overton, retired chief justice of the Supreme Court of Tennessee, climaxed a long career of speculation in land by founding the town of Memphis on the lower Chickasaw bluff where they owned five thousand acres. The project was not the inspiration of a moment, nor was its accomplishment a matter of a few months' effort. On the contrary, Overton and Jackson, partners for thirty years in land deals that were sometimes questionable,[1] had acquired title to this site in the 1790's. From that time on, though they had their fingers in other pies, the possibilities of their holding on the bluff were never forgotten.[2] The occupation of West Tennessee by the Chickasaws long blocked the realization of their ambition, but when that tribe ceded its remaining land in Kentucky and Tennessee in 1818, the last obstacle in their path was removed. The course of events immediately preceding the founding of the town reveals a careful premeditation, for which Overton, the brains of the trio, was undoubtedly responsible. In October, 1818, Isaac Shelby and Andrew Jackson as commissioners of the United States negotiated the treaty of cession; the following January the proprietors entered into an agreement to lay out a town; and by May 1 Overton and Winchester were at the bluff having a survey made.[3]

In the long prenatal period of Memphis various influences were at work which were to affect the circumstances of its birth and to determine somewhat its future character. Certain earlier events, consequently, must first be considered, as they pertain directly or indirectly to the village which arose in the twenties on the bluff.

Before the break with England, the numerous plans for the colonization of the trans-Allegheny West were received with coldness if not outright hostility by the British Board of Trade. As early as 1701, Daniel Coxe, physician to Charles II and Queen Anne, having purchased the earlier Heath grant to "Carolana," sent out a party of Huguenots with the intention of forming a colony on the Mississippi within the bounds of his territory, but the French in Louisiana prevented the ship from reaching its destination.

Coxe's project was but the first of many similar attempts in the course of the century, chief of which were those of Samuel Hazard of Philadelphia in 1755, later revived by Phineas Lyman of Connecticut; and of the Mississippi

Company of 1763, composed of Virginia and Maryland gentlemen like the Lees, Washingtons, and Fitzhughs.[4] Though none of these schemes materialized, the strategic and commercial advantages to the mother country of such colonization were not overlooked by all Englishmen. Thomas Pownall, one of the most far-sighted colonial governors, and James Adair, an unofficial but capable Indian agent, both urged a barrier colony on the Mississippi.[5] The *Gentleman's Magazine* of London stated in 1742 that several Virginians who had recently descended the river to New Orleans, "saw more good land on the Mississippi and its many large branches than they judge are in all the English colonies as far as they are inhabited."[6]

The Proclamation of 1763 temporarily dashed prospects of fortunes in western land, but during the Revolution North Carolina showed signs of an incipient interest in its western region, soon to become the state of Tennessee. Settlements were made in the Watauga valley about 1770 by Virginia Scotch-Irish and Carolinians under James Robertson, the Dan Boone of Tennessee, all of whom thought they were on Virginia soil. Like Boone, Robertson was probably connected with Richard Henderson, organizer of the first large land company in North Carolina,[7] and it was land, not freedom, which beckoned to these early settlers from the wilderness. The year 1779 found Robertson in the vanguard that established a colony at French Lick on the Cumberland, which in time became the town of Nashville.

Throughout this era the politics of North Carolina were tainted with speculation in land. Politicians in league with surveyors and Indian fighters controlled the state government and divided among themselves the spoils. Their master, William Blount, empire-builder of the Southwest and prince of speculators, who organized the second great Carolina land company, held the balance of power between Conservatives and Radicals within the state. Having anesthetized the rival parties, in 1783 Blount pushed a bill through the legislature reopening the land office for eight months, so that only those who were prepared, like himself, could get the choice land.[8] Though the price named was ten pounds per hundred acres, provision was made for payment in state and continental bills as well as in specie certificates, which were so depreciated that the actual cost was less than five dollars for that amount of land.[9] The Cumberland region had been reserved for compensation to the state's continental line; yet even excluding grants within the several reservations four million acres were entered in eight months, two and a half million of which were in the Chickasaw country in violation of the recognized Indian title.[10] To reduce further the actual cost of land, Blount had more state notes issued, and all the while his agents were purchasing military grants from their shortsighted owners at a fraction of their real value.

His next move was to secure a stable government for the western country by getting it ceded to the United States. The legislature of 1784 obediently passed a bill to that effect, stipulating, however, that all previous state grants be honored. With free protection against the Spanish and the Indians assured, North Carolina suddenly rejected Blount's leadership for the moment and repealed the act of cession. To pull the chestnuts out of the fire he was forced to turn to John Sevier, governor of the new State of Franklin which had been formed in the ceded territory, and Sevier played his part with skill. In spite of the activity of another group of speculators under one Arthur Campbell, who realized what an opportunity they had missed, and in spite of the efforts of the Radical party to save the land for the state, the Blount interests remained untouched. Sevier was working from the inside, and his apparent failure as governor of the rebel State of Franklin was actually a clever victory. What has long been considered and much praised as the conspicuous example of the frontier's demand for autonomy was thus in reality only a smoke-screen for Carolina speculators.

Appreciating the possibility of a strong government for the frontier, in 1788 Blount favored the adoption of the Constitution, but again his enemies defeated him. His supporters in the West thereupon made overtures to Spain in order to protect their trade outlet and to frighten the state into ratification. Not this threat, however, but the acceptance of the Constitution by the required number of states in 1789 and the inclusion of the first ten amendments brought North Carolina into the Union. Immediately the western country was again ceded to the national government, and Blount was rewarded for his efforts with the position of governor of the Southwest Territory. In this capacity, through Sevier and Robertson, he ruled the frontiersmen with an iron hand, though the anticipated federal aid was not forthcoming, and he succeeded in discouraging attacks on the Indians in order to allow the state department at Philadelphia a free hand in dealing with Spain.

When Tennessee entered the Union as the sixteenth state in 1796, a decade of confusion and litigation ensued because she denied the claims of Congress and North Carolina to her land. Finally, by the settlement of 1806, Tennessee agreed to satisfy the North Carolina claims and to surrender to Congress all land west of the Tennessee River, though parts of that area were later used to satisfy early warrants. In fact, so many Carolina warrants had been issued, numbers of them illegally, that every new area bought or otherwise secured from the Indians was immediately consumed in satisfying them. The new state found itself faced with the task of bailing out an ocean.[11]

To the colony on the Cumberland had come in the late eighties two young lawyers, John Overton and Andrew Jackson, who soon threw in their lot with Blount. Their fortunes rose with his, and they shortly became trusted lieutenants, for the Governor knew how to pick his henchmen. Upon the expulsion of Blount from the United States Senate in 1797, Jackson as heir-apparent was selected to fill his place, and with the aid of his chief's brother, Willie, he was able to control the political forces of what was then West Tennessee for a generation. By 1810 the development of sectionalism had produced bitter rivalry between the eastern region around Knoxville, whose hero was the popular "Nolachucky Jack" Sevier, a hotspur like Jackson, and the more fertile section around Nashville, represented by the Blount-Jackson faction.

Overton and Jackson formed an excellent team. The former possessed a good education and innate craft, qualities which made him in time the richest man in Tennessee,[12] while "Old Hickory" supplemented these attributes with the ability of a man of action to get things done, regardless of opposition, by fair means or foul. That Overton was one of the General's few intimate friends to remain on cordial terms with that fiery individual throughout forty stormy years is indicative of the former's power over men. Before his death he burned all his correspondence with Jackson, reputedly to prevent the curious from prying into the details of the campaign of 1828.[13] Hailed as a gesture fitting such a Damon-Pythias relationship, this act was by no means purely altruistic, for the destroyed letters undoubtedly contained information as damaging to the reputation of Overton as to that of the Hero of New Orleans.

Since many of the details concerning the paternity of Memphis are obscure, the story has to be reconstructed much in the manner of a paleontologist who creates a dinosaur from a fossil jawbone. Fortunately there remain enough facts for at least a skeleton.

In October, 1783, just before the land office at Hillsborough, North Carolina, closed, two entries were recorded

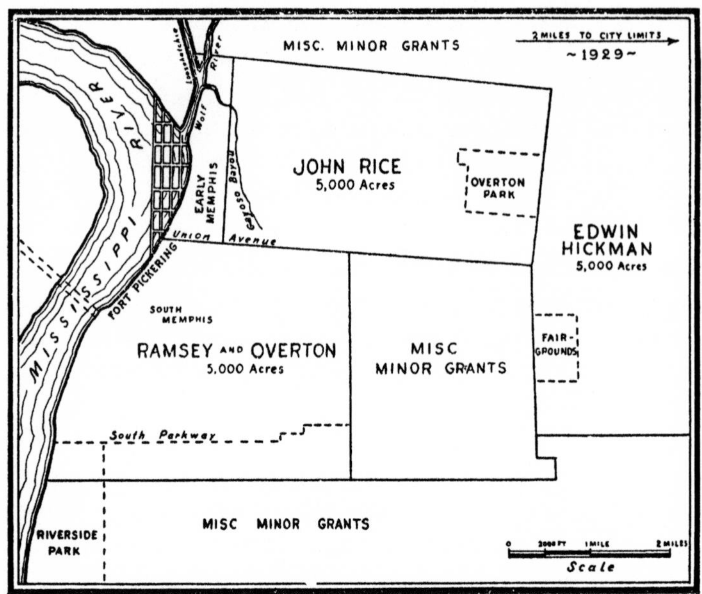

EARLY LAND GRANTS IN THE MEMPHIS AREA IN RELATION TO PRESENT-DAY LANDMARKS

The checkered area, upper left, shows the region which was constantly changing because of variations in the river, and over which there was consequently considerable litigation.—Adapted from the *Memphis City Planning Commission Report, 1924,* page 22.

for riparian land on the lower Chickasaw bluff: one for five thousand acres adjacent to Wolf River, by John Rice, and another for a similar amount of land immediately to the south, by John Ramsay.[14] Because of the red tape connected with the legal process of securing title to land, Rice did not receive his deed until 1789, and it was 1823 before Overton, who had purchased one seventh of the Ramsay tract, and the Ramsay heirs received theirs.[15] North Carolina had no right to sell this land, for until 1818 the Chickasaws were recognized as its owners by the United States government, and any court would have declared the Rice and Ramsay grants illegal.[16]

In 1794, probably at the suggestion of Jackson, who was aware of the excellence of the location, Overton bought the Rice tract for five hundred dollars from the heirs of the original holder, who had been killed by Indians several years before.[17] Two years later Overton sold half of it to Jackson for one hundred dollars, and he, in turn, during the next two decades disposed of parts of his interest to the Winchester brothers at prices which varied from $312.50 for one eighth of the tract in 1797, to $5,000 for the same amount of land in 1818 after the cession.[18] After numerous transactions, in 1819 Overton still owned half, James Winchester one fourth, and Andrew Jackson and the heirs of William Winchester one eighth each.

With the price of cotton rising yearly and available land on the frontier being rapidly occupied by settlers from the East, the value of the land in the Western District of Tennessee gradually increased, as the Jackson-Winchester transactions reveal. As mentioned above this district had become a congressional reservation in 1806, but the Indian title was not extinguished until a dozen years later. Anticipating the purchase by the federal government of this territory, for which Kentuckians had long been clamoring, and the rush for land that would inevitably follow, Overton prepared for the tide which, in its flood, would lead to fortune. Through his agent Cage he made every effort to purchase the other tracts on the bluff, and in the autumn of 1818 he sent Marcus Winchester, son of his fellow proprietor, to explore the region and to serve as his representative there when the boom should start.[19]

When James Robertson died in 1814, the last friend of the Chickasaws in Tennessee was gone. A petition from the Tennessee legislature for the relinquishment of the Chickasaw claim was presented to Congress in the spring of 1818, and within six months Jackson and Shelby had secured their treaty. During the negotiations the American commissioners were often at each other's throats, and at the conclusion of the treaty Shelby in anger declared Jackson's conduct corrupt.[20] That the General, however honest his intentions, was guilty of equivocation in regard to the two reservations in the document cannot be denied,[21] nor can it be overlooked that as a direct result of the cession he was able to sell one eighth of the Rice tract, for which he had paid twenty-five dollars, for the fat sum of five thousand.

According to the standards of his own age and his own conscience, Jackson should not be charged with deliberate dishonesty in this instance. What to the socially-conscious twentieth century seems an outright fraud was, to the less sensitive early nineteenth, legitimate reward for commendable craft. During those halcyon days of the New West, life was much of a dogfight, with no quarter asked and no quarter given. Overton and Jackson violated only the spirit of the law, never the letter, nor were they ever guilty of the wholesale swindling perpetrated by John Sevier.[22]

With the announcement of the purchase in October the boom began. Land formerly sold at five dollars per hundred acres now brought one thousand, and by June, 1820, there were more than one hundred surveyors in the district locating claims.[23] The normal movement westward about this time was accelerated by the Panic of 1819 and the ensuing years of depression in the Carolinas and Virginia. In 1827 an Asheville correspondent of the *Western Carolinian* reported that "during the last four months the flow of immigration has surpassed anything of the kind the writer has ever witnessed. It was not uncommon to see eight, ten, or fifteen wagons and carts passing in a single day . . . to the more highly favored climes of the West."[24]

Overton was determined to let no rival get ahead of him. "We must proceed," he wrote General Winchester in

October, "to lay off a town by this time twelve months [hence]. I suspect [if] the country settles as fast as I think it will . . . we must not let the owners of property on the Bluffs of the Mississippi above us be beforehand in laying off towns, as it might damp the sale of ours."[25] As soon as General Winchester received power of attorney from the heirs of his brother William, the proprietors entered into an agreement in regard to the town, which was to be binding for ten years regardless of changes in ownership.[26] On May 1, 1819, Overton and General Winchester, with William Lawrence, their surveyor and attorney, laid out the little town to which the general gave the name of Memphis.[27] Difficulty was experienced in locating the Rice entry, for the mouth of Wolf River, one of the landmarks, had moved north half a mile in the thirty years since Rice had staked his claim, causing much uncertainty as to the southern boundary of the tract and similarly affecting the Ramsay grant to the south.[28] The proprietors discovered, to their dismay, that the narrow batture which had extended along the northwestern extremity of the bluff in the previous century and which had made an excellent flatboat landing had been completely swallowed by the river. The eddy also had moved south two miles to the site of old Fort Pickering, now part of the Ramsay tract, where the blockhouse was still standing.[29] Here the flatboats chose to land in the early twenties rather than in the swift water at the base of that section of the bluff on which the new town was located.

For a day when city planning had not been thought of west of the Alleghenies, the village was excellently laid out—at least on paper. Three hundred and sixty-two lots were surveyed on the northwestern edge of the Rice tract with wide streets running toward the cardinal points of the compass and with four public squares, named, according to their purpose, Auction, Court, Exchange, and Market. Pro-

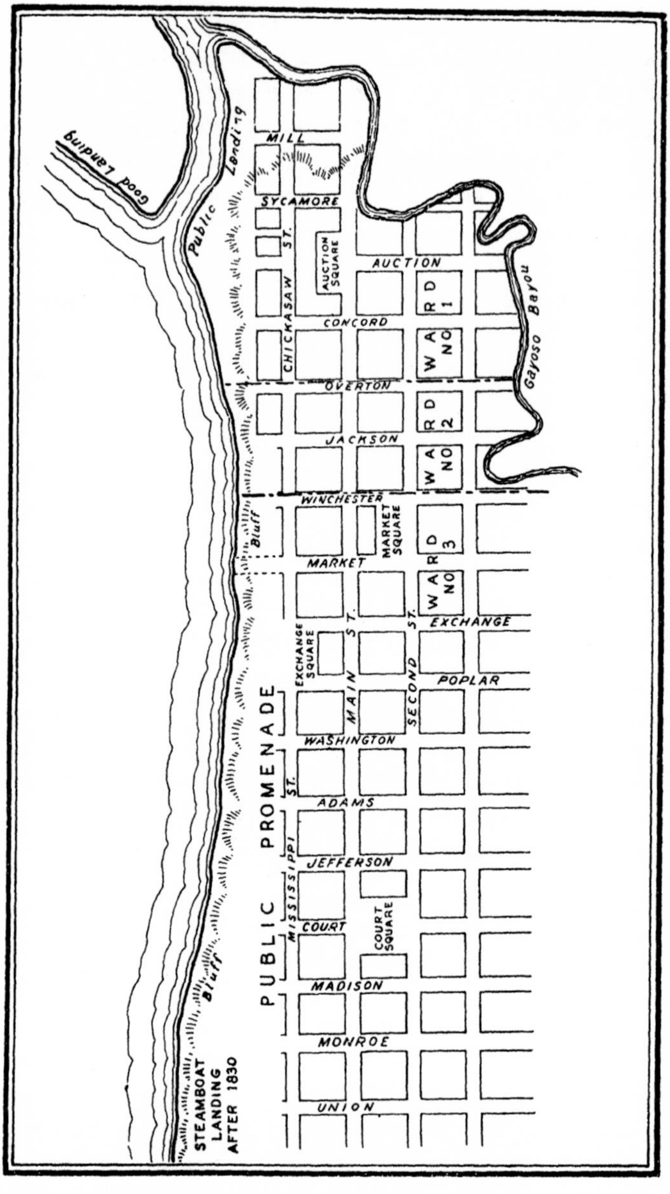

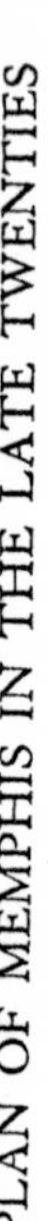

PLAN OF MEMPHIS IN THE LATE TWENTIES

vision was also made for a spacious promenade extending along the summit of the bluff for the entire length of the river front. Lots were to be sold only to actual settlers, and payment on them had to be completed within five years.[30]

Upon his return to Nashville Overton directed his attention to the organization of a new county along the Mississippi. As a result of his efforts the state legislature in November, 1819, created Shelby, the first county to lie wholly within the Western District, and the act stipulated that court be held at Chickasaw Bluffs, at that time the only village west of the Tennessee River.[31] The eager proprietor then embarked on a publicity campaign, sending a flowery description of the site and an announcement of the sale of lots to the Nashville *Whig,* New Orleans *Gazette,* Natchez *State Gazette, Arkansas State Gazette,* St. Louis *Enquirer,* Louisville *Public Advertiser,* Cincinnati *Western Spy,* Pittsburgh *Gazette,* and the Nashville *Clarion.*[32] In spite of publicity the sale of lots in 1820 at prices from thirty to one hundred dollars each, though accompanied by a generous distribution of whisky at the proprietors' expense, proved definitely disappointing.[33]

The three speculators early met spirited opposition from the few squatters on the bluff, led by Isaac Rawlings, who had resided there for some years, and this antipathy continued to exist between citizens and the heirs of the proprietors until the middle of the century. Many of these settlers were veterans of the War of 1812, some of whom had bought cabins from the Indians and consequently had a better legal claim to the land than the purchasers of the Rice tract.[34] Those who had no legal basis for their claims of course talked much of pre-emption rights. To prevent litigation and to dispel hostility, therefore, the proprietors gave lots to many of these old settlers.[35]

Yet the hostility of the squatters remained so pronounced that Jackson, who was then clearing deck for the 1824 presidential campaign, was forced to deed his remaining one-eighth interest to John C. McLemore in exchange for other land in Tennessee.[36] "Old Hickory" well knew what capital his enemies would make of this apparent lack of generosity to his former soldiers, particularly since ugly rumors about his part in the Chickasaw Cession of 1818 were still current.[37] Actually, Jackson had little to do with the founding of Memphis. While proprietor of the Tennessee town he also had interests in Pensacola, Florida, and Florence, Alabama. What was most noteworthy about his connection with Memphis was his profit on the deal of five thousand, five hundred and twenty-five dollars in addition to the tract of land he received from McLemore, which was worth at least that much more.

Overton soon had to face the rivalry he had anticipated. The Big Creek settlement, founded in the early twenties a few miles north of Memphis under the leadership of Jesse Benton and the Boltons, became temporarily more prosperous than the village on the bluff.[38] Jealousy of the better-located but less wealthy river site led the Big Creek people to make a determined attempt to have the county seat moved elsewhere, a development which Overton had foreseen and viewed with apprehension as early as 1822.[39] Failing to realize that the riparian location of Memphis guaranteed its ultimate victory over any inland site, the Judge considered that its growth was dependent upon keeping the court. Upon this issue, he thought, hung its future, "whether it shall be a decent little town in our day (say in 20 or 30 years) or a harbor for a few drunken boatmen (besides those now there)."[40]

In spite of ill health, therefore, he spent most of November, 1823, lobbying night and day in the legislature at Murfreesboro, where his influence was considerable.[41] His efforts were rewarded by the passage of a bill naming four commissioners to select sites for seats of justice in the Western District and providing for an election to be held in Shelby County the following February to determine the wishes of its citizens. The act, however, contained a joker permitting the commissioners to disregard the public sentiment expressed by this vote if they were of the opinion that some location, other than that chosen, was superior.[42] Overton also secured an amendment allowing the violation of the current practice of placing county seats within three miles of the geographical center, and he succeeded in getting commissioners named whom he considered friendly to his project.[43]

To be doubly sure, Overton arranged for generous donations of land to the county by owners of the Rice and Ramsay tracts and for the shipment of two hundred gallons of whisky to Marcus Winchester, now in permanent residence on the bluff, in case the voters needed a little stimulus.[44] The replacement of Jackson at this point by the energetic John C. McLemore gave the proprietors much more power, for the General had been dead timber in the partnership, and it may have been due to the activity of McLemore that the population of the settlement doubled in 1824.[45] His first assignment was the management of the election in question; but there is no record of its being held as scheduled and the following year a new act was passed directing the commissioners to fix the seat of Shelby County where they pleased, regardless of any law to the contrary.[46]

To Overton's surprise, in 1824 the commissioners selected Sanderlin's Bluff on Wolf River ten miles east of Memphis, and there the town of Raleigh was laid out, though the court was not actually moved until 1827.[47] That the population of Raleigh reached fifteen hundred in a dozen years, much of it coming from Memphis,[48] suggests that Overton was partially justified in his conviction about the court. Thus a Memphis lobby received its first defeat, ominous for the future, in the Tennessee legislature. Worse than that, instead of becoming a "decent little town" which could boast of some refinement like Raleigh, Memphis remained for a score of years a tough river town overrun by "drunken boatmen." The prediction of the Judge proved correct.

Yet all was by no means lost. To offset the transfer of the county court, in December, 1826, the legislature was induced to grant the town a charter of incorporation.[49] When they read the notice in the Nashville papers, those citizens who abhorred the thought of taxes immediately raised a howl of protest. At a public meeting over which he presided, Isaac Rawlings spoke for the malcontents of the anti-proprietary element. Since the majority of the settlers, however, seemed to favor incorporation, narrow strips to the south and east, supposedly belonging to the disgruntled minority, were left out of the city, but it was later discovered that 98 per cent of the excluded area belonged to the proprietors.[50]

The following spring Marcus Winchester was elected mayor, though had Rawlings not withheld his own name he would probably have been chosen for that office.[51] Two years later, the enemies of Overton in the legislature amended the charter by giving Memphis all the powers of Nashville and subjecting it to the same restrictions. This was a clever attack upon Overton, for, since one of these restrictions disqualified the holder of a federal position for the office of mayor, Winchester as postmaster immediately surrendered the mayoralty because it paid no salary.[52] Rawlings was elected to succeed him, and for two years the proprietors faced an administration headed by their worst enemy. With the termination of the original agreement in 1829, the courts, in response to a petition from the owners of the Rice tract, divided the land among them.[53]

In the early decades of its existence Memphis faced competition both from towns in Shelby County and from other villages along the middle Mississippi. Raleigh was the metropolis of the county, Randolph on the second Chickasaw bluff was the chief river town of the Western District, while Commerce, Mississippi, and three Arkansas towns which arose just opposite Memphis—Mound City, Pedraza, and Hopefield—vied with it for the river trade.[54] Yet it was not the rivalry of these towns so much as that of the competing projects on the Ramsay tract to the south of his own grant which worried Overton most. In an attempt to lessen the danger from this source, he himself bought a portion of it and persuaded General Winchester and McLemore to do likewise. After the re-election of Marcus Winchester as mayor in the spring of 1828, anti-proprietary sentiment resulted in an attempt at the organization of a new town, South Memphis by name, on the northern edge of the Ramsay tract.[55] This project was sponsored by Robert Fearn and a land company to which he sold part of his holding in 1828. Overton attempted to placate Fearn by appointing his partner, Robert Lawrence, joint agent with Marcus Winchester in 1830.[56]

McLemore eventually became more interested in Fort Pickering, the area which he owned in the Ramsay tract, than in Memphis, and he was apparently willing to double-cross Overton. "Get the property out of his [Overton's] hands," he wrote to Marcus Winchester. "It is to his interest as well as that of the town that he sell. He is getting very infirm and can't last long. My lots are not for sale at present prices."[57] The Judge, however, did not fear McLemore since he had a mutual grant with him for ferries at Fort Pickering and owned half the landing as well. McLemore outbid Memphis for the western terminal of the first Memphis-to-LaGrange railroad, but its failure in 1832 put an end to his project and almost ruined him financially.[58]

Little is known of the history of these early projects on the Ramsay tract, which later became the towns of Fort Pickering and South Memphis, for until 1840 they are shadowy entities. Apparently few people lived there at the time, and it was the potential rather than the actual threat of these settlements which worried the proprietors of Memphis. All that can be stated with any certainty is that McLemore and Overton owned part of the riparian section, and that Fearn owned a number of acres in the interior which he sold to a land company. As has been mentioned, there was an unsucccssful attempt by this land company to organize a separate town on the Fearn tract in 1828, as well as a similarly ill-fated attempt by McLemore several years later to launch a third enterprise on his riparian property. Communities known locally as South Memphis and Fort Pickering did exist during this period, but in spite of their competition with Memphis for the flatboat and steamboat trade they hardly possessed sufficient organization to be considered bona fide towns.[59]

The constant changes in the topography of the river front and the difference between the type of landing favorable to flatboats and that favorable to steamboats must always be borne in mind when this period of Memphis history is under consideration. Flatboats required an eddy and shallow water in which to dock, while deeper water was necessary to steamboats and the speed of the current did not bother them. In 1783 an eddy existed at the northern extremity of the bluff along the edge of a narrow batture; consequently Rice located his grant there with an eye to the flatboat trade. By 1819, however, the water at this point, because of the vagaries of the Mississippi, was deep and swift, while the eddy had moved south a mile or so off Fort Pickering, leaving the town of Memphis temporarily under a handicap.[60] When the eddy again moved north to its original position in the late twenties and a broader batture began to form along the northwestern base of the bluff, the flatboats immediately favored that point as a landing place. Yet as steamboats became more numerous in the thirties, they deserted the wharf along the batture at which they were accustomed to dock, and moved to the deep water just below the southern line of Memphis.[61]

Overton was troubled by considerable litigation resulting from the uncertainty of boundaries caused by the shifting of the Wolf and the Mississippi rivers. Soon after the high water of 1828 it became apparent that the batture was reappearing.[62] Several individuals, anxious to secure ferriage and wharfage rights which possession of the batture insured, staked claims on it for which they received federal warrants. Both the proprietors and the corporation regarded it as their property, and the three-cornered lawsuit which resulted was settled by compromise only when further discord would have meant the loss of the proposed navy yard in 1843.[63] Later R. K. Turnage, displaying a legal insight that would do credit to the twentieth century, insisted that there was a space between the western line of the Rice tract and the batture grants. Support was given this contention by the error of a clerk who in copying the map had sought to improve it by drawing a meandering rather than a straight line. Turnage caused local officials much worry and actually collected hundreds of dollars from gullible tenants until the courts decided the case against him.[64]

Yet the issue which engendered most hatred between inhabitants and proprietors was the question of the promenade.[65] The original agreement stated that this tract was donated as public ground to which the proprietors relinquished all claims for themselves and their heirs, "but all other rights not inconsistent with the above public rights incident to the soil, it was never the intention of the proprietors to part with, such as keeping a ferry or ferries."[66] Overton contended that the owners had not surrendered their ferriage, wharfage, and other riparian rights by the donation—in fact, he declared that he had been of the opinion, even prior to his purchase of the Rice tract in 1794, "that someday the water privilege attached to the banks would be worth more than all the lots."[67]

The first clash on this question occurred in 1828, when the populace was in an angry mood over the re-election of Winchester, upon the Judge's discovery that a road had been cut across the promenade. He offered the citizens three alternatives: the street could remain and all that part of the promenade to the north would revert to the proprietors. Should this proposal not be accepted, the street would be filled in and the promenade enclosed. If, however, they desired access to the river, he was willing to permit the construction of two streets down to the Mississippi, dividing the promenade into three equal parts, but under no condition should these streets be built upon by the corporation, proprietors, or individuals.[68]

Among the residents these proposals produced the impression that the proprietors regretted their earlier liberality and were trying by underhand means to recover their donation.[69] Overton was undoubtedly attempting to preserve a monopoly of the river front, though from his actions his immediate objective is not always clear. In 1834 a strong agitation arose for the conveyance of the promenade to the Mississippi and Atlantic Railroad Company in return for the road which Fort Pickering also desired.[70] This earlier struggle over the promenade reveals the true significance of the later litigation for the batture, which served to complicate the matter further. By a decision of the chancery court the proprietors retained their ferriage but practically lost their wharfage and other riparian rights.[71] The two blocks of river front between Poplar and Market streets became public property through which streets and alleys were cut to the water's edge. As a matter of fact, the proprietors were fortunate to come out as well as they did, for the Rice grant was really defective in that it never specifically mentioned the Mississippi River as the western boundary.[72]

In the thirties the Chickasaw Indians and the state of Mississippi made a determined attempt to wrest the bluff from Tennessee on the grounds that the southern boundary of the latter state had been incorrectly run, but a re-survey proved that the line was actually four miles too far north.[73] The outcome of the controversy disappointed Memphis citizens, who were anxious to become part of Mississippi because its cotton rated higher than that of Tennessee.[74] Jealous of Nashville and considering themselves neglected by their own state, the residents next lent their support to the project of a new state along the river which would include parts of Kentucky, Tennessee, and Mississippi.[75] That Memphis, as well as Jackson and Chickasaw, was suggested as a possible name proved no small factor in securing their support, but no action was taken at the moment. When this movement was revived in 1841 it seemed for a while that the Tennessee legislature would enact legislation favorable to the creation of a new state, but after prolonged debate the measure was finally defeated.[76]

During this long struggle Marcus Winchester became quite discouraged. "It matters little," he wrote in 1834, "whether the railroad terminates at Fort Pickering . . . or Randolph or Fulton. In either event the young Memphis must be merged into its greater rival. . . . As a town, it is not probable that we have anything the advantage over Fort Pickering. As a landing place it has decidedly the advantage over the one we now use."[77]

To such despondency, however, Overton never succumbed, even if he was "getting very infirm."

It is obvious from the preceding pages that, to the extent that one man can make a town, John Overton made Memphis. Jackson did next to nothing; General Winchester provided little besides money; and McLemore strayed off after other gods. But Overton, working through Marcus Winchester, the Tennessee legislature, and every medium which happened to be at hand, was ever a watchful and devoted patron of the little village. No matter was too petty for his attention. At one time he is found writing a glowing description of the new town for the Philadelphia *Portfolio;* at another, he is chiding Winchester and Carr for failing to provide wood for the steamboats; berating Memphis editors for lack of publicity regarding the town; or trying to buy Widow Foy's property across the river before she learns that an act in Congress for a projected Memphis-to-St. Francis railroad will increase its value tenfold.[78] In the formative period of Memphis the energy of Overton was the determining factor. Once such an enterprise were well established the efforts of a single individual would count for little, but in its initial stages, particularly under the conditions peculiar to the Western District in the twenties, the genius of the Judge meant much.

Yet it must be said that Overton's motives do not seem to have included any concern for the welfare of the people or the future of the country, but to have been the mere desire for the accumulation of wealth. In his nature there was not an iota of magnanimity or generosity; if he rendered a trivial service to Jackson and Winchester, his closest friends, he, the richest man in Tennessee, demanded his pound of flesh.[79] Working for Memphis, he was working for himself, and that was the limit of his horizon. Small and almost mean though he was, John Overton alone begot, played midwife to, and nurtured the childhood health of the town upon the bluff.

CHAPTER III

FLATBOAT TOWN

In the first stage of American urban development all cities, such as Boston, New York, Philadelphia, and Charleston, lay adjacent to the Atlantic coast. When the advent of the steamboat and of the railroad in the first half of the nineteenth century made rapid transportation possible in the interior, urban growth entered its second phase, and inland towns, such as Louisville, St. Louis, Chicago, Buffalo, Memphis, and Atlanta, came into being. After the Civil War the final era of American urban history began; as the Industrial Revolution progressed in the United States during this epoch, proximity to deposits of coal and iron converted older towns like Pittsburgh and Detroit into large manufacturing centers and produced new industrial cities like Birmingham.

The history of Memphis in the nineteenth century falls into three definite periods. From 1820 to 1840, though a tough and uninviting hole overrun by the scum of the river, it bested its local rival Randolph in a life-and-death struggle and put itself in a position to profit fully from the technological development in transportation that was soon to reach its height. In the next three decades, in spite of the blighting effect of war upon its hinterland in the sixties, Memphis enjoyed a riotous progress which was the direct product of the steamboat and the railroad. During these thirty years its population increased from eighteen hundred to forty thousand. In 1860 it was the first city of Tennessee in size and the acknowledged mistress of the Mississippi between New Orleans and St. Louis. By 1870 it was fifth in population in the entire South and, together with Louisville and New Orleans, a metropolis of the region south of the Ohio between the Ozarks and the Appalachians. Just as it had about recovered from the war, Memphis was smitten in the seventies by three devastating epidemics of yellow fever, a catastrophe which cannot be overemphasized in its effect upon the city's future. After a remarkable recovery, however, in 1900 it emerged with a population of more than a hundred thousand, third in rank among the towns of the New South.

TABLE I

LEADING SOUTHERN CITIES, 1820-1930

1820	Rank in Nation	Population	1840	Rank in Nation	Population
1. New Orleans...	5	27,176	1. New Orleans...	3	102,193
2. Charleston.....	6	24,780	2. Charleston.....	10	29,261
3. Richmond.....	12	12,067	3. Louisville......	16	21,210
4. Norfolk........	16	8,478	4. Richmond.....	20	20,153
5. Savannah......	18	7,523	5. Mobile........	30	12,672
6. Petersburg.....	28	6,690	6. Savannah......	34	11,214
7. Lexington, Ky..	36	5,229	7. Petersburg.....	35	11,136
8. Louisville......	..	4,012	8. Norfolk........	38	10,920
9. Natchez.......	..	2,184	9. Lexington......	..	6,997
10. Russellville, Ky.	..	1,712	10. Nashville......	..	6,929
1860			**1880**		
1. New Orleans...	6	168,675	1. New Orleans...	10	216,090
2. Louisville......	12	68,033	2. Louisville......	16	123,758
3. Charleston.....	22	40,522	3. Richmond......	25	63,600
4. Richmond.....	25	37,910	4. Charleston.....	36	49,984
5. Mobile........	27	29,258	5. Nashville......	40	43,340
6. MEMPHIS......	38	22,623	6. Atlanta........	49	37,409
7. Savannah......	41	22,292	7. MEMPHIS......	..	33,592
8. Petersburgh....	50	18,266	8. Savannah......	..	30,709
9. Nashville......	..	16,988	9. Norfolk........	..	21,966
10. Covington, Ky..	..	16,471	10. Augusta.......	..	21,891
1900			**1930**		
1. New Orleans...	12	287,104	1. New Orleans...	16	458,762
2. Louisville......	18	204,731	2. Louisville......	24	307,745
3. MEMPHIS......	37	102,320	3. Houston.......	26	292,352
4. Atlanta........	43	89,872	4. Atlanta........	32	270,366
5. Richmond.....	46	85,050	5. Dallas.........	33	260,475
6. Nashville......	47	80,865	6. Birmingham....	34	259,678
7. Charleston.....	..	55,807	7. MEMPHIS......	36	253,153
8. Savannah......	..	54,244	8. San Antonio....	38	231,542
9. San Antonio....	..	53,321	9. Richmond.....	44	182,929
10. Norfolk........	..	46,624	10. Fort Worth....	48	163,447

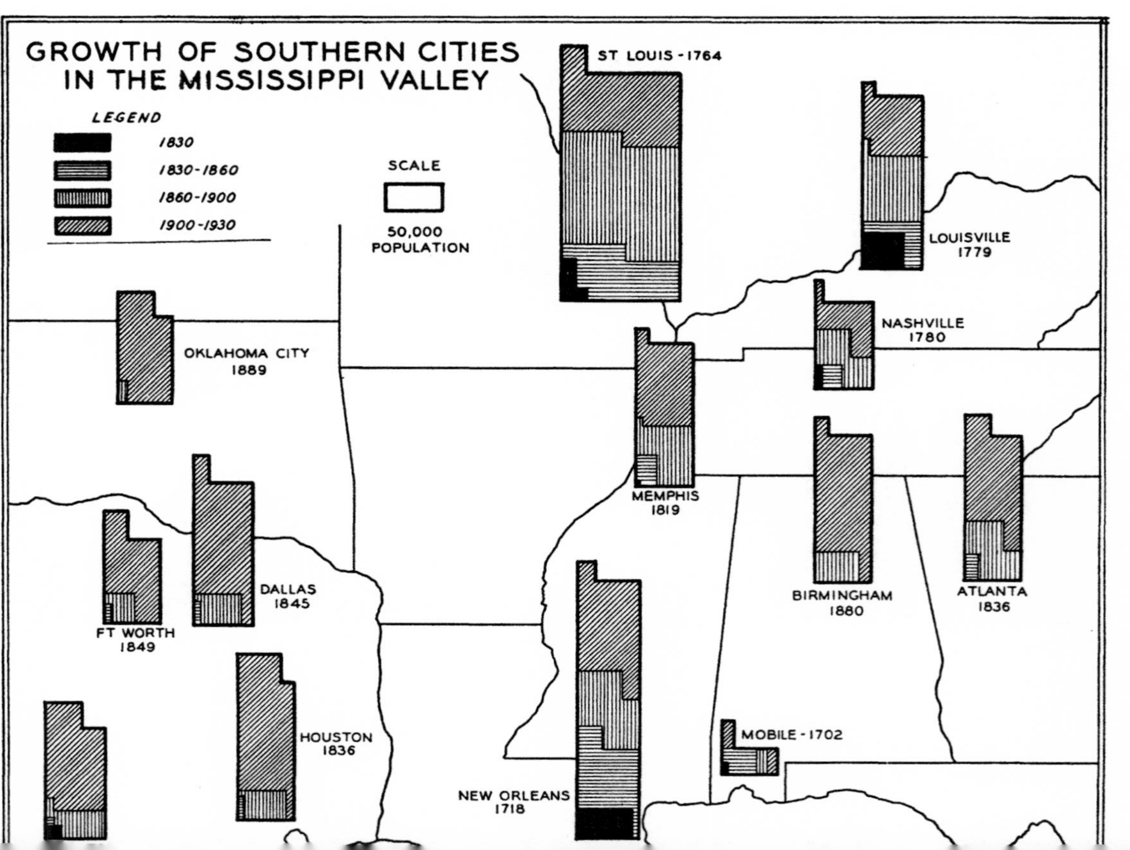
GROWTH OF SOUTHERN CITIES
IN THE MISSISSIPPI VALLEY
LEGEND
1830
1830-1860
1860-1900
1900-1930
SCALE
50,000
POPULATION
ST LOUIS - 1764
LOUISVILLE
1779
NASHVILLE
1780
OKLAHOMA CITY
1889
MEMPHIS
1819
BIRMINGHAM
1880
ATLANTA
1836
DALLAS
1845
FT WORTH
1849
HOUSTON
1836
MOBILE - 1702
NEW ORLEANS
1718

EXPLANATION OF CHART

Name	Date of Origin	Population 1830		Population 1860	Population 1900	Population 1930
St. Louis*	1764	16,469	(1840)	160,773	575,238	821,960
New Orleans	1718	46,082		168,675	287,104	458,762
Louisville	1779	30,289		68,033	204,731	307,745
MEMPHIS	1819	663		22,623	102,320	253,153
Nashville	1780	5,566		16,988	80,865	153,866
Mobile	1702	3,194		29,258	38,469	68,202
Atlanta	1836	.....		9,554	89,872	270,366
San Antonio	1716	5,000	(approx.)	8,235	53,321	231,542
Houston	1836	.....		4,845	44,633	292,352
Dallas	1845	.....	(1871)	5,000	42,638	260,475
Fort Worth	1849	.....	(1873)	4,000	26,688	163,447
Birmingham	1880	.....		.....	38,415	259,678
Oklahoma City*	1889	.....		.....	10,037	185,389

* Not southern, but included for purposes of comparison.

When Marcus Winchester arrived at Chickasaw Bluffs early in 1819, he must have been dismayed by the sight which greeted him.[1] Buried in the thick wilderness that then covered most of West Tennessee, the settlement contained only half a dozen white men—Ike Rawlings, Tom Fletcher, Paddy Meagher, and Joab Bean, who traded with the Indians, and the Carr brothers who had recently stopped there upon hearing rumors of the Jackson Purchase.[2] The only roads leading to the bluff were the Cherokee Trace from North Alabama and the Chickasaw Trace from Mississippi. With the exception of Foy's Point across the river, there was no other white settlement within seventy-five miles, and the few steamboats on the river rarely stopped at the place.

After the removal of the garrison a few years earlier, the little community had disintegrated as rapidly as had the fort. Isaac Rawlings, sutler for Jackson's army, had tarried there in 1813 to set up a store for Indian trade. Prospering in this pursuit, thanks to the exorbitant prices he was able to charge ignorant natives, Rawlings, like Foy across the river, soon became a person of authority.[3] When Marcus Winchester arrived in 1819 and founded a trading establishment of much superior quality, not only was Rawlings' social position threatened but his commercial future as well. It is not strange that for the next fifteen years the rivalry between them, though not always bitter, was intense and unchanging.

The population of Memphis in its first decade was 53 in 1820, 308 in 1825, and 663 in 1830, though these estimates may have been padded with Indians.[4] Until 1824 the efforts of Overton to attract settlers met with little success. Business was restricted to the activities of three firms, Rawlings, Winchester and Carr, and Henderson and Fearn, whose total trade of less than two thousand dollars a month was entirely with Indians. Barter was the method of exchange, and in return for peltry of deer, cow, bear, beaver, wildcat, and coon the red men received clothes, whisky, and sundry articles that appealed to their naïve tastes.[5]

In 1824, a year which witnessed the visits of two such different figures as La Fayette, who came in state, and Davy Crockett, who was rescued from a sinking flatboat, occurred an influx of immigrants possessed of more means and more ability than the earlier inhabitants.[6] The resulting diversity of trades made the town practically self-sufficient for its simple needs; yet for some years the Jackson (Tennessee) *Gazette* continued to refer to it as "the village on the Mississippi better known as Chickasaw Bluffs."[7] About this time Memphis became an entrepôt for flatboatmen, who for a score of years were to be its chief source of wealth and, next to mud, its greatest menace.

Before the heyday of the steamboat and the advent of turnpikes, when water was the sole means of transportation in the valley, farmers built rude but easily assembled flatboats or "broadhorns," in which they floated their produce downstream to various markets along the Mississippi, where they sold the cargo for whatever it would bring. Then the boats would be broken up for lumber, and after a carousal which often lasted as long as their money held out, the boatmen returned home, usually on foot, through a robber-infested country. New Orleans, Natchez, and Vicksburg were distant markets, but on the middle Mississippi Memphis battled with Randolph, thirty miles to the north, for this trade.

Barges and keelboats were larger craft engaged in upstream as well as downstream traffic, which required the services of a skilled crew. The flatboat, however, floated only with the current, requiring no exertion on the part of its occupants, but it was very difficult to steer. It derived its name from the fact that its bottom, in contrast to that of the keelboat, was perfectly flat; in reality it was little more than a raft with perpendicular sides and a roof for protection against the elements. In early days whole families emigrated down the Ohio in flatboats. Later their chief use was in floating produce from the back-country of the lower valley to the nearest market at high water.[8] In the Memphis region they carried largely cotton, but corn, hogs, whisky, tobacco, and anything else that was salable might be included in the cargo.

These flatboatmen must be distinguished from the lawless professional rivermen like Mike Fink, who boasted of being "half horse and half alligator." On the contrary, the former were respected and often religious members of their own communities, though on the long voyage to market they often assumed different personalities and became veritable Mr. Hydes.[9] They despised the "barbarians" of the river towns, whose attempts to collect wharfage fees they considered postively "onconstitutional."[10] Arriving in Memphis singly or in groups, they completely controlled the settlement, and citizens retired for safety as soon as business was transacted.[11] Until their suppression in 1842 these transients ruled the town, refused to pay wharfage, and violated laws at their pleasure. Only low water could give harassed Memphians a temporary, but not even then complete, respite.

Some attempts to bring order out of this chaos were initiated, but all in vain. The county court which met on the bluff from 1820 until 1827 was a conservative force, but its attention was devoted more to such matters as fining Paddy Meagher one dollar and costs for retailing spirits without license.[12] With the incorporation of 1826 the residents elected Winchester mayor, swearing that they "would never again be run over by flatboatmen,"[13] but they were forced to eat their words many times. The opposition of Rawlings and the anti-proprietary faction denied local officials any real support, and they faced their problems under a handicap that no amount of ability on Winchester's part could have offset.

Winchester and Rawlings, around whom most of the early history of Memphis is woven, deserve more than passing mention, though now a century after their day they have become somewhat mythical characters. Ike Rawlings, possessed of meager education and no background, was one of those inexplicable geniuses occasionally found in out-of-the-way places. His native common sense, shrewdness, and acute sense of equity made him at once the leader of his fellows, who carried to him for judgment all of their problems. Never was there an appeal from his decisions, and the punishments he ordered were executed thoroughly without the aid of any police. When organized government came to the Western District, the legislature recognized his talent by conferring on him the title of magistrate. In spite of this honor, the "Squire," cursed with an inordinate vanity, was subject to a lifelong jealousy of the more polished Winchester, though the latter continued to treat him with the utmost fairness and generosity.

The superiority of his young rival's establishment and location forced Ike to move his store from the northern extremity of the town (Anderson's Bridge on Gayoso Bayou) down into the center where the little commerce of the day was transacted. He then proceeded to buy a new lot of supplies, which he carefully marked with the prices he had charged the Indians. Out of stubbornness, not necessity, since he was well off, he insisted on maintaining "mark and price which neither time nor decay could alter,"[14] and soon his store became a mere magistrate's office.

The enmity of Rawlings to the proprietors and to Winchester personally was the foremost obstacle to the progress of the town. Much to everyone's surprise, when because of

Winchester's ineligibility Rawlings became mayor in 1829, he supervised its affairs with minute care, becoming as active a supporter of its development as he had formerly been an enemy. Serving in this capacity for five terms with a single interval from 1831 to 1833, he entered the campaign for delegate to the state constitutional convention of 1834, pronouncing himself, as did his three opponents, opposed to slavery and in favor of some feasible plan of removing its curse.[15] Unsuccessful in this attempt, he continued his private activities, among them the organization of the town's first bank and first insurance company. The last public appearance of this eccentric but colorful figure was in 1840, when he was carried to the polls in a chair by two Negroes to cast his vote for "Tippecanoe and Tyler too." There, since his doctor had given up hope for his life, the Democrats challenged his vote on the ground that he was a dead man, but the judges compassionately ignored the protest.

Winchester was all that Rawlings was not. Mild in disposition, modest, handsome, and well educated, he was one upon whom the world must thrust its honors. As a major on his father's staff in 1812, he was captured by the British in the disaster at Raisin River. His reputation, in contrast to that of Rawlings, was more than local—in fact it was rumored that he could have obtained from Jackson any position he desired. As will later appear, he was radical in his attitude toward the Negro, and he kept a strict account for all his slaves with a view to their eventual emancipation. That he was no provincial is apparent from the fact that Mrs. Trollope, who delivered a tirade on domestic manners in America at that time, considered him a "gentleman-like man . . . misplaced in a little town on the Mississippi."[16] Mrs. Anne Royall, editor of *Paul Pry,* the contemporary "Washington Merry-Go-Round," never tired of singing his praises.[17]

Tragedy early entered Winchester's life when Thomas H. Benton of Missouri, seeing visions for the first time of a political future, decided to cast off his mistress, a beautiful French quadroon, for the socially more valuable institution of matrimony. Making liberal provisions for her future, he placed her in the care of Winchester as trustee, who to Benton's amazement took her to Louisiana, where the law permitted such unions, and married her. This was too much for young Memphis, liberal as it was in its attitude toward the Negro. Rawlings lived with his housekeeper, but she was a slave and he did not dignify the relationship with a formal title; Winchester's wife was a free quadroon, beautiful and accomplished, whom he chose to recognize as an equal. The social stigma under which this marriage placed him preyed constantly upon his sensitive nature, and as he grew older he sought escape from the trying situation in drink.[18]

During the first few years of his residence on the bluff, Winchester was much in demand as a financial expert because of the complicated currency of the frontier and the wide prevalence of counterfeit money. Later, as a result of his proprietary connection and his unfortunate marriage, gamblers and other undesirables whom he held in check joined with respectable puritans, a paradoxical union not unknown to later generations, in an attempt to drive him from the community. There were those, however, who appreciated his true worth, for when he became a Democratic candidate for the legislature, the Whigs made no allusion to his personal affairs. As is often the case, the same society which had made his life unbearable canonized him after his death. "There was never a member of any community," wrote the *Appeal* in the seventies, "more esteemed while he lived or more honored at his death than Major Marcus B. Winchester, the most graceful, courtly, elegant gentleman that ever appeared on Main Street."[19]

The Western District of Tennessee, a rectangular area between the Tennessee and Mississippi rivers containing roughly eleven thousand square miles, slopes gently westward from an elevation of almost 700 feet above sea level on the east to little more than 200 feet on the west. It falls into three natural divisions: the extremely narrow valley of the Tennessee at the foot of the rocky ridge on its eastern edge; the wide central plateau of sandy loam soil; and the alluvial bottoms along the Mississippi, rarely more than twelve miles in width and generally only two or three. The mean annual temperature of this region is 62 degrees, 43 for winter and 78 for summer. Its annual rainfall of from 48 to 52 inches, the heaviest along the Mississippi, produces a long growing season of from 190 days in the northeast to 219 days in the more fertile southwest.[20]

The low central plateau, which includes practically the whole district, is drained by several medium-sized rivers, which flow westward into the Mississippi. The four main streams, the Obion, the Forked Deer, the Hatchie, and the Wolf, separate in the interior into numerous branches, so that early settlers, regardless of their location, were able to float their crops down to market at high water. The bluff region in the southwest requires detailed description. Between Nonconnah Creek, near the boundary of the state of Mississippi, and Wolf River several miles to the north, stands the fourth or lower Chickasaw bluff. The Wolf, perhaps one hundred miles in length, was never navigable to steamboats for any considerable distance. Near its mouth it is joined by the Loosahatchie, a somewhat smaller stream. Forty or fifty miles north of the lower bluff by water the largest river of the district, the Hatchie, empties into the Mississippi. Here to the north, at Fulton, the first Chickasaw bluff rises; to the south is the second, the site of Randolph; and halfway between Randolph and Memphis stands the third.[21]

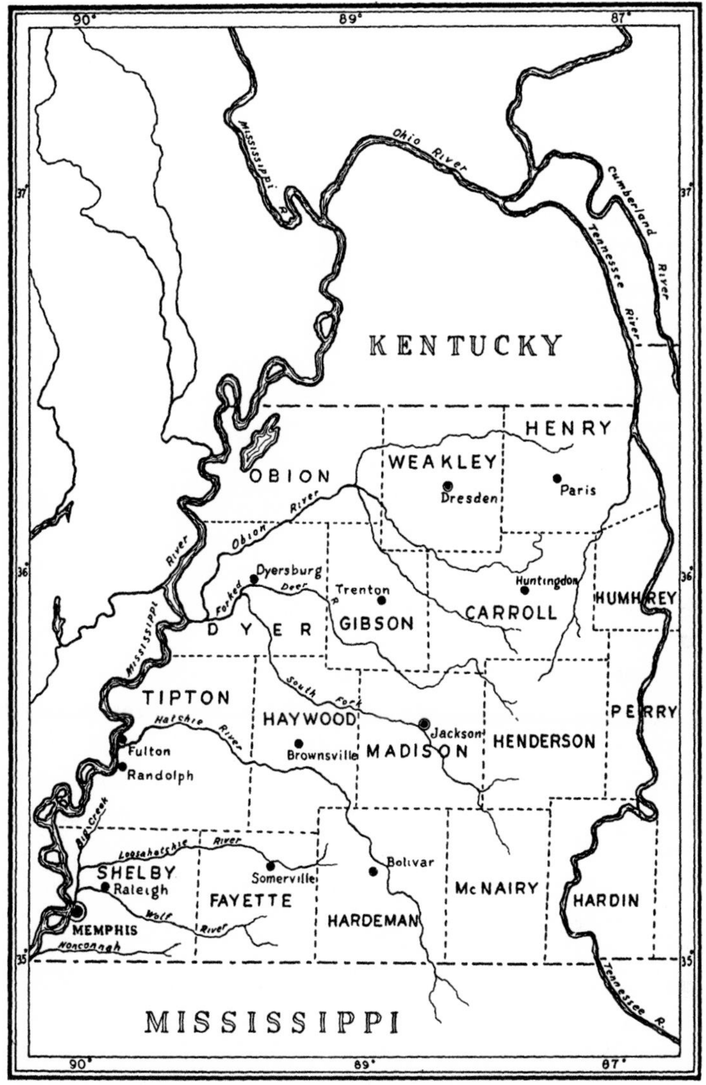

THE WESTERN DISTRICT ABOUT 1830

The first white settlers of the district were not all perennial transients on an eternal hegira toward the setting sun, for many of them were emigrants from the settled regions of Virginia, North Carolina, South Carolina, and Tennessee,[22] whom hard times at home and the soaring price of cotton had sent westward in search of richer land. Not inferior to the average Americans of their day,[23] often they were so poor that they could not retreat from the hard life of the wilderness, much as they might desire to do so, and for several years they barely succeeded in keeping their families from starving.[24] In most cases they were squatters, not by choice but by necessity, for the speculators and the state of North Carolina had early grabbed all the valuable land in the district, and until 1841 Congress refused to cede the remainder to the state.[25] It was this group of squatters for whom Crockett fought and from whom he derived support.

The district filled so rapidly after 1819 that there were fourteen counties wholly within its limits by 1823. The increase of its population from roughly twenty-five hundred in 1820[26] to approximately one hundred thousand in 1830 and to almost two hundred thousand in 1840 made Tennessee one of the larger states of the Union. Corn, wheat, tobacco, and cotton were its principal crops, but the last was soon raised in such quantities that it consumed most of the acreage. Though the majority of Tennesseans in 1860 owned few slaves or none at all, nevertheless in that year West Tennessee had three blacks for every five whites, while the ratio for Middle Tennessee was one to three and for East Tennessee only one to twelve.[27] With this increasing concentration on cotton, the river counties, which earlier had been shunned because of the universal belief that they were unhealthy, began to fill up in the thirties when it was discovered that the riparian region was little if any more sickly than the rest of the valley, and Shelby cotton won the medal at a London Exposition as the best in the world.[28] In need of a sound currency and of internal improvements to bring markets closer, these rich southwestern counties gave Henry Clay and his American System their whole-hearted support.

Though the town of Jackson was the political and cultural center of the district, its trade outlet, determined by the pull of gravity, was toward the southwest. Memphis in the extreme corner, with Indian land to the south, a dense wilderness to the east in the direction of Nashville, and fifty miles of overflowed bottoms to the west, had little chance at first of becoming its point of export.[29] Randolph, founded in 1823 farther north on the second bluff at the mouth of the Hatchie, which, navigable as far inland as Bolivar, drained the heart of the most populous section of the district, was a location much superior.[30] Boasting twenty-two business houses during its prime in the thirties, Randolph until 1836 not only shipped more cotton than Memphis[31] but also served as the steamboat depot of West Tennessee. Much of this prosperity was the result of several epidemics which occurred on the lower bluff, cholera in 1826 and 1832, the dengue or break-bone fever in 1827, and yellow fever in 1828.[32] This first attack of the disease which was to prove the near-destruction of Memphis fifty years later produced fifty-three deaths in one hundred and fifty cases in 1828 and gave the town a reputation for unhealthiness, which frightened flatboatmen and steamboats away to Randolph.[33] In the next decade the only cotton received on the lower bluff came by wagon from the immediate vicinity, and the number of flatboats decreased considerably. In fact, had the much-discussed Hatchie-Tennessee canal been constructed,[34] Memphis would probably have become a mere village and Randolph a metropolis, but Jackson's veto of the Maysville Road bill doomed projects for internal improvement which required financial aid from the federal government.

The victory of the town on the lower bluff, noticeable only after 1838, was the result of a series of events which had begun a decade earlier. In 1829 a tri-weekly mail line of four-horse coaches was established between Jackson and Memphis by way of Bolivar, Somerville, and Raleigh, while only a weekly one-horse mail was set up between Jackson and Randolph by way of Brownsville and Covington.[35] Both routes passed through sparsely settled regions, but soon the heavier traffic on the Somerville road caused that section to grow more rapidly than the back-country of Randolph. The purchase of the remaining Chickasaw land in northern Mississippi by the federal government in 1834 and the ensuing removal of the Indians gave Memphis a rich new hinterland, which throughout its history has proved a constant source of prosperity. As the area south and east of the town developed, so did the town.

The Panic of 1837 hit the river counties hard, and Randolph, their commercial center, suffered in particular.[36] As a final blow, in 1838 extremely low water diverted steamboats and the cotton trade to Memphis. Even before this last catastrophe an exodus of the former's merchants, led by Frank Latham, editor of the *Randolph Recorder,* had started toward the lower bluff.[37] There was to be but one town in the district, a town that was certain to be on one of the Chickasaw Bluffs, and by 1840 it was apparent that the lower bluff would be its location.

While it is true that natural forces like soil, climate, and topography determine the general location of a town, the personal equation often determines the specific site. The middle Mississippi stood in need of a port between St. Louis and New Orleans; in 1835 it seemed that Randolph, a spontaneous settlement, would be that port; yet a decade later there was no doubt that Memphis, its proprietary rival, had succeeded it. This victory of the town on the lower bluff may have been the direct or indirect result of Overton's efforts, but the future of the metropolis that would arise on one of the Chickasaw Bluffs was predestined in prehistoric times when the waters receded from the ocean which then covered most of the Mississippi Valley.

A better example than Memphis of the importance of location is hard to find. In wealth, culture, political influence, and calibre of citizens, Nashville, with forty more years of tradition behind it, was far superior to the village of the twenties on the bluff; yet by 1860 the latter, because of its more advantageous location, had outstripped the state capital in population and volume of business.

The geographical influences affecting the growth of Memphis are numerous. Firmly entrenched on one of the few available river sites south of the Ohio, it early became a river town second only to New Orleans and St. Louis. Its position in the center of the South later made it a terminal of almost every railroad, thus placing it on the east-west trade route as well as the north-south. Located in the heart of the richest cotton region in the world and one of the most extensive hardwood lumber forests in the United States, it has long served as a shipping point for these raw products. To a hinterland, huge because of the vast distance between cities in the South and always able and anxious to buy because of its staple economy, Memphis has annually distributed quantities of manufactured goods and food products. In any analysis of its economic development there must be constant mention of cotton and lumber, river and railroad, marketing and distribution.[38]

Competition from Randolph was not the only threat to the permanence of Memphis in the flatboat era. The potential danger of Fort Pickering and South Memphis, rival communities on the same bluff, long a source of worry to the proprietors, was accentuated by an internal schism in the town itself, which arose early and lasted long. To a particularly wide part of Gayoso Bayou near its junction with Wolf River on the northern extremity of the village was given the name Catfish Bay, and here flatboats and houseboats gathered to escape the swift waters of the Mississippi. Here, too, the poorer folk came because of the quantity of rubbish lumber about. Early in its existence this neighborhood acquired the name of Pinch,[39] a sobriquet at first resented by its residents, as it was later cherished. Always sound on the "poor-man question," in early days its denizens were ever harangued by Davy Crockett and local demagogues.[40] Throughout the city's history Pinch has been noted for its poverty; the Irish congregated there in great numbers during the fifties, and when the fever decimated them in the seventies the Negroes succeeded them as residents.[41]

That Crockett wooed Pinch is sufficient proof of its early political power, but there is evidence even more convincing. Mayor Rawlings, objecting to the pungent stench of dead fish in its hot and almost stagnant waters, caused a nuisance ordinance to be passed in 1831 to remove that condition. The cause of the Pinchites, who declared the ordinance a broadside at themselves because of their poverty and a violation of their constitutional rights, was taken up by Seth Wheatley, a young lawyer who possessed all the qualifications of the demagogue, and together they easily defeated Rawlings in the next election. Their triumph was short-lived, however, for a few nights later a sheet of tan-ooze and filth, released from Carr's tannery by unknown parties, floated down the bayou upon the unsuspecting victors. All human life was forced to leave the neighborhood at once, and with the help of fellow citizens the houseboats were moved to an eddy in the Mississippi which fortunately had formed along the northern extremity of the bluff.[42]

Feeling died down until 1837, when the practice of addressing aldermen by the name of the ward they represented revived the issue on a new and larger basis. The third ward, from Winchester Street south to Howard's Row (Union Street), though sparsely settled was larger in area than the first two wards together,[43] which the name Pinch now included. Because of the constant enlargement of the batture in the river off Pinch, there was a strong tendency for the steamboat landing and the related business to move south to the deep water of the third ward, which the Pinchites in derision had named Sodom.[44] To prevent this natural southward movement city officials refused to allow any roads to be cut from Front Street down the bluff to the river south of Market Street, thus cutting the third ward completely off from the river, and they discriminated against it in other ways. The matter came to a head in 1837 when Hart, a United States mail agent, moved his wharf boat south to Howard's Row just below the corporation line, half a mile from the nearest hotel. Municipal officials haughtily but vainly ordered him to return, and the bitter feeling thus created led to a powerful agitation in Sodom, encouraged by South Memphis, to secede from the town.[45]

Pinch made several determined attempts to save the steamboat landing. A high levee was built along the bluff, and a huge bridge and wharf were constructed over the batture, but neither device proved successful.[46] Though W. A. Bickford erected an entire block of three-story buildings on Exchange Square, many merchants moved to Front Row in Sodom.[47] When Pinch, frightened by the ardor of the secession movement, finally realized that the flatboat trade, which it retained, was far more valuable than that of the steamboats, it hastened to make concessions to Sodom. As evidence of its desire for reconciliation it even allowed the third ward to be divided into three new wards, thus giving the southern section of town the controlling vote in the corporation.[48] That Pinch was partially holding its own can be seen from the fact that investors who came in during 1841 preferred property in the first two wards.[49] The emotional disturbance accompanying this strife, however, was not alleviated, and a contemporary remarked with surprise that there could be so much fervent hate with so little bloodshed.[50]

As might be gathered from this Pinch-Sodom affair, life in a flatboat town was rude and rough, for few of the conservative forces of organized communities were present. In the twenties there was no "society" worthy of the name, since the few respectable white women dared not appear in public for fear of drunken Indians or boatmen, to say nothing of the male residents themselves. Because of a lack of females of their own race, a few men married Indians or Negroes, but most of the male population were content merely to live with them in a state of concubinage.[51] The number of red and black women to be had for the taking prevented any demand for white prostitutes which might otherwise have arisen; consequently Memphis was a "pure town" until 1830, when a tavern proprietor, in imitation of urban ways, established a bawdy house.[52] Every frontier settlement had its "doggery," or whisky store, and with Dean's Best selling at twenty-five cents a gallon, many declared that they never intended to drink water while whisky sold at that price.[53] Perhaps their decision was wise, for throughout the ante-bellum period Wolf River furnished the water supply of Memphians.

Houses were mere cabins of roughhewn logs until sawmills in the thirties permitted architectural improvement, and bears occasionally roamed in the streets, which were so full of deep holes that as late as 1843 an ox team pulling a wagon on the main street drowned in one.[54] Meal was made in the primitive manner of pounding corn in a mortar with a pestle, and before the advent of a physician several white settlers resorted to the treatment of Indian medicinemen.[55] Full beards were considered indecent, only a narrow strip of whiskers from the temple along the edge of the jaw to the mouth or chin being customary.

In 1824 there was not enough silver in Memphis to "buy a coonskin," a situation which forced merchants to resort to "cut money"; that is, quarters were cut into "bits" (twelve and a half cents) and bits into "picayunes" (six and a quarter cents).[56] The only coins in circulation were the Mexican dollar, the old Spanish dollar, and the French five-franc piece, while the only paper currency consisted of Tennessee, Georgia, and North Carolina state notes which the Tidewater would accept only at a considerable discount.[57] It is hardly necessary to add that this condition made counterfeiting easy and profitable, and that banking in a frontier town was rather crude. Because of this shortage of currency and specie, merchants extended credit freely until the trek to Texas forced them to restrict that privilege. Indians, incidentally, proved ideal customers, for they never abused the credit so lavishly extended them nor did they ever dispute accounts.[58]

Though it was held the deadliest of sins by the devout,[59] dancing was a popular diversion. He who played a fiddle or a banjo was welcome everywhere, and the favorite songs of the day were "Old Zip Coon," "Row, Boatman, Row," and "Arkansas Traveler."[60] Militia musters were occasions on which everyone turned out to see the drill to the strains of "Yankee Doodle" and "Jay-Bird Died of the Whooping-Cough." An abundance of pies, cakes, cider, beer, and "red-eye" prepared the crowd for the real event of the day —the fights in the late afternoon. Before the advent of the formal duel these musters were the usual place to settle all grievances, and combatants fought with hands, teeth, and feet until one of them was "whipped."[61] In cases where the insult was of a deeper nature, knives, pistols, or rifles might be used.

Horse racing was even then an amusement of a more or less élite group, but nothing approached the camp meeting as a social gathering for all ages, regardless of sex. "Races, fairs, and monkey-shows," says Davis, "were comparatively small concerns, as these drew only the wicked and were suspended on Sundays, while the camp meeting drew all sorts, particularly the women, who of course drew the men."[62] The services, which lasted a week, were held out from town in a shady grove on the Raleigh Road where a stage and a "bull-pen," filled with straw to prevent injury to the mourners who got the "jerks," had been constructed. Certain features of the Memphis meetings may have been unique. Within a quarter of a mile from the main shed were a dozen piles of brush beneath which were concealed barrels of whisky for the convenience of the congregation. Courting was the chief occupation of the younger folk at these gatherings: "For a mile or more around the camp-ground the woods seem alive with people; every tree or bush has its couple, while hundreds of others are seen prowling around in search of some cozy spot."[63]

Before the community was opulent enough to afford church buildings it was served by "journeymen-soulsavers," but the chief significance of the camp meeting lies in the fact that it was the center of social and not merely religious life. Davis, an excellent and at times objective critic of his own day, saw it in this light, but there were those who thought otherwise. "At no former period in this state," commented the Jackson *Gazette* in 1829, "has there been such a general revival of religion as is now going on in the Western District. . . . Under its influence the beastly practice of drunkenness will be driven from the county."[64] This may have been true in the conservative interior around Jackson, but in early Memphis religious activity was as crude as the town itself. He who felt the call of God did not lack listeners, and no community of a dozen families or less was without its Jeremiah. "Strange to say," observed a contemporary, "the call generally fell on those most ignorant in matters of this world, but most astonishingly knowing in reference to the world to come."[65] The visit of the circuit rider was a signal for a holiday of prayer and feasting, marked by the cessation of work by all hands, white and black, and by a wholesale massacre of fowls. Hellfire-and-brimstone ranting by the "shepherd" and "jerks" on the part of the flock were accepted conventions,[66] and piety seemed a matter of strong lungs and bodily antics.

Many settlers came to the district in the twenties from regions where the church was a central institution, and the majority of them were Methodists or Baptists.[67] As might be expected, wicked Memphis was less susceptible to the religious impulse than the interior; yet it had its voices crying in the wilderness. Uncle Harry Lawrence, a Negro who often preached to mixed congregations, was the first in point of time of these amateur exhorters on the bluff,[68] but his fame was soon eclipsed by two white competitors, Elijah Coffey and Silas T. Toncray. Coffey, a shoemaker and a Freewill Baptist, who left a wife and an unsavory reputation behind him in Illinois, arrived in Memphis on a Sunday morning in March of 1822, and he had hardly landed before he was reproaching the residents, at a service in the cabin of Barney Flynn on the batture, for their sinful lives.[69] During his career he belonged to all denominations, even the Catholic, but he severed his connection with the latter when he discovered that it did not encourage preaching by laymen. Toncray, a Hard-shell Baptist as well as a silversmith, watch-maker, engraver, sign-painter, druggist, dentist, and doctor, preached mostly to Negroes, constructing an African church at his own expense later in his career. Both Elijah and Silas served on the board of aldermen, and Coffey even discharged the duties of mayor for a brief period.[70]

Yet there was evidence of the beginnings of organized religion in the twenties. A. J. Crawford of the Methodist Forked Deer Circuit probably preached in Memphis in

1822, and W. C. Blair, a Presbyterian missionary to the Chickasaws, followed him a year or so later.[71] Thomas Davidson, a Methodist circuit rider, appeared in 1826, as did the eccentric free lance, Lorenzo Dow, who returned to keep an appointment made two years before.[72] The Reverend Sam Wilkinson of the Presbyterian Church and the Reverend William Whitsett of the Cumberland Presbyterian arrived in 1829 to "labor for the Lord."[73] About 1830 two Methodist ministers, P. T. Scruggs and F. A. Owen, were stationed regularly in Memphis, but they were too reserved and too intelligent to be popular in a flatboat town.[74]

These pioneer labors resulted in the formation of the nuclei of future congregations, forced by poverty to use as temples of worship the meetinghouse in Court Square, erected in 1826, or private homes, warehouses, saloons, carpenter shops, and whatever structures were available.[75] In a rude cabin on Wolf River Davidson began preaching in 1826 to a small group which ultimately became the First Methodist Church. Under the pastorate of Owen, this congregation in 1832 completed the construction of Wesley Chapel, the first church erected in the town. Two years later the First Presbyterian, organized by the missionary Blair in 1828, announced the completion of a similar structure. After eleven years of effort Whitsett assembled a Cumberland Presbyterian congregation, and the previous year witnessed the formal inauguration of the First Baptist.[76] In 1832 Bishop Ives of North Carolina sent to the district its first Episcopal clergyman, the Reverend Thomas Wright. Before Wright died of yellow fever three years later he organized and became rector of Calvary Church in Memphis.[77] In 1839 mass was celebrated by Father Stokes of Nashville in the home of the Irish schoolmaster, Eugene Magevney, and Father McAleer, sent to Memphis soon afterwards to guide the spiritual life of its ten Catholics.

erected St. Peters Church, which was placed in the care of the Dominicans.[78]

Near Memphis in the late twenties was conducted one of the strangest social experiments America has witnessed, an experiment which has been described by one critic as "Brook Farm plus a Negro basis," and by another, who saw it only in the days of its decline, as "one great brothel."[79] Miss Frances Wright, a Scots woman who in 1818 had visited the United States, where she became a protégée of General La Fayette, returned in 1824 to found a model society for the emancipation of slaves. Through La Fayette's friend, Andrew Jackson, she purchased two thousand acres of land on Wolf River a few miles outside of Memphis.[80] This estate she named Nashoba (Chickasaw word for "wolf"), and here she established a co-operative community which was an eclectic product of Economie, Pennsylvania, Rappite teachings, and bits of Benjamin Lundy, Robert Owen, and La Fayette. Negroes were bought, and as soon as the profits of the co-operative labor system equaled their purchase price, they were to be freed and the process repeated.

The illness of Miss Wright in 1826, which forced her departure the following spring, and her poor choice of associates transformed Nashoba in its later days into an experiment in free love, racial equality, and amalgamation. Discouraged, she abandoned her project in favor of work on Robert Owen's *New Harmony Gazette,* and in December, 1829, she emancipated the thirty remaining Nashoba slaves, whom she colonized in Haiti.[81]

Nashoba sprang entirely from external sources and is pertinent to the history of Memphis only in regard to the reaction of its citizens, by whom Miss Wright, tall and mannish but not unattractive, was well received. Winchester assisted her in many ways, and Davis, who thought she "lived full half a century before her time," defended her character quite ferociously.[82] Public sentiment at the time was strong for emancipation, but racial equality would not be stomached—as Winchester and this Scots Diana both discovered. Since Negro women were then commonly accepted by Memphians as concubines,[83] the stigma associated with a dark skin was certainly not as pronounced as it became in the fifties, when such a practice would not have been tolerated.

It has been mentioned that the four local candidates for delegate to the constitutional convention of 1834 were in favor of emancipation, but, with a single exception, their attitude was premised on the understanding that deportation would immediately follow. This Tennessee convention, similar in sentiment to the famous session of the Virginia legislature three years earlier, rejected a proposal for gradual emancipation because it failed to include a program of colonization. Despite the efforts of a determined minority from the eastern section of the state, by a vote of thirty-three to twenty-three it disfranchised free Negroes, who possessed the right to vote under the existing constitution drawn up in 1796.[84] Branches of the American Colonization Society were formed in Memphis and elsewhere in the district, but after Nat Turner's Rebellion the motive was rather the desire to rid the section of a potential menace than concern for the welfare of the Negro.[85]

Flatboat Memphis had more than its share of the gamblers and robbers with which the valley teemed. The saga of John A. Murrell, outlaw of the Hatchie country, and his powerful clan reads like a tale from the *Arabian Nights*. The "Great Western Land Pirate," as Murrell was called, stole Negroes, horses, and land, and passed counterfeit money, but the wholesale murder and the grandiose schemes described in the confession that Virgil A. Stewart alleges to have received from the famous outlaw are obviously Stewart's own fictitious contribution.[86]

The Old Bell Tavern, operated by the jovial Paddy Meagher, was the town's most colorful institution. Paddy when in his cups claimed to be a bosom friend of Andrew Jackson, and his pretty daughter Sally was actually quite a favorite of the General's.[87] The tavern was a rendezvous not only for the élite of the village but occasionally for some of the leading figures of the state, since it was the local headquarters of the Bentons, Jackson, and Crockett. Upon the death of Paddy, Sally married a gambler, and after a succession of barkeepers each worse in character than the preceding, the once proud tavern became a dive full of confidence games patronized only by the sots of Catfish Bay. During the severe winter of 1831-32, it was half torn down by the poor for fuel.[88]

The situation in Memphis was worse than it otherwise would have been because of the proximity of Hopefield and the Pedraza Hotel just across the river, which after the death of Judge Foy deteriorated into one of the leading hangouts for criminals on the Mississippi. Encouraged by the hanging of gamblers in Vicksburg during the summer of 1835, Memphians banished their most notorious public enemies, only to have them cross over to Hopefield. For a while there were constant rumors that the exiles were planning to burn the town, but with the wisdom of their kind they waited until the spasm of moral uplift had passed and then returned in safety.[89] The large transient population which its location renders inevitable has ever been a characteristic of Memphis life responsible for the excessive number of murders in its annals.

This large vicious element among its inhabitants undoubtedly kept respectable settlers away from the town for many years, and it is often commented upon by contemporary travelers, whose impressions of the community in comparison with the world outside are valid testimony as to its real nature—if occasional allowance is made for their individual prejudice. Reuben Davis, the later famous Mississippian, while a youngster in the twenties considered Memphis as a possible residence, but finally decided against it. "Memphis was then," he wrote, "a small town, ugly, dirty, and sickly. . . . Everything pointed to the certainty that in a short time this squalid village must grow to a great and wealthy city . . . but for many years the population would be rough and lawless, and the locality and sanitary conditions of the town promised that disease and death would hold high carnival there."[90] A. Levasseur, who accompanied La Fayette on his visit in 1824, was more severe in fewer words: "From Natchez to St. Louis," was his comment, "we did not meet with a single assemblage of houses that deserved the name of town or even of village."[91] The Duke of Saxe-Weimar on his way up the river in 1826 saw a "group of rather miserable houses; it is the town of Memphis."[92] Toqueville was impressed with the stoicism of some Choctaws waiting there in 1831 for transportation to the Indian Territory.[93] Captain J. E. Alexander of the Royal Highlanders, who was at the bluff about the same time, enjoyed the cleanliness of the frame houses, the cheapness of hotel rates, and a Negro religious service which he witnessed. He made the perennial observation of tourists in regard to the inconvenience of travel, though he cheerfully accepted the poor roads and all other hardships as quite normal in a new country.[94] Mrs. Trollope, who arrived in 1828 with Frances Wright to visit Nashoba, had breakfast at the Bell Tavern with the leading men of the community. Their manners probably irked her as much as those of the rest of America, but her chapter on Memphis was so full of Miss Wright that there was little space for criticism of the town.[95]

In spite of the prediction of Reuben Davis that Memphis in a short time would be a "great and wealthy city," the signs of progress during its first two decades were relatively few. Roads that were impassable half the year were completed to Taylor's Mill on the way to Forked Deer in 1821 and to Jackson by way of Randolph and Somerville in 1829; by 1831 a rude stage line was in operation between Nashville, Jackson, and Memphis.[96] The variety of bank notes thus brought in necessitated some form of a clearinghouse, and in 1834 the Farmers and Merchants Bank was founded.[97] From the first 300 bales in 1826 cotton receipts increased until Memphis in 1840 handled 35,000 out of the 41,468 bales produced in the district that year.[98] One of the most progressive and far-sighted of its residents, General E. P. Gaines, who secured the western military road starting at Hopefield which the federal government spent more than a score of years in building, was the first to catch a vision of the town as a railroad center, and to this end he devoted all of his efforts after his arrival in 1831.[99] In 1834 a line of packets was inaugurated between Randolph, Memphis, and New Orleans, which made about two trips a month; but until the middle forties the town was served largely by independent steamboats.[100]

Cultural advancement was likewise slight. In 1826 Tom Phoebus, probably as a result of Marcus Winchester's efforts to interest the proprietors in such a project, began publishing his *Memphis Advocate and Western District Intelligencer,* a weekly sheet by no means as impressive as its name.[101] Several years later Phoebus faced competition from the *Western Times and Memphis Commercial Advertiser,* but both papers were soon discontinued. Their place was taken by the *Memphis Gazette,* a Jacksonian organ of which P. G. Gaines was editor. When the Whig White-for-president agitation started in Tennessee in 1836, the *Memphis Intelligencer* appeared almost immediately on White's behalf, but after several weeks it was taken over by F. S. Latham. This journalist, who had just sold his *Randolph Recorder,* made a decided impression upon his adopted community, and his rivalry with the *Gazette* was the beginning of the Whig-Democratic contest for the vote of Memphis.[102]

In this period there was occasional evidence of an increasing diversity in popular amusements and perhaps in the intellectual interests of the inhabitants. Sporadic attempts at establishing a school were made about 1830 by Messrs. Garner and Williams, but the first educational institution of any permanence was taught by Eugene Mageveny, fresh from Ireland, in the meetinghouse in Court Square.[103] The Thespian Society, organized in 1824, was host the following year to Sol Smith, a popular contemporary comedian, and as a result of the ensuing enthusiasm an old frame building was converted into a theater, accurately named "Blue Ruin."[104] In 1836 a track was laid off on the Hernando Road by a group of race-horse owners, and a meet was held there in the spring.[105]

Perhaps the best instance of the town's growing pains was the purchase by an alderman, who happened to be in Cincinnati, of "Little Vigor," a three-foot fire engine which he proudly presented to the surprised citizenry. It was soon applied to a perverted use, however, when a self-appointed moral uplift squad filled it with soapsuds and lampblack, which they proceeded to squirt on the prostitutes who rode along Chickasaw Row in hacks in quest of gallants.[106] A volunteer fire brigade had been organized before the purchase of the engine, but its chief function, prophetic of the future, was to keep the municipal administration in office and only secondarily to fight fires.[107]

Outwardly, Memphis in 1840 was still a flatboat town, slightly larger but not appreciably different from what it had been fifteen years before. Since its incorporation in 1826, which was the culmination of Overton's efforts, the little settlement had experienced many vicissitudes. The loss of the county court had doomed it to a continuous bondage to the flatboatmen. The epidemics of 1826 and 1828 had driven trade to Randolph, and the potential competition of rival projects on the lower bluff had made its future even more uncertain. At the close of the first two decades of its existence Memphis had barely regained the economic status it had held in the late twenties, though the basis for its future growth had been established in the rapid development of the surrounding area. In 1840 its population was a mere eighteen hundred, while Vicksburg, founded at the same time, had more than three thousand inhabitants, Natchez almost five thousand, and Nashville seven thousand.[108]

In 1841 Memphis began to pay its mayor a salary, and in the following year it began to call itself a "city";[109] yet these are but superficial matters when compared with the conquest of the flatboatmen which occurred simultaneously, the first indication that law as well as trade had come to the young community. From the hordes that docked at their landings during high water, none of the river towns north of New Orleans was able to collect the customary charge for wharfage. The life of wharf master along the Mississippi was not a happy one. In fact it was a common sight to see him being chased up the hill by irate boatmen—if indeed he were lucky enough to escape more severe injury than the mere indignity of flight.[110] A "reform" ticket won the annual Memphis municipal election in 1841, and as the town was yet young the new administration was forced to do some honest reforming. William Spickernagle, the mayor, decided that able men could be attracted to public service only by ample reward, and on this basis he reorganized his small staff. To a wharf master, selected because he would not be squeamish about a little blood-letting, was offered a commission of 25 per cent on all collections. Two volunteer military companies, the Guards and the Blues, were immediately formed to assist in enforcing the law, and with such organization wharfage receipts became for the first time the chief source of municipal revenue.[111]

The situation was complicated by the activity of Fort Pickering and South Memphis, which, jubilant over their acquisition of the steamboat landing, now made a strong bid for the flatboat trade. The stern measures of Memphis had little effect on the boatmen as long as her rivals below catered to them. These Argonauts of the Mississippi correctly interpreted this strife as an indication of weakness, and after a year of submission to Spickernagle's men they determined to regain their old supremacy. The 1841 season had been unusually productive and in May, 1842, there were five hundred flatboats in Memphis at the same time. One Trester from the Wabash region, considering the time ripe for action, refused to pay his fee and threatened to assault the wharf master if he persisted in his attempt to collect it; whereupon that dignitary secured a small force of deputies and soon returned with a warrant for the trouble-maker's arrest. In the scuffle which ensued Trester was slain, and for a while the town was in danger of being destroyed by some two thousand irate boatmen. The citizens, however, stood firm and order was preserved, in spite of rumors that the Indiana legislature had passed hostile resolutions against Memphis in retaliation.[112]

Here the flatboat days end. Like the vigilantes of a later day in the Far West, by this spontaneous and unanimous action citizens announced to the valley that the reign of law had come to Memphis. The conquest of the flatboatmen is significant because it indicated a new attitude and the beginning of a new era. For the first time, apparently, the town considered itself permanent; it must become a community safe for its children and its children's children. More than that, Memphians had caught a vision of autonomy, and to achieve it they had been willing to risk their economic security and even their lives.

CHAPTER IV

BOOM DECADES

When lots were first sold by the proprietors of young Memphis in 1820, the Southwest was sparsely settled. The region which now includes Alabama, Mississippi, Arkansas, Louisiana, and West Tennessee had only two thirds as many inhabitants as the state of Kentucky alone. Mobile and Natchez, the only towns of the territory in question besides New Orleans, were mere villages, according to modern standards, for their combined population amounted to less than three thousand. Indeed, in the whole South only New Orleans, Charleston, and Richmond boasted of more than ten thousand citizens. Yet in a brief forty years this southwestern region, with the addition of Texas, became three times as populous as Kentucky, whose density of population had meanwhile doubled; and by 1860 seventeen southern cities, nine of them west of the Appalachians, had more than ten thousand inhabitants.[1] The figures showing this remarkable growth of the Southwest are given in Table II.

This westward movement, which became alarming to the Tidewater soon after the War of 1812 and which continued for a century with but occasional interruptions until it had penetrated Texas and Oklahoma, is to be explained largely in terms of cotton. As soon as Whitney's gin made the cleaning of short-staple cotton possible, there began a mad rush for richer land to produce raw material for a foreign and later a domestic market which were long insatiable. Even a drop in price from twenty-six cents in the

TABLE II

GROWTH OF THE SOUTHWEST, 1820-1860[2]

	1820	1860
Kentucky	564,317	1,155,684
Tennessee	422,823	1,109,801
Total	988,140	2,265,485
West Tennessee	2,500	293,088
Alabama	127,901	964,201
Mississippi	75,448	791,305
Louisiana	153,407	708,002
Arkansas	14,273	435,450
Texas	....	604,215
Total	373,529	3,796,261
New Orleans	27,176	168,675
Mobile	1,500	29,258
Natchez	2,184	6,612
Memphis	53	22,623

second decade of the century to seven cents in the forties failed to discourage seriously its cultivation. Because of this low price of cotton and the lack of a corresponding drop in the price of slaves, however, such cultivation became profitable only in the more fertile areas. There were, to be sure, other southern staples—indigo, replaced by rice in the Southeast, sugar in Louisiana, and tobacco in the border states—yet seldom has any region as large and as rich as the ante-bellum South been so devoted to one crop as it was to cotton, and seldom has one crop so completely determined the economic and social life of so large a section.

Memphis was the child of cotton and this westward expansion of the South. During the twenty years following its victory over Randolph, the town on the lower bluff experienced a 1200 per cent increase in population and an even greater increase in wealth. There was much demand in the valley during this period for cotton buyers and factors, since southwestern planters learned early that they lost money by shipping their own crop. Because of its size and location New Orleans at first had no rivals as a cotton market, but by the fifties Memphis, having far outstripped Vicksburg and Natchez, was causing the Louisiana city much concern.

The prosperity of these boom decades was in itself an epic in transportation. Planked roads were bringing neighboring Tennessee towns nearer and were winning much of the cotton of the hill region of North Mississippi from Vicksburg. Each new year saw larger and more numerous steamboats plowing the waters of the great river and its tributaries. With four railroads under construction in the early fifties to complete its transportation system, the Tennessee metropolis became the largest inland cotton market in the United States.[3] The Yazoo Delta to the south, for the first time able to raise its crop behind a protecting wall of levees constructed by state and private funds, increased its production between 1850 and 1860 from 42,000 to 220,000 bales. Its northern counties were beginning to turn to Memphis as a market; here North Alabama sent its cotton, as did also the fertile valleys of the White, the St. Francis, the lower Arkansas, and even the Red River in Louisiana.[4] So heavy did the traffic become that in 1857 twenty-six buyers of cotton and twenty-eight factors were listed in the city directory;[5] three years later roughly 400,000 bales, valued at $16,000,000, were handled in a single season. Table III makes clear the development of Memphis as a cotton market.

The cotton interests of Memphis were primarily responsible for its transportation program, but other commercial houses were equally benefited and the bluff became a depot which supplied a large and ever-expanding hinterland with all its necessities. Even New Orleans began to take notice: "If Memphis already begins to attract the trade of Arkansas," commented the New Orleans *Crescent* in 1850, "we may kiss it goodbye, for when the Mississippi and Atlantic railroad is completed Memphis promises to be the most important town in the Southwest after New Orleans."[6] The

TABLE III

A. MEMPHIS COTTON STATISTICS, 1826-1860*

Year	Bales	Value	United States (Bales)	New Orleans (Bales)
1826	300	....	957,281	....
1830	1,000	$ 3,500	976,845	....
1835	50,000	....	1,360,725	....
1840	35,000	1,400,000	2,177,835	....
1845	75,000	3,000,000	2,394,503	....
1846	130,000	....	2,100,537	....
1849	140,000	....	2,866,938	....
1850	150,000	7,520,000	2,333,718	....
1850-51	163,000	6,500,000	2,454,442	....
1851-52	172,000	6,880,000	3,126,310	....
1852-53	202,000	8,080,000	3,416,214	....
1853-54	188,151	8,520,000	3,074,979	....
1854-55	202,000	8,000,000	2,982,634	....
1855-56	295,246	11,800,000	3,655,557	1,661,433
1856-57	281,000	14,050,000	3,093,737	1,435,000
1857-58	243,000	12,150,000	3,257,339	1,576,409
1858-59	325,720	16,250,000	4,018,914	1,669,274
1859-60	398,721	16,000,000	4,861,292	2,272,500
1860-61	360,653	18,500,000	3,849,469	....

B. COTTON PRODUCTION (BALES) IN SOUTHERN STATES, 1820-1900

	1820	1840	1860	1880	1900
South Carolina	169,561	175,985	353,416	522,548	876,545
Georgia	165,000	450,076	701,840	814,441	1,296,844
Alabama	68,500	391,495	989,955	699,654	1,103,690
Tennessee	50,000	76,305	296,464	330,621	215,175
Louisiana	48,000	411,224	777,738	508,569	708,508
Mississippi	43,000	532,871	1,202,507	963,111	1,264,048
Virginia	32,000	9,628	12,727	19,595	9,239
North Carolina	30,000	143,034	145,514	389,598	473,155
Florida	....	33,359	65,153	54,997	56,821
Texas	....	6,970	431,463	805,284	2,658,555
Missouri	....	271	41,188	20,318	19,377
Oklahoma	....	....	....	17,000	244,359

*The information in this table has been taken from *Rainey's Directory, 1855*, p. 68; *Memphis Cotton Exchange Directory, 1897*, p. 55; *The Cotton Plant* (U. S. Department of Agriculture), pp. 41-42; and J. L. Watkins, *King Cotton*, numerous tables.

editor of the *Railroad Record* of Cincinnati, a fairly impartial critic in spite of his zeal for railroads, surpassed the *Crescent* in enthusiasm for the city's future.

"We begin with Memphis," he wrote in the fifties, "because it is the most promising town in the Southwest. . . . We visited it in 1851 and were struck with the superiority of its position. . . . It is destined in our opinion to be the largest city in the Southwest *not excepting New Orleans.*

. . . Memphis as the port of that region will be chiefly a commercial town, but if it would grow to be a really large place it must seek to manufacture, and this it may. By railroads through Tennessee and Kentucky it may be supplied with coal and iron, and then iron factories, steam machinery, and cotton mills may be readily carried on. If Memphis would be great she must make railways and build factories."[7]

A glance at the figures in Table IV suggests that there were ample grounds for such a prediction:

TABLE IV

GROWTH OF MEMPHIS, 1840-1860[8]

	1840	1850	1860
Population	1,799	8,841	22,623
Taxable Wealth	$ 679,200	$4,600,000	$18,297,545
Bales of Cotton	35,000	163,000	398,791
Value of Cotton	$1,400,000	$6,500,000	$16,000,000
Value of Annual Trade	....	....	$51,500,000

Real estate and slave values reflected this general prosperity. A piece of property worth $200 in 1850 sold five years later for $2,000.[9] Buildings were erected by the block, and the extensive construction of the fifties caused the local price of slaves to soar. While field hands cost only from $750 to $1,000, carpenters were selling for $2,500, blacksmith's hammerers for $1,114, and painters for $1,005. In many cases even unskilled Negroes were hired out annually for $150 or $200.[10]

Though infant Memphis was the child of cotton, the mature city of the fifties cannot be explained so simply. Economically, the settlement on the bluff was West before it was South; it did not become rabidly southern until it was caught in the emotionalism of the early months of 1861. Situated upon the Mississippi, it was vitally interested in trade between the upper and the lower valley. Its complete dependence upon the river for transportation before the advent of the railroad made it all the more concerned in the early period that proper economic relations with the upper valley be preserved. As a matter of fact, on the eve of the war Memphis was both a southern and a western town. Cotton, railroads, and the Negro bound it to the South; the Mississippi River and pristine industries bound it to the West; and it attained commercial fame because nature had made it the logical depot for the distribution of upper western produce to southern planters.

Though it has not generally been recognized as a separate and distinct section of the United States, that part of the South west of the Alleghenies was in ante-bellum days a unit to itself. Bound to the Tidewater by ties of tradition and certain common factors, cotton and the Negro, the Southwest in its economic interests was quite different from and often opposed to the older region. In Mississippi as well as in Illinois the welfare of the West depended upon improved means of transportation; yet South Carolina and Virginia, not merely Massachusetts, rejected the proposal that the national government should bear the expense of internal improvements, projects which none of the western states was rich enough to finance independently. If parts of the lower West often refused to vote for Henry Clay for the presidency, he was, nevertheless, generally regarded by the propertied element of that section as its champion. When in 1860 the western South chose to fight, as it thought, in defense of the "peculiar institution" about which it had recently become so sensitive, its decision was dictated not by enlightened self-interest but by sentiment and uncontrolled passion.[11]

There is ample evidence that the Memphis of these boom decades was considered nationally as well as locally a western town. A gateway to Texas and the Far West over the only route open the whole year round, it received considerable attention in the plans of the war and navy departments for defense of the frontier against possible ag-

THE MEMPHIS COTTON LEVEE IN THE 1840's

A reconstruction sketched for *Harper's Weekly* by Porte Crayon (D. H. Strother), who was in Memphis during the Civil War. Note the oxen and the covered wagons. The city proper is just back from the bluff, as may be seen in the picture of Colonel Ellet's ram approaching the city of Memphis, facing page 150.

Harper's Weekly

STEAMBOAT LANDING

In the 1840's this landing was located just below the southern boundary of the city. The houses in the distance are the rival town of South Memphis.

GENERAL VIEW OF MEMPHIS IN 1862, FROM HOPEFIELD ON THE ARKANSAS SIDE

From left to right may be seen the Navy Yard, Overton House, Exchange, Washam House, Episcopal Church, Odd Fellows Hall, and the Gayoso House.

gression from Mexico or the Gulf. In the commercial convention of 1845 at Memphis, the West joined the South in a demand upon the federal government for assistance in the development of that great "inland sea," the Mississippi and its tributaries. Throughout the fifties Memphis merchants disputed bitterly with their rivals in Chicago, St. Louis, and New Orleans as to the route of the proposed railroad to the Pacific. Each of these movements must be examined closely, not merely as proof that the city was consciously West as well as South, but also as integral parts of the purely local history of the place.

In 1840 the frontier was hardly a hundred miles west of the Mississippi, and as the possibility of war with England or Mexico increased much attention was given to the problem of national defense by the officers of army and navy. In this connection both Memphis and St. Louis received careful consideration. No military man was so convinced of the immediate necessity of adequate means of transporting troops to the frontier as General Edmund P. Gaines, whose headquarters were established at Memphis in 1831.[12] In 1835 and again in 1838 Gaines submitted to Congress elaborate schemes of railroads for this purpose, in both of which the city figured prominently. His first plan called for five roads: from Lexington to Pensacola, from Memphis to Baltimore, from Memphis to Savannah, from Louisville to Mobile and Pensacola, and from Memphis to the Sabine River on the eastern edge of Texas. His later proposal dealt only with the trans-Mississippi region, where he suggested seven railroads connecting the eleven frontier posts between the Sabine and Lake Superior, the two main lines running from Memphis to the Sabine and from St. Louis to Fort Gibson.[13]

Neither of these projects materialized, but they did create local enthusiasm and attract attention to the advantages of the town's location. As a result of Gaines's earlier activity,

Colonel S. H. Long, an army engineer, had been sent there in 1834 to survey three possible routes to the seaboard, one to Baltimore, a second to Charleston, and a third to Savannah. "I know of no place in the valley of the Mississippi," wrote Long concerning the lower Chickasaw bluff, "combining so many advantages for speedy and cheap concentration of all the elements of force and supply—of men and rations—whether for military, naval, or commercial purposes . . . a position where formations of ice never occur to interrupt navigation . . . a position which is destined soon to become the seaport and the principal commercial emporium of the state."[14]

Stimulated probably by Gaines's proposals, Lieutenant Matthew F. Maury of the United States navy began in 1839 a series of articles in the *Southern Literary Messenger* to arouse the South to the possibilities of direct trade with Europe and South America, and to convince the federal government of the need for adequate preparations to defend the Gulf of Mexico against Great Britain.[15] Three years later in an article in the *National Intelligencer* of Washington, Maury, writing under the pseudonym of "Union Jack," suggested the Memphis batture as a proper site for an inland navy yard. Such a suggestion was immediately scoffed at by citizens of that town,[16] but soon its officials, encouraged by later articles of Maury's in the Chicago *Democrat,* gave the proposal enthusiastic support. Plans were discussed for a Wolf River canal to provide power, the Tennessee legislature was induced to send a memorial to Congress, and Mayor Hickman belabored the national body with a lengthy report enumerating the advantages of Memphis.[17]

These efforts resulted in the passage of a bill by the Twenty-seventh Congress authorizing the examination of the site.[18] In May, 1843, a naval commission submitted a report not altogether favorable,[19] but after a second inspection it gave the location its approval. Meanwhile local litigation over the batture had ended in compromise; and by public meeting the land between Front Row and the river, Auction and Market streets, was donated to the government.[20]

In a letter submitted to Congress in December, 1843, Maury introduced the argument that the South had been neglected in appropriations for defense.[21] When this cry was taken up immediately by southern members, their northern colleagues were forced to make some concession, regardless of the fact that Vicksburg had a lighthouse and Helena a government hospital.[22] At first the whole Southwest had supported Maury's proposal for a navy yard on the batture, but once the project seemed likely to succeed, Natchez, Cairo, and even inland towns of Tennessee entered the competition.[23] Memphis, however, had previously joined Illinois and Indiana in their agitation for improvement of the Wabash, and, in spite of opposition from certain western senators, in 1844 Congress voted an appropriation of $100,000 for the navy yard.[24]

The call of bids for construction by the secretary of the navy in October, 1845,[25] apparently produced no satisfactory response, for the following year Representative F. P. Stanton of Tennessee was complaining loudly about what he considered deliberate delay on the part of the federal government. At this point George Bancroft advised Polk against spending more money on the project because of its extravagance.[26] Congress seems to have agreed with Bancroft at the moment, for, despite a protest from the Tennessee legislature demanding execution of the original program, the appropriation of 1846 required that work be confined to the mere construction of a rope-walk.[27] Thereafter, however, funds continued to be voted annually, totaling roughly a million dollars,[28] until the grant for 1854 was reduced by the House from the $60,000 allowed by the Senate to $13,000. When the bill returned to the chamber in which it originated, an amendment was inserted, at the suggestion of the disgusted J. C. Jones of Tennessee, ceding the yard to the mayor and aldermen of Memphis. Southern members had grown tired of having "Stanton's Pet," as the navy yard was called, thrown in their faces whenever they rose to speak of the neglect of the South.[29]

The matter did not end here, for the amazed Memphians refused to accept the gift. In opposition to the wishes of city officials, who probably sensed that extensive opportunities awaited them for plundering, the *Appeal* by editorials and public meetings led a campaign to induce Congress to reconsider the proposition, with the understanding that no mere rope-walk but a real shipbuilding yard should be constructed.[30] "Let us unite," it urged, "Whigs, Democrats, Know-Nothings, and Know-Somethings, in refusing acceptance of the bribe to deprive the Southwest of its rightful share of the favors of the Federal Government."[31] After two years of agitation so intense that enraged citizens had an injunction issued against municipal officials to prevent the sale of the yard, at last it was realized that Congress was beyond persuasion and the donation was reluctantly accepted.

The project of a navy yard at Memphis was doomed from the start. The machinery and buildings constructed cost the government, as usual, several times the necessary amount. The youngest and poorest officers were stationed there, and naturally men used to the roving life of the sea soon grew to hate the bar on the Mississippi, which was to them little less than prison. One ship of war, the *Allegheny,* was built at a cost of a half a million dollars, but her speed was such that she was considerably annoyed in the course of her maiden voyage in the river by little boys in skiffs, who paddled around and around her. On her way to New York she was forced to put in at Norfolk for repairs, and there she was condemned before reaching her first destination.[32]

The acquisition of the navy yard in the forties merely whetted the ambition of the little town. Besides the enlargement of the yard the program of progressive Memphians included a western armory, railroads, the completion of the military road to Texas, a Wolf River canal to provide power for future cotton mills, rope foundries, flour and sawmills, and the general improvement of the Mississippi waterway.[33] Yet these men were astute enough to realize that the welfare of the whole valley was of vital importance to a town so centrally located as theirs, and that alone they could do little. Consequently, they must throw in their lot with other western towns, whose needs were similar, to force co-operation from Washington. The upper West and the lower West spoke the same language, and the experience of both with horses had taught them the value of a trade.

By 1845 the military road from Memphis to Little Rock, which had been begun in 1816 and over which more than twelve hundred persons traveled west in a single month as early as September, 1837,[34] was well on its way to completion. In the middle forties a company was formed in Little Rock with the purpose of bridging the Arkansas River at that point in order to extend the road to Texas.[35] In the spring of 1845 Major Bingham, the company's architect, went to Memphis to secure its co-operation. Here Memphians saw their opportunity. After several meetings with Bingham, a committee of fourteen was appointed to encourage subscriptions to the stock of the company and to call a convention in July to consider the "general improvement of the valley."[36]

Much is heard of the Nashville Convention of 1850, at which South Carolina made a vain attempt to induce her sister states to secede from the Union, but the Western and Southwestern Convention at Memphis five years earlier, where the western South joined the upper West in a demand that certain projects necessary to the development of the Mississippi Valley be instituted at national expense, has been buried in oblivion. This Memphis Convention is one of several events of the mid-nineteenth century which boldly give the lie to Seward's hypothesis of the "irrepressible conflict." In essence it was a mart where various representatives of the South and the West came to trade their influence in return for particular projects of their own, hoping by thus pooling resources to wrest from the East what had long been denied them. In fact, had the resolutions of the meeting been enacted by Congress, there might have been no Nashville Convention, and it is unlikely that the western South would have followed South Carolina into secession in 1861.[37]

In spite of complications, largely political, the first session of the convention met on July 4 with delegates present from Tennessee, Louisiana, Mississippi, Arkansas, and Pennsylvania.[38] Though a series of resolutions were passed, the chief function of the gathering was to arrange for a greater session to be held in the fall. Memphis and Little Rock received their strongest support for a second convention from Illinois, where in the preceding month several meetings had been held at Springfield, in which Stephen A. Douglas had played the leading role, to agitate for the acquisition of Oregon, the defense of the West, and a Michigan-Illinois canal.[39]

The second convention opened on the 12th of November. By the 13th, 476 delegates had arrived, representing the fifteen states of Louisiana, Texas, Arkansas, Mississippi, Alabama, Tennessee, Kentucky, Missouri, Illinois, Indiana, Ohio, Pennsylvania, Virginia, North Carolina, South Carolina, and the territory of Iowa.[40] Of the several southern groups besides those from Memphis and Little Rock who hoped to use the prestige of the convention for private ends, John C. Calhoun and his South Carolina friends were the most important. Ignored by Polk, Calhoun was undoubtedly eager to take advantage of the occasion to unite the South and the West and to ride upon the crest of the wave in 1848 into the coveted presidency.[41] More significant economically was the presence of another Carolinian, Colonel James Gadsden, the South's most active railroad promoter, and representatives of the related Georgia railroad interests, who were anxious to divert western trade from New Orleans by way of Nashville and Memphis. From these eastern groups must come the capital for railroad construction in the Southwest, and they were as anxious to secure the co-operation of the Memphians who called the convention as the latter were to give it.[42] Also in need of funds for similar purposes, Nashville was forced to take an active part in the proceedings, in spite of jealousy of its younger Tennessee rival.

No national statesmen of first rank besides Calhoun attended the meeting, but the list of delegates included the governors of several states and individuals of economic and intellectual fame: notably, B. B. Minor, editor of the *Southern Literary Messenger;* J. D. B. DeBow, soon to start his widely read review; Henry Shreve of Missouri, who had almost cleared the Mississippi of snags; J. C. Jones of Tennessee, who deserves more credit for the first railroads of the Memphis area than any other man except Gaines; and General Gaines himself, whom the gathering treated with special honor as the earliest advocate of its principal objectives.[43] Calhoun as chairman sounded the keynote of the convention in his speech on the second day when, after enumerating the needs of the "Inland Sea," as he aptly termed the valley, he declared that federal aid should be evoked for the projects agreed upon as steps vital to national and not merely sectional welfare.[44]

Unanimous refusal met the proposal of one individual who enthusiastically declared that the time had come for the removal of the seat of the national government across the Alleghenies, but all sections represented were satisfied with the twenty resolutions adopted.[45] Each group got what it wanted in the document, though it was indicative of how far the convention had risen above its origins that the committee on resolutions forgot to include the Arkansas military road in its first draft—an omission that was hastily remedied.[46] The measures advocated fall roughly into three categories: (1) those concerning the economic development of the Mississippi and its tributaries, such as deepening the mouth of the river and the construction of a canal from the Great Lakes to that stream; (2) those providing for adequate defense of the valley, and the gulf and lake coast; (3) those encouraging the building of railroads.[47]

The committee of five appointed by the convention to memorialize Congress to incorporate these resolutions into a bill accomplished little. Ill feeling engendered by the dispute over Oregon in 1846 divided the lower and the upper westerners, causing the rejection of the memorial by the House. Calhoun introduced several bills in the Senate, but his personal unpopularity nullified whatever chance they had of passing.[48] Had any of the proposed legislation been passed by Congress Polk would probably have resorted to veto, for following the strict-construction precedent of Monroe and Jackson he refused to sign the river-and-harbor bills of 1846 and 1847. In the latter year a second western convention, purged of all southern connection, met at Chicago, but it was equally unsuccessful.[49] Yet the Memphis men who had called the earlier meeting had some cause for satisfaction, for it was probably at the Convention of 1845 that the Tidewater promoters selected Memphis as the terminal of their railroad from Charleston to the Mississippi,[50] a dream which became a reality twelve years later. Railroad construction throughout the entire

Southwest was greatly stimulated, and no city of that region benefited as much therefrom as did the metropolis of West Tennessee.

The three other conventions which met on the bluff before 1860, while not so comprehensive in purpose or patronage or so pertinent to the national scene as that in 1845, were nevertheless its direct offspring. Beginning in 1845 Asa Whitney plagued Congress incessantly with petitions for land grants to aid construction of a railroad from Lake Michigan to the mouth of the Columbia River.[51] Upon the conclusion of the Treaty of Guadalupe-Hidalgo in 1848, Memphis, Natchez, and Vicksburg all entered the competition for the eastern terminal of the, as yet imaginary, transcontinental road. About the same time Senator Benton introduced a bill in Congress specifying a St. Louis-San Francisco route. As for the other chief contestants, New Orleans preferred a road across the Isthmus of Panama, while Chicago supported the "compromise route" of Douglas through the Southern Pass to the Pacific.[52]

At the suggestion of the state of Arkansas, Memphis planned to hold a Pacific Railroad Convention in July, 1849, but a cholera epidemic necessitated a three months' postponement. This delay proved disastrous, for St. Louis meanwhile held a convention of its own, which resulted in a tacit understanding with the New Orleans group. Consequently, at its meeting in November Memphis found both of these rivals unbending; yet regardless of their opposition the convention resolved that the transcontinental route should run from San Diego to El Paso and strike the Mississippi somewhere between the mouths of the Red and the Ohio rivers. This recommendation, of course, left both New Orleans and St. Louis out of consideration, and their representatives charged that the resolution had been passed by resort to questionable tactics.[53] Memphis had spurned their offer of an "olive branch," said the St. Louis men sadly; no, replied a local delegate, what had actually been offered was not an olive branch but a railroad branch.[54]

In June, 1853, a third Memphis convention discussed cotton, trade with South America, and improvement of the Mississippi, but the underlying issue was still the location of the Pacific road. Foreshadowing the bargain soon to be made between the South and the upper West—the extension of slavery for the continental railroad—the body advocated "that route which scientific exploration shall show to combine in the greatest degree . . . temperate climate, fertility of soil, cheapness of construction, and accessibility at all seasons from all portions of the union."[55] The last of these Memphis conventions in February, 1859, showed clearly the change of temper that had occurred in six eventful years. It stated frankly that the best route to the Pacific was from Memphis through Little Rock and El Paso to San Diego.[56]

The prosperity of Memphis in these boom decades has been described above as an epic in transportation. Nature had made it largely a western town, but man proceeded to bind it to the South. While the ports along the north Atlantic coast in the forties and fifties were striving to extend their railroads to Chicago, those along the south Atlantic at the same time were trying to reach Memphis, the Chicago of the lower West. As a result of the extreme emphasis on the planter and the slave in southern economic history, the activities of the cities of the ante-bellum South have largely been ignored; yet urban ambition, not the efforts of the planters, produced a network of railroads by 1860 in the Land of Cotton that was more systematic than, if not so extensive as, that in the North.[57]

It is apparent from a glance at a relief map of the United States that as long as there was no alternative to transportation by water, New Orleans possessed a monopoly of the export trade of the area south of the Great Lakes between the Rockies and the Appalachians—a monopoly to which canals in the thirties offered a challenge but which only the railroads of the fifties were able to destroy. The rivalry of Bienville's day between the St. Lawrence and the gulf settlements was resumed in the early nineteenth century by New York and New Orleans. By 1836 the latter, though it attracted but a fraction of its competitor's import trade from Europe, was incontestably the leading export city of the Union.[58]

During the year 1836-37, the steamboats docking at its wharves numbered 1,372 and the 401,500 tons of freight carried by them was valued at $43,515,402.[59] The steamboat tonnage of the valley in the forties, exclusive of New Orleans, exceeded that of Atlantic ports, exclusive of New York, by 15,000 tons, while the tonnage of the Crescent City was more than double that of its rival on the Hudson.[60] The value of western produce was estimated at $220,000,000 in 1845; of the one third of this produce exported, New Orleans handled twice as much as all other ports together.[61]

Not only New York but southern Tidewater cities, particularly Charleston and Savannah, viewed the rise of the Louisiana colossus with dismay. That Virginia, South Carolina, and Georgia were the first southern states to construct railroads on a large scale is an indication that they did not sit idly by while this western port took more and more of the trade which they hoped would be their own. Simultaneously Mobile yearned for the commerce of North Alabama which went down the Mississippi by way of the Tennessee, while Memphis and Vicksburg were quite willing to become depots where western produce would be transferred overland to the South Atlantic. All of these cities, consequently, joined in an attempt to divert trade, by means of railroads, from its natural course down the river.

South Carolina made considerable progress in railroad construction during the thirties, and in the following decade Georgia carried on the work with Chattanooga as its destination, planning to use the Tennessee River from that point to the Mississippi.[62] In September, 1845, Atlanta was reached, giving Charleston a 307-mile artery to the West.[63] Long before connection was made with Chattanooga in 1849,[64] however, eastern interests realized that their road could not stop short of the Mississippi. The choice for western terminal lay between Vicksburg, Nashville, and Memphis, an issue which the Convention of 1845 indirectly settled in favor of the last. It is somewhat ironical that one of the few tangible results of a Memphis convention for the development of the West should have been the binding of that town by bars of iron to the eastern cotton belt.

The western South was roused from its lethargy by the Convention of 1845 and by the fact that in 1850 Charleston and Savannah had received together 35 per cent of the annual cotton crop to New Orleans' 38 per cent.[65] Early attempts at construction in the Southwest during the thirties had ended abruptly with the Panic of 1837,[66] and as late as 1850 little more than two hundred of the twenty-four hundred miles of southern railroads lay west of Georgia. Ten years later, however, the eleven thousand miles of railway in the South were equally divided between the Tidewater and the transmontane region.[67] The Mobile and Ohio, chartered in 1847, was completed, after a long struggle, to Columbus, Kentucky, in April, 1861.[68] The New Orleans, Jackson, and Great Northern never reached Nashville, its original destination, but by connection with the Mississippi Central and other intervening routes it reached Columbus a year ahead of its Alabama rival.[69] The Nashville and Chattanooga was finished in 1854, but the Louisville and Nashville and the road between Richmond and

Chattanooga by way of Knoxville were not completed until the end of the decade.

The Tidewater did not succeed in its scheme to tap the trade of the West, nor did New Orleans retain its monopoly. Competition from the Erie Canal had been felt as early as 1835. Eleven years later Buffalo passed New Orleans in receipts of western flour, and in the fifties northern railroads and the Great Lakes took from the southwestern port all but 18 per cent of western exports.[70] Though the year 1859-60 was its best season in river traffic, prosperity now came from exports of four southern staples: cotton, tobacco, sugar, and molasses.

What, then, is the significance of this thirty-year period of southern railroad construction? It means that there was commercial enterprise in the cities of the South as in those of the North; that there was in the South, besides a planter aristocracy, a second economic group possessed of power, though it chose usually to act with that aristocracy. In view of its eleven thousand miles of railroad and its pristine industries, was not the South, on the eve of its debacle, about to enter an era of prosperity similar to that which the North enjoyed in the sixties?

With this outline of the history of ante-bellum transportation as a background, the problem must be approached briefly from the purely local viewpoint of Memphis. Since half of its population lived inland during the thirties, the Western District of Tennessee stood in real need of railroads. There was constant talk of a Paris-to-Randolph road and of one from Jackson to some point on the river other than Memphis; yet only the latter town made any effort in the direction of actual construction.[71] With Muscle Shoals as its goal, the Memphis Railroad Company was chartered in 1831, but it was soon discouraged by cholera and other adverse conditions.[72] In 1833 the same project was revived as the Mississippi and Atlantic Company and again two years later as the Memphis and LaGrange. When two thirds of the capital stock had been subscribed in 1836, the state contributed the remaining $125,000 in accordance with the provisions of its Internal Improvement Act of that year.[73] Impeded by lack of funds, the LaGrange Company in 1840 foolishly accepted an offer from John McLemore to combine real estate speculation with railroad construction. Two years later cars were operating over six miles of track, but in 1845 a state investigating committee pronounced the road bankrupt.[74]

In the fifties Memphis had four roads under construction toward each of the cardinal points of the compass. After the Convention of 1845 the LaGrange project was resumed as the Memphis and Charleston, which in 1857 opened its entire line from the Mississippi to the Atlantic amid much celebration.[75] A Memphis and Ohio Company was chartered in 1842 and again in 1848, but it did not commence building until after the war.[76] The Memphis and Nashville, begun in 1852, and known locally as the Memphis and Ohio, departed from its original program when the Louisville and Nashville agreed to build a western branch from Bowling Green, Kentucky, to Paris, Tennessee. Working northeast instead of east, as was originally planned, the Memphis road met the Louisville and Nashville at Paris.[77] The Mississippi and Tennessee, chartered in 1852 to provide a connection with New Orleans by way of the Mississippi Central at Grenada, reached its destination nine years later.[78] The Memphis and Little Rock, uncompleted until the seventies, received grants amounting to $350,000 from Memphis during this decade, but in 1861 only the thirty-nine miles through the swamps to the St. Francis had been completed on its western end.[79]

Though these early railroads were important to the future Memphis, throughout the ante-bellum period the Mississippi remained its lifeblood. According to a census in 1843 there were four thousand flatboats on the river and four hundred and fifty steamboats; the flatboats carried one fifth of the total tonnage, and at Memphis, as Sodom discovered, their trade was still far more valuable than that of the steamboats.[80] Not until the middle of the century did steamers displace smaller craft on the middle Mississippi. By 1850 packet lines were in operation from Memphis to New Orleans, Louisville, and Cincinnati. Within the next five years a local company began to run two boats to St. Louis, making the round trip in ten days, and in 1857 a similar schedule was started to Nashville on the Cumberland. Soon a new three-packet line was established between the bluff and St. Louis; and the Memphis and Ohio Packet Company, as well as smaller lines to Vicksburg, Little Rock, and several villages on the White River, was organized. By 1860 the New Orleans company had increased its fleet to nine of the most palatial steamers on the river, and in the same year it has been estimated that thirty steamboats were either owned in Memphis or made it their home port.[81]

The first receipts of cotton in Memphis came from Fayette County by wagon in 1826,[82] and during the ascendancy of Randolph most of the bluff's staple continued to come by land over roads which, bad at their best, were rendered almost impassable by the autumn rains that fell just when harvest was being carried to market. The process of "turnpiking" these roads, begun about 1830, improved them only slightly as it merely meant filling them with dirt that was scarcely better than the original surface.[83] Until 1852 all cotton which came to Memphis by land was hauled by ox teams, sometimes as far as one hundred miles, and each night during the autumn and the early winter hundreds of campfires burned where teamsters were encamped along the bluff.[84]

When planked roads became popular in the early fifties,[85] several construction companies, encouraged by the Tennessee Internal Improvement Act of 1852, were formed in Memphis. This new device began to be applied on highways to Horn Lake, Chulohoma, and Hernando in Mississippi, and to Raleigh, Big Creek, Germantown, Somerville, and LaGrange in Tennessee. Before the entire program was completed, however, the cost of upkeep and the competition of the railroad brought the experiment to an early end.[86]

These developments in transportation, national and local, enlarged the hinterland of Memphis and brought it in touch with a once distant world. It by no means suffered from New Orleans' loss of western export trade. Rather, since the portion of western produce which continued to come down the river was for southern consumption,[87] Memphis, because of its central location and its superior railroad connections, began to compete with New Orleans as a distributing point. The same railroads which proved the latter's undoing became the chief asset of the metropolis of the middle Mississippi. More intimate business relations were formed with Louisville and Cincinnati, while Charleston, Norfolk, and St. Louis began to appear on the economic horizon. Prior to the late fifties the little up-river trade that existed had gone to Louisville and Cincinnati by way of the Ohio, but a sudden rapprochement with the Missouri town in 1858 led the *Appeal* to prophesy that "the shallow Ohio must be changed for the profound Mississippi and Cincinnati must give way before the superiority of position occupied by St. Louis."[88]

Time proved this prediction a bit premature, but there was some justification for it at the moment. A St. Louis observer in October, 1858, discovered to his surprise that during his several weeks' visit in Memphis, over half the cotton received went to New York and Boston by way of

St. Louis at a rate of from seventy-five cents to one dollar cheaper, disregarding the saving of time, interest, and insurance, than by way of New Orleans.[89] Upon investigation the *Appeal* found that while only 786 bales had gone from Memphis to St. Louis the entire previous year, yet during only the first twenty-three days of October, 1858, 10,204 bales had been shipped to that point.[90] Cincinnati and Louisville soon regained their ascendancy, but not before a brisk trade had sprung up between the two Mississippi River towns. In return for cotton and small amounts of wheat and cottonseed, Memphis received from St. Louis bagging, rope, whisky, manufactured articles, bacon, lard, vegetables, and fruit. It is not surprising, then, that the Memphis and St. Louis Railroad Company opened its books for subscriptions in 1860.[91]

Prior to the era of the railroad, cotton, received from every direction but shipped to a few definite markets, left Memphis only by river. The new means of transportation, strange to say, by enlarging the city's receipts actually increased the absolute amount of cotton exported by the Mississippi. Of the 369,000 bales handled in the season of 1860-61, the steamboat was responsible for only 18 per cent of the receipts but carried 95 per cent of the shipments. Though the Memphis and Charleston hauled increasing quantities of the crop to Atlantic ports annually,[92] that road did not offer serious competition to river traffic. On the eve of the war cotton reached Memphis by train, boat, and wagon, but continued to leave as formerly by the Mississippi. Yet by 1860 the East and the upper West had diverted much of the trade of the central South from New Orleans.[93] Table V, showing these facts statistically, is based mainly upon a two-page report in the *Appeal* of September 4, 1861, a report by far the most valuable single document on the economic history of Memphis. Heretofore its existence has been unknown.[94]

Table V

A. Receipts of Cotton at Memphis, 1860-1861
(number of bales)

Wagon		23,339
Steamboat		67,678
Train		
Memphis & Charleston	164,413	
Memphis & Ohio	52,316	
Memphis & Little Rock	3,784	
Memphis & Tennessee	58,103	
	278,616	278,616
Total		369,633

B. Destination of Memphis Cotton, 1857-1861
(number of bales)

	1857–58	1858–59	1859–60	1860–61
New Orleans	....	241,546	263,589	184,366
Ohio River	28,104	57,827	111,144	153,894
St. Louis	786	23,724	16,769	13,802
European and Northern Ports	....	....	160	14,989
Interior Points	....	....	256	2,806

Shipments Up River to Immediate Points

1851-52	16,706	1856-57	34,184
1852-53	22,251	1857-58	28,800
1853-54	23,156	1858-59	84,139
1854-55	16,427	1859-60	128,329
1855-56	34,306	1860-61	167,696

Within a single decade the simple flatboat town had become a river port complex in economic structure. In the thirties its inhabitants had subsisted by bartering with Indians and flatboatmen; less than a generation later its new and much larger populace consisted of bankers and manufacturers, cotton buyers and factors, wholesale grocers and slave traders, doctors and lawyers, editors and railroad presidents. These were dynamic years, and the transition to the metropolis of the fifties cannot be explained merely in terms of transportation and cotton.

Long before the war, far-sighted southerners like DeBow recognized the weakness in their economic system with its extreme dependence upon cotton, a dependence by no means necessary, since their section possessed raw materials, water power, and labor in sufficient quantities to support extensive manufacturing. As a result of the efforts of certain progressive individuals, a system of factories sprang up, in spite of the Panic of 1857, which gave much promise for the future.

For a metropolis of an agrarian district, Memphis in 1860 had an amazing industrial output valued at four million dollars.[95] This manufacturing was largely the result of the acquisition of the navy yard and the steady influx of foreigners after 1850, since much of the nation's mechanical skill was imported in the nineteenth century. When the price of cotton dropped to seven cents a pound early in the forties, the *Appeal* boldly proposed that Memphis abandon her cotton trade and specialize in the manufacture and distribution of articles necessary to the surrounding area. "The prosperity of this community," said the *Appeal* "has heretofore rested mainly upon the production of one article—cotton. It is evident to all . . . that we are deprived of this resource now and in all time to come; that a sufficient amount . . . can be produced by other portions of the country . . . cheaper than it can be produced here in the Western District. It therefore becomes absolutely necessary that we resort . . . to the production of some other material for export."[96] For years, therefore, this Democratic paper carried on a cogent and continuous campaign for a Wolf River canal, which it predicted would make the city the "Manchester of the South."[97] At last municipal officials were induced to call for bids in January, 1847, but the lowest estimate of $104,000 was rejected as being too costly. The city council seems to have favored the project, but the strenuous opposition of many influential taxpayers and the Whig paper, the *Eagle,* doomed it to defeat after five years of agitation.[98]

The *Appeal* was not alone in encouraging Memphis and

the South to turn to manufacturing. The Conventions of 1845 and 1853 both discussed the matter and included it in their resolutions,[99] and DeBow constantly harped on that theme. In the latter's *Review* for 1846 appeared an article entitled "Memphis and its Manufacturing Advantages," which observed among other things that Ohio coal sold for $2.40 per ton in Memphis while eastern cities were paying $5.00 per ton for it.[100] "If Memphis would be great," wrote the editor of the Cincinnati *Railroad Record,* in the next decade, "she must make railroads and build factories.[101]

These appeals did not go unanswered. In 1846 there were two flour mills and two machine works in Memphis, and three years later an extensive foundry was erected (Curtis and Knapp) which launched two steamboats within the year.[102] Besides other minor enterprises a rope and bagging factory was then in operation, and a plant for the manufacture of cotton goods, which had been in the process of construction since 1846, was soon turning out cotton yarn and osnaburgs.[103] The myriad uses of cottonseed were not known at the time, but quantities of it were crushed for oil. As early as 1844 M. E. Cochran and Company operated a planing mill and a sash, door, blind, and box factory.[104] Bohlen and Wilson stored ice on the Illinois in the winter and sold it in Memphis during the summer.[105] The fabrication of carriages, harnesses, tools, soap, lard oil, candles, flour, and other relatively simple products might be expected in a western town, but it is surprising to discover that such delicate instruments as pianos were made there, and that its shops built most of the coaches for the Memphis and Charleston.[106] The German immigrants proved excellent craftsmen, specializing in metalwork, watchmaking, tailoring, and other trades which required a high degree of skill.[107] The industrial activity of the city in 1860 is indicated in Table VI.

Table VI

Manufactures in Memphis in 1860[108]

	Capital Invested	Value Raw Material	Value Added
Sash, doors, blinds, etc.	$158,000	$268,000	$635,000
Steam engines, cars, wheels, iron works	367,000	259,000	541,000
Flour and corn meal	100,000	237,000	300,000
Bricks (5,000,000)	20,000	7,500	300,000
Carriages and buggies	75,500	33,500	143,101
Tinware, roofing, sheetiron	33,000	81,600	142,000
Lumber (sawmills)	87,000	68,600	124,000
Furniture (staple articles)	125,000	32,000	100,000
Wagons, carts, and drays	151,000	32,000	90,000
Soap, lard oil, candles	32,000	45,000	88,000
Boots and shoes	5,000	30,000	78,000
Gas (15,000,000 cu. ft.)	200,000	20,520	68,800
Cottonseed oil	102,000	30,600	61,000
Saddlery and harnesses	9,000	28,500	60,100
French, buzz, and saw mills	28,000	15,000	59,000
Steel, iron, copper, brass	12,000	20,000	42,000
Boilers	13,000	8,500	35,000
Agricultural and ornamental iron works	7,000	17,900	29,500
Laths	8,000	13,500	27,250
Plantation machinery	10,000	10,000	20,000
Mineral water	5,250	4,900	19,900
Hats and caps	3,500	4,700	10,500
Total	$1,551,250	$1,263,320	$2,974,151
Total value of manufactured goods			$4,237,471

Telegraphic connections were completed with New Orleans in 1843, with Nashville in 1847, and with Tuscumbia, Alabama, and Little Rock and Helena, Arkansas, in 1857.[109] As for banking, the Panic of 1837 introduced further confusion into a polyglot medium of circulation consisting of state notes, foreign coins, shinplasters (due bills issued in place of change), and counterfeit bills. The crisis of 1837 did not hit Memphis with full force, since its commerce was still negligible, but the financial disturbance of the middle fifties caused the suspension of specie payment by all its banks.[110]

Prior to 1850 Memphis had only three banks: the Farmers and Merchants (1834-48), and branches of the Union

Bank (1839) and the Planters Bank (1842) of Nashville.[111] The bluff city undoubtedly suffered from discrimination on the part of the state, for Jackson received a branch of the Union Bank in 1832, and though divisions of the Whig state bank of 1838 were located at Somerville and Trenton in the district, not until 1858 was a branch established in Memphis.[112]

The most striking evidence of the prosperity of the fifties in Memphis was the organization of eleven new banks between 1853 and 1858. Encouraged by the Tennessee Free Banking Act of 1852, a Whig measure, new financial institutions appeared yearly: three in 1853, two in 1854, two in 1855, one each in 1856 and 1857, and two in 1858.[113] Three of these banks failed before 1860, and the others were disrupted by the outbreak of the war or survived the hostilities only to collapse during reconstruction.

The transportation system which made Memphis the largest inland cotton market in the United States gave it similar advantages as a distributing center. Over the same rails, rivers, and planked roads that brought in cotton, went out an endless stream of food, provisions, and manufactured goods of every description. J. F. Frank & Co. established the first wholesale grocery in 1846, and by 1860 there were almost as many such houses as there were doctors or lawyers.[114] Other pioneer firms in the jobbing trade were Orgill Brothers, wholesale hardware, 1840; S. Mansfield & Co., wholesale drugs, 1840; C. W. Goyer & Co., produce, 1846; Shepard and Moore (W. R. Moore), wholesale dry goods, 1859; Bransford, Goodbar & Co., wholesale boots and shoes, 1860; and B. Lowenstein and Brothers, wholesale dry goods, 1861. Table VII shows the variety and extent of the activities of Memphis as a distributing center.

As the largest slave market of the central South, Memphis in 1857 had a dozen traders who advertised regularly in its papers.[116] Slaves were brought to the bluff by river

TABLE VII

RECEIPTS IN MEMPHIS FOR THE YEAR ENDING AUGUST, 31, 1861[115]

	Value		Value
Apples.....$	30,943	Limes.....$	107,495
Alcohol.....	16,800	Lemons.....	9,000
Agric. Implements....	55,150	Liquor.....	119,000
Ale and Beer.....	110,984	Lumber (16,527,670 bd. ft.).....	320,000
Bagging.....	372,460	Molasses (19,094 bbls.)	248,500
Beans.....	14,340	Nails.....	90,000
Boots and Shoes.....	123,030	Oats.....	55,600
Butter.....	99,612	Onions.....	18,200
Beef.....	56,242	Oakum.....	1,200
Bacon.....	1,710,070	Oranges.....	16,000
Cotton.....	18,481,650	Oil (3,107 bbls.).....	90,000
Cottonseed.....	70,124	Pork.....	806,680
Cotton gins (198).....	42,000	Potatoes.....	87,000
Cotton Yarn.....	34,020	Powder.....	29,500
Corn (1,137,546 bu.) ..	682,527	Rice (3,493 tierces)....	110,000
Cattle (7,332).....	219,660	Rope.....	249,500
Crockery.....	34,000	Sugar.....	898,000
Cloverseed.....	16,900	Salt.....	130,000
Cement and plaster...	40,000	Seed Grass.....	6,800
Cheese.....	73,800	Stoves.....	73,000
Coal (1,065,725 bu.)...	639,400	Sheep (3,236).....	11,500
Coffee.....	823,000	Shot.....	18,000
Dry Goods.....	4,012,800	Soap.....	30,600
Dried Fruit.....	22,400	Tobacco.....	689,100
Drugs.....	305,000	Tea.....	20,000
Eggs.....	108,000	Tar.....	6,000
Flour (155,000 bbls.)..	1,020,000	Turpentine.....	20,500
Furs.....	50,000	Wheat (140,054 bu.) ..	134,000
Fish.....	60,000	Whisky (31,471 bbls.) .	378,600
Furniture.....	375,000	Wool (1,880 ba.).....	47,500
Gunny Sacks.....	23,500	White Lead.....	9,300
Gunny Cloth.....	49,000	Wine, bbls. (364).....	29,120
Glass.....	25,000	Wine, casks (355).....	12,400
Glassware.....	40,000	Wine, boxes (4,204)...	21,000
Hay (32,300 ba.).....	150,000	Wine, baskets (1,452) .	21,780
Hides (60,860).....	152,000		
Hogs (5,582).....	67,000		
Hats.....	98,000	Total.....	$38,787,687
Horses (1,615).....	400,000		
Hardware.....	2,122,220	Articles manufactured.	4,000,000
Iron (2,827 tns.).....	234,000	Articles necessarily omitted.....	9,000,000
Ice (19,654 tns.).....	395,000		
Lead.....	112,800		
Leather.....	142,900		
Lard.....	151,500	Grand total.....	$52,787,687

from Kentucky, Virginia, and Missouri, or by rail from North Carolina, Tennessee, and northern Georgia to be sold to planters in West Tennessee, Arkansas, Mississippi, and northern Louisiana. The dean of local traders was Isaac Bolton, who with his numerous brothers and his partner Dickens did a lucrative business.[117] A feud in the Bolton family caused the decline of Bolton, Dickens & Co.,[118] and its place in the slave-trading world was soon taken by Nathan B. Forrest, an illiterate but energetic individual who had graduated from horse trading to traffic in real estate and blacks. The myths which have gathered around this guerrilla chieftain of the Confederacy have permanently obscured what must have been a unique character. Forrest applied himself to his profession, and by shrewdly keeping his pens more sanitary than most of his competitors and by honest dealing with his customers, he sold roughly one thousand Negroes annually in the late fifties. When he retired with a comfortable fortune in 1859 to become a planter in Gayoso County, Mississippi, Forrest was recognized as one of the richest and most popular traders of the South.[119]

In closing this description of the complex economic structure of ante-bellum Memphis, it should be emphasized that its outstanding characteristics were the rapidity of its evolution and a certain indescribable but effervescent dynamic quality, both of which differentiate it sharply from Charleston and Richmond in the southeast, and classify it definitely with western cities like Chicago. In fact, a comparison of Memphis and Chicago in the period before the war brings out striking similarities. Both began as Indian trading posts; both were incorporated about the same time, Memphis in 1826 with a population of three hundred, Chicago in 1833 with two hundred. Though their growth in the ante-bellum era was disproportionate, the Lake Michigan port and its southern counterpart on the lower Mississippi faced the same basic problems, and their development tended to follow a similar pattern. Chicago, too, was menaced by mud, gamblers, prostitutes, disease, and filth; it also had local rivals whom it vanquished by the construction of canals, planked roads, and railroads. In 1845 Memphis held a convention for the development of the West; two years later Chicago was the scene of a second meeting for the same purpose. In both cities during the fifties an influx of foreigners evoked a virulent nativism, and the Know-Nothings captured the municipal government in the Illinois as well as in the Tennessee metropolis.[120]

Perhaps the best example of the optimistic and dynamic spirit of the Memphis of the boom decades is the paragraph written by Rainey in conclusion to his city directory for 1855-56: "This is the four and five story era," he proclaimed. "The steamers on the rivers are grander than the stateliest ships that rode the deep a few years ago. Turnpikes are common roads, canals are antiquated, and the railroad spirit is at its height. [Soon] we shall be within forty hours of the Atlantic Ocean. . . . Hardly a house is put up in the business portion of the town that has less than four stories. Every modern invention and improvement is brought into play, and . . . structures whose spendor and capacity are not exaggerated by calling them palaces are reared upon the sites of humble cabins. We are arriving at a dizzy height, but our foundations are sure—our gaze is over the immensity of the Southwest, which our railroad arms will soon comprehend. What Era of Stories Next?"[121]

CHAPTER V

MEMPHIS COMES OF AGE

In the forties Memphis was in its adolescence, but in the fifties the city reached maturity. By the victory over Randolph and the conquest of the flatboatmen, it acquired an economic and social security soon reflected in a gain in population both quantitative and qualitative. Between 1840 and 1845 the number of inhabitants doubled; during the next five years it doubled again.* The twenty thousand people who arrived between the close of the flatboat era and the Civil War were of two classes: native Americans, many of whom were propertied and educated individuals from the Tidewater and from older sections of the Southwest, who realized the possibilities of the city; and European immigrants, chiefly Irish and Germans, who were drawn westward by the demand for labor in a growing town.[1]

The prosperity of the boom decades produced in Memphis an élite bourgeoisie, composed of the former class, a *petite noblesse* of southern society which fell short of being a full-fledged aristocracy, not because it lacked the manner of southern aristocrats, but only because it did not possess sufficient age, family background, and landed estates. West Tennessee had its own bona fide planter aristocracy, large numbers of whom resided in Shelby County, but they came to Memphis only for the winter season of music and drama. Urban life became so transitory on the bluff after 1840 that new names appear in the city's annals each year; yet many

* See map of the territorial growth of Memphis, on p. 125, below.

of its merchants and professional men in the fifties had undoubtedly acquired much of the polish of the county aristocracy of which they considered themselves a part. They patronized concert and theater with enthusiasm and with genuine appreciation;[2] their intellectual scope was surprisingly broad, for they were not bigots except for the minority that was rabid on the slavery question. They dueled at Hopefield across the river or beneath the oaks on Hernando Road, though Mayor Baugh and Dr. Dickinson in a moment of passion shot it out in front of the Exchange Building.[3] They discussed the topics of the day at their coffeehouses and gathered at rich banquets to pay homage to national figures like Clay and Douglas; they placed their money on favorite horses during the height of the racing season at Montgomery Park.[4] They filled their fine houses with ornate furniture and stocked their cupboards with the best of wines and whiskies; they left the city in the heat of the summer for popular watering places.

In contrast to this merchant and professional class of native Americans must be placed the large foreign element which also arrived in the boom decades. It is surprising that the homogeneous twentieth-century metropolis in 1860 should have contained 6,938 foreign-born persons out of a total population of 22,623; in other words, in that year 30 per cent of all Memphis citizens and 36 per cent of its white citizens were born outside of the United States.[5] This percentage, it should be noted, was entirely normal for the average American town in 1860, and even unusually low for the Mississippi Valley, since foreign-born inhabitants composed 60 per cent of the population in St. Louis, 50 per cent in Chicago and Milwaukee, 46 per cent in Cincinnati, 38 per cent in New Orleans, and 34 per cent in Louisville.[6] Obviously, in a description of any American city in the fifties these foreign groups require careful analysis.

Of the 22,623 persons in Memphis on the eve of the war,

11,803 were native whites; 4,159 were Irish; 3,882, Negroes; 1,412, Germans; 522, English; 140, British-Americans; 120, French, 113, Scots; and 472, of other foreign stocks.[7] Two thirds of these foreigners were Irish who, driven westward by famine in the old country, had followed river and railroad camp to the Chickasaw bluff. Though only a third as numerous as the Irish, the Germans proved far more valuable to their adopted community than all the other foreign groups; yet the number of exclusive organizations which they formed indicates a jealous preservation of a consciousness of their racial heritage. The English were amalgamated without difficulty, but smaller foreign groups, such as the French and the Swiss, preserved a certain clannishness.

If the Germans proved a valuable addition to the community, so much cannot be said of the Irish. They arrived years before the former and by congregating in Pinch gave Memphis a large proletariat which remained ever orthodox on the "poor-man question." They must have been numerous as early as 1844, for the Whigs of Shelby County were defeated in a local election that year, as they charged, "because of the God Damn Irish!"[8] The arrival of two hundred sons of Erin in 1854 to build levees in Mississippi frightened the mayor into calling out the militia, and the intensity of the nativistic upheaval then in progress indicates the existence of a deep-seated fear and hatred of the Irish.[9] By no means as sober or as ingenious as the Germans, their social needs were easily satisfied by the Catholic Church; the only secular organizations they formed were the Hibernian Relief Society and the St. Patrick's Literary Society.

The first influx of Germans apparently came soon after the Revolution of 1848 and continued throughout the next decade.[10] At any rate, they figured prominently in the economic and social life of the fifties, for during those years they founded the *"Unterstützung Verein"* (a benevolent society), the German Casino Club, and the so-called "German Turners' Gymnastic Association."[11] Their influence was soon felt in religious circles as well. In 1852 German Catholics, previously members of the Irish St. Peter's, organized the Society of St. Boniface which shortly became the St. Mary's German Catholic Church, and three years later their countrymen of Protestant faith formed the Evangelical Lutheran Trinity Church.[12] Their participation in commercial affairs is evident from the appearance of such concerns as B. Lowenstein and Brothers in 1861, the German National Bank in 1866, and the German Savings Institution in 1867.[13]

Although they clung to their language and certain other customs of the fatherland, German immigrants readily adapted themselves to their new environment. In response to the current trend towards military companies they formed the Steuben Artillery in 1858.[14] Opposed to slavery and permeated in many instances with the rationalism of the Old World, their chief contribution to Memphis was a broadening of its intellectual scope and an improvement of taste in esthetic matters. In 1854 August Kattmann, graduate of the University of Giessen and a Carl Schurz in miniature whom the Revolution of 1848 had forced into exile, started *Die Stimme des Volks* (Voice of the People), a weekly sheet with definite liberal tendencies. Four years later Louis Wundermann issued the first number of *Der Anzeiger des Südens* (Southern Advertiser), an independent paper popular for the next twenty years. Shortly after the capture of Memphis by the Federal army in 1862, P. Walser began publishing *Die Neue Zeit* (The New Era), which was frankly agnostic and radical unionist in sentiment.[15]

Nationalities other than the Germans and the Irish scarcely presented a real ethnic problem, because of their small numbers. The Swiss had their *"Gruetli Verein,"* in which German was adopted as the official language in order to exclude French and Italians. In 1855 Messrs. Pelegrin, Leclerc, Lavigne, Faquin, and Dupuy formed the *"Société Française de Secours Mutuel,"* and eleven years later the Scots, not to be outdone, started a St. Andrew's Society.[16] Nevertheless, it is hard today to believe that a city afflicted since the eighties with an unbroken provincialism could have once been so cosmopolitan.

While the ante-bellum Negro was considered neither by contemporary Americans nor by foreigners as a distinct social class, the objective critic can hardly classify him, along with cotton and mules, as mere property. Yet the social significance of the urban black was slight, for there is little evidence of his having affected contemporary institutions. Demand for slaves in the city was limited since their utility depended upon skill in some manual trade or in household service.[17] Usually they were too valuable to employ in such pursuits as digging ditches, particularly when there were hordes of Irish available who would work for a pittance. According to United States census reports there were 2,486 Negroes in Memphis in 1850, representing 28 per cent of its population, and ten years later their number had increased to 3,882, though at the later date they formed only 17 per cent of the population.[18] Comparing the percentage of Negroes in the city in 1860 (17 per cent) with the figures for the rest of Shelby County (52 per cent) and for West Tennessee as a whole (37 per cent), it is evident that the colored population of ante-bellum Memphis was unusually small.[19] The number of free Negroes, 126 in 1850 and 198 in 1860, was negligible.[20]

Slavery did not become an issue in Tennessee politics until the Wilmot Proviso, but Memphis was not immune to the general hysteria in regard to Negroes which arose in the South during the forties. In 1856 ordinances were passed to govern their conduct. According to these regulations blacks were required to return home immediately when curfew was tolled on the Court Square bell; all persons and institutions were forbidden to teach them to read and write; their meeting at night was prohibited except by written consent of the mayor and under the strict supervision of the police; and it was declared unlawful for any black person to preach in the city.[21] Still these regulations were laxly enforced and Negroes were on the whole well treated, since they represented an investment of which West Tennesseans had cause to appreciate the value.[22] In response to the dictates of good business if not humanitarian instincts, Memphis slave dealers tended to follow the example of Forrest rather than that of Bolton.

By the fifties the inhabitants of Memphis were divided into two distinct social classes with a large and less distinct neutral group in the middle. At the top was a prosperous bourgeoisie, composed of native Americans and largely of native southerners, bound by tradition to the Tidewater but becoming more and more affiliated with the commercial interests of the upper West. At the botton was a propertyless proletariat, primarily Irish in composition. Between these two extremes were numerous categories, including the German shopkeepers and shiftless southerners who became day laborers like the Irish. Society was not strictly stratified, since individuals were constantly passing from the lower to the upper levels, but its members, even in a day when the doctrines of Marx were known to few in America, were quite conscious of the struggle between economic classes.

In a city that passed from infancy to maturity as fast as Memphis did in its boom decades, it was inevitable that social organization should become hastily and increasingly complex. During these years arose various institutions characteristic of urban life, determined and modified by the fundamental clash between bourgeoisie and proletariat, natives and foreigners. Nowhere is this clash so apparent as in the politics of the period.

To understand the political situation in Memphis between 1840 and 1860, one must consider briefly the origins of Jacksonian Democracy and the Whig party in Tennessee. Andrew Jackson, though he bitterly fought the democratic movement in the state under Governor Cannon which the Panic of 1819 produced, was supported by the people because the memory of his victory at New Orleans was vivid despite its remoteness in point of time, and because they considered it no mean honor to have a son in the White House. Jacksonian Democracy, in Tennessee at least, was not an agrarian crusade with a definite program like that of the Populists sixty years later—it was rather an emotion. Had his appeal not been to the heart instead of the head, Jackson would never have survived eight years of the most extreme executive inconsistency in the history of the presidency; in fact, his straddling of issues before 1828 would have prevented his election in the first place. As president he opposed internal improvements and sound banking, both necessities to a state that was inland and commercial; yet Tennessee continued to support him.

By arbitrary acts, however, the Hero of New Orleans had alienated certain of his followers in Tennessee—Newton Cannon, John Bell, David Crockett, and Hugh Lawson White—men who had supported him only because the public had forced them to do so. Realizing that Jackson could be displaced only by the use of his own weapons, for years these new enemies of his waited for a false move on his part which they could use to discredit him with the people. Their opportunity came in 1836 when he attempted to force Van Buren upon his supporters in place of White, who was almost as popular with Tennesseans as Old Hickory himself. This move was fatal, for it caused the President to appear in his own state as dictator as well as traitor to his own friend, and the frontier had little use for either.[23]

Thus out of enmity to Jackson arose the Whig party in Tennessee, a party that remained a power in the state until secession disrupted it. The Whigs were strong enough to defeat Polk in 1844, though he was a local planter of whose platform Tennessee highly approved, and they insured the failure of the Nashville Convention in 1850.[24] These political alignments, formed in the thirties, changed little before the war, except temporarily during the brief Know-Nothing upheaval. Though such alignments were often determined by individuals and personalities, they were based after 1836 on a fundamental conflict between commercial interests and agrarian. The Whigs represented the towns and their hinterlands against the back country, and the planters sided with the merchants and the bankers, upon whom they were dependent, against the small self-sufficient farmer.[25]

The rich counties in the Southwest were a Whig stronghold. In every presidential election from 1836 through 1860, with the exception of 1856 when Buchanan defeated Fillmore by sixty-seven votes, Shelby gave the Whig candidate a majority, as shown in Table VIII, below.[26] Anti-Jackson sentiment appeared quite early in Memphis, and as soon as White's candidacy was announced in 1836 a paper started there in his behalf.[27] As the town's commercial interests increased in the forties one would expect it to have become even more attached to the conservative party. On the contrary, though but two or three records of the actual vote in the city have been preserved, there is every indication that the Democrats were almost as powerful as the Whigs.[28] Yet no Democratic or Whig machines existed in Memphis, for except in 1855 and 1856 party lines were drawn not in municipal, but merely in state and federal elections.

This abnormal Democratic strength in the metropolis

of a rich cotton region can be accounted for only by the size of its poorer class and the increasing number of foreigners, who usually became members of the party of Jefferson. The denizens of Pinch were wooed by Crockett when he was defending the rights of West Tennessee squatters, with whom they had little in common but poverty. These poorer folk were numerous enough to defeat the popular Rawlings in 1832 because he had displeased them, and Seth Wheatley was not the only demagogue in whom they aroused ambitions. As commercial interests grew stronger, the tendency toward conservatism was offset by the number of Irish immigrants who flocked to the Democratic standard, as is evident from the Whigs' assertion that the Democratic victory in the state election of 1844 in Shelby County was due to the urban Irish vote. The Memphis Whigs had their revenge, however, for they won a majority of two hundred votes for both Taylor in 1848 and Scott in 1852.[29]

The arrival of the Germans during the early fifties tended at first to increase the numerical strength of the local

TABLE VIII

VOTE OF MEMPHIS AND SHELBY COUNTY IN ANTE-BELLUM PRESIDENTIAL ELECTIONS

Memphis		
1848	Taylor (W) 1,147	Cass (D) 892
1852	Scott (W) 1,171	Pierce (D) 976
1856	....	....
1860	Douglas (N.D.) 2,319 Bell (C.U.) 2,250 Breckinridge (S.D.) 572	

Shelby County		
1836	White (W) 488	Van Buren (D) 310
1840	Harrison (W)	
1844	Clay (W) 1,625	Polk (D) 1,352
1848	Taylor (W) 1,828	Cass (D) 1,607
1852	Scott (W) 1,824	Pierce (D) 1,628
1856	Buchanan (D) 2,083	Fillmore (K) 2,016
1860	Bell (C.U.) 3,048 Douglas (N.D.) 2,959 Breckinridge (S.D.) 744	

Democratic party, but later this same immigration weakened it because the influx of foreigners created nativistic sentiment among the older settlers, regardless of their party affiliation, with whom the new arrivals competed economically. The vigorous sectionalism of the decade before the war, which later split even the older and more unified Democratic party, disrupted the Whigs early in the fifties. This development left Memphis conservatives somewhat at sea. In view of this situation it is easy to understand the swift transition of most of the local Whigs and many of the local Democrats to the new Know-Nothing party, as that comet of the American political galaxy was dubbed by its opponents.

For two decades nativism in the Mississippi Valley had been approaching a boiling point because of the hordes of immigrants who were descending upon the river towns.[30] As in New Orleans, St. Louis, and Louisville, so also in Memphis the setting was favorable to a rabid outburst of anti-foreign emotion when the American (Know-Nothing) party appeared on the national scene. On June 17, 1854, the *Appeal,* as the official organ of the Democrats and therefore the self-constituted protector of the foreigners who filled the ranks of that party, fulminated against the "deadly fanaticism" of the revived "Native-Americans"; yet already many Know-Nothing lodges had been formed in Memphis.[31] The ignorance of the Democratic paper in regard to the local strength of the Know-Nothings was cruelly and cogently dispelled when, a fortnight later, it was forced to announce that the new party had emerged victorious in the recent municipal election. No more conclusive proof of the strong nativistic sentiment in the city could be advanced than the fact that Mayor Taylor, a candidate for re-election, made known his allegiance to the Know-Nothing organization a few days before the public went to the polls.[32]

For several years the Democratic sheet bombarded the Know-Nothings by sarcasm and frontal attack, but for a while all its efforts were in vain because it was attempting to check a tide that was fast approaching flood. Even its own followers did not prove steadfast, for Solon Borland, a leading Democrat, deserted to the enemy. Memphis Whigs had gone over early; the *Eagle and Enquirer* became as staunch a Know-Nothing organ as it had formerly been Whig, quite in contrast to the course of its upstate colleague, the Nashville *Whig,* controlled by the old-line or Scott wing of the party, which would have no truck with the Americans. By seducing the temperance party, which was just becoming a factor in state politics, in 1855 the Know-Nothings won a sweeping victory in Shelby County, and in the state as a whole they succeeded in electing their candidates to the principal offices with the single exception of the governorship, which the popular Democrat, Andrew Johnson, acquired by the small margin of two thousand votes.[33] They retained control of Memphis in 1855, but the following year, according to mutual agreement, national politics were divorced from the municipal election.[34] In the presidential contest of 1856 the American party, though its popularity was already on the wane, cast 2,016 votes for Fillmore in Shelby to Buchanan's 2,083.

The nativistic movement in Memphis was the product of definite economic and psychological factors. The antipathy of Whig for Democrat had grown bitter by the early fifties, since conservative merchants undoubtedly regarded the success of their new competitors from across the sea with fear and envy, and this hostility was tremendously accentuated when the newcomers joined the party that spoke for the masses. For those southerners, regardless of party extraction, who realized that much of the political strength of the East and the upper West was due to the votes of an endless wave of immigrants, nativism was a welcome cloak with which to hide a conscious sectionalism which they did not care to admit outright. In Memphis the movement was colored by religious prejudice which, though the principal characteristic of Americanism in the northern states, was absent in the South at large.[35] A local Baptist minister delivered a sermon extolling the virtues of the Know-Nothing program, and a subscriber of the *Appeal,* who probably expressed the attitude of many citizens, discontinued his subscription because the paper had "too much to say in favor of those damnable Catholics."[36]

The downfall of the American party, in Memphis and in the nation, was as swift as its meteoric rise. With southern Know-Nothings pro-slavery in sentiment and their northern brethren Free-Soilers, the same force that had disrupted the Whigs soon proved their own nemesis. The first local indication of this fatal development was the conversion of ex-Governor J. C. Jones, a leading old-line Whig, to the Democratic party. At a political rally in 1856 Jones spoke for four hours, declaring in all earnestness that if Frémont were elected the South ought not to remain in the Union. To prevent such a catastrophe he was transferring his allegiance to the party he had fought all his life, for he was convinced that "Black Republicanism" could be defeated only by a merger of the southern Whigs with the Democrats.[37] Jones's views carried considerable weight with the Know-Nothings of Memphis and with the former Whig planters of the surrounding area, for he was known to be a conservative Union man and anything but an alarmist.[38] The decline of the Know-Nothings was precipitous, and in 1857 the Democratic ticket swept the county in the state election.

The American party served as a bridge which led many Memphis Whigs temporarily into the camp of the Democrats, but once the latter seemed to be leading the nation into disunion and war, the conservatives returned in haste to their former affiliation. It is highly significant that in the presidential election of 1860 the city gave Bell 2,250 votes to Douglas's 2,319, and that 90 per cent of the electorate pronounced themselves opposed to Breckinridge and the secessionists.[39]

The transition from the simple life of the flatboat town to the relatively complex society of the river port is quite apparent from developments in journalism, religion, and education which occurred in the forties and fifties.

In a day when library facilities were narrowly limited if not unknown and even an elementary education the possession of a minority, the newspaper, as the only source of information for the vast majority about the world outside, occupied a more influential position than, with its broadened scope, it does today. Since its existence has always depended upon sufficient circulation, the newspaper has ever been compelled to cater to public opinion; therefore it was quite natural that the ante-bellum press should become obsessed with politics to such an extent that the support of a particular party seemed its chief excuse for existence. Prior to 1860, in the South at any rate, politics held the center of the stage, and economic affairs were definitely of secondary importance.

The history of the press in Memphis during this era, then, is concerned largely with a Whig and a Democratic succession, and its significance lies not so much in journalistic excellence as in its sensitivity to changes in public sentiment. During the forties this Whig-Democratic rivalry, begun in the flatboat era, became more pronounced. Latham of the *Enquirer* left that paper in 1841 to his colleague, Colonel McMahon, and the new year found him in Fort Pickering starting a weekly, the *American Eagle,* which two years later became the first daily on the bluff. One year after Latham's retirement in 1850 the two Whig papers sired by him merged and took the name of the *Eagle and Enquirer*. The Democrats, meanwhile, had not been idle. Shortly after the demise of the *Gazette* in 1838, Solon Borland issued the first number of his *Western World and Memphis Banner of the Constitution,* which in 1840 was purchased by Henry Van Pelt, who changed its name to the *Appeal*. Under the editorship of this ablest of local ante-bellum journalists the *Appeal,* too, became a daily.

When the rivalry between the *Enquirer* and the *Appeal* became bitter in the fifties as party strife increased, broadside met broadside in a Gargantuan battle of words. The fate of the proud Whig journal is pathetic, for in the month before Sumter fell it was absorbed by the *Avalanche,* the antithesis of all that it had held sacred. Yet there must have been a substantial group of citizens who were neither Democrats nor Whigs nor Know-Nothings in sentiment, since McMahon withdrew from the *Enquirer* in 1855 and formed an independent paper, the *Morning Bulletin,* which was also taken over by the *Avalanche* after the outbreak of war. The latter, started in 1858 by M. C. Gallaway, a Mississippi fire-eater, outdid the *Appeal* in its defense of the South. The *Evening Public Ledger,* which appeared late in the decade, was a mere rehash of the four morning papers.[40]

By 1840 congregations of all the denominations represented in ante-bellum Memphis, except the Disciples of Christ and the Jews,[41] had been formed, but only the Methodists and the Presbyterians had actually erected churches. The prosperity of the following years resulted in the construction of numerous church buildings and in a general institutionalization of religion. As the town grew, offshoots and missions of the earlier congregations became churches in their own name, and with the steady influx of Irish and Germans the Catholics became incontestably the most powerful single denominational group. On the eve of the war an imposing church directory included Wesley Chapel, Asbury Chapel, McKendree Chapel, and Davidson Chapel of the Methodists; the First, Second, and Third Presbyterian churches; the First, Beale Street, and Fort Pickering Mission churches of the Baptists; the Cumberland Presbyterian, the South Memphis Cumberland Presbyterian, and the South Memphis Presbyterian Mission; Calvary, St. Mary's, and Grace Episcopal churches; St. Peter's and St. Mary's Catholic churches; the Trinity Lutheran church, the Linden Avenue Christian church, and the Jewish Synagogue.[42]

In acquiring respectability and becoming conventionalized, however, religion suffered from a loss of much of its pristine spontaneity. No longer was it the center of social life as in the early flatboat era, and the church was forced to take its place merely as one of the numerous institutions in an intricate and a worldly society. In spite of the example of wives and families, many influential men of the community refused to affiliate with any church,[43] and those who found themselves seized with the holy spirit usually compromised by joining the Episcopal, since it was less likely to offend esthetic temperaments and was less strict in its demands upon the chosen. Indeed, Memphis merchants and professional men seem to have taken their religion as they took their liquor—in the easy manner that marks the gentleman. What one scholar has said of the ante-bellum planter applies equally well to this *petite noblesse:*

"The planters and the lawyers—the educated classes—though formal Episcopalians in many cases, were inoculated with the skepticism or indifference which came down from the eighteenth century, and a man could not be a 'gentleman' under the 'code duello' and the decanter and a pious church member at the same time."[44]

Education in West Tennessee, as in the ante-bellum South at large, was only for those who could afford it. In the secondary field it was provided by the private academy, preparatory to entrance to southern colleges or to Yale, Harvard, and Princeton in the East. Reputable academies were founded at Jackson in 1825 and at Raleigh four years later, but Memphis contented itself until the forties with the elementary institution of Eugene Magevney. With the prosperity of the middle of the century, private schools of more extensive scope came into existence, of which Mr. Whitehorne's grammar school for boys and the Misses Young's school for girls were typical.[45] In 1851 St. Peter's Church organized the St. Agnes Academy for girls, an institution which was immediately placed in the care of the Dominican Sisters.[46] Soon this church set up a more comprehensive parochial school that four years later boasted a membership of a hundred and twenty-six.[47] The Mechanics' Institute offered a library, a night school, and lectures to those who were interested in technical training, and the Mercantile College specialized in vocational studies.[48]

Higher education was not neglected. Though the elaborate plans of Rev. B. F. Farnsworth, founder of Union University in Tennessee, for a similar institution in Memphis came to grief, the Botanico-Medical School and the Memphis Medical School were founded in 1846 and 1849 respectively.[49] Upon its reorganization in 1851 the latter became a first-class institution, conducting a dispensary for the poor to supplement the service of the Memphis City Hospital.[50] Ample attention was given the education of girls, for several women's seminaries were formed in the forties, and the Memphis Female College (1854) and the State Female College (1858) earned a wide reputation[51] as finishing schools.

Education in Memphis, however, was distinguished not so much by the number of its private institutions as by the inauguration of a public school system; in all the South only a few of the larger cities took any step in this direction before 1860. The size of its proletariat and the number of foreigners among its inhabitants forced such an enterprise upon the busy and none too willing town—in fact the affair has the earmarks of a struggle between the poor and the well-to-do. In spite of opposition from the wealthy[52] and lack of co-operation from those who were to benefit therefrom, the first public schools were opened in March, 1848, as a result of the efforts of Professor McGevney, J. W. A. Pettit, G. B. Locke, and a few other enlightened individuals. During the four years in which Pettit served as superintendent (1848-1852), at first without pay, the city spent for education a meager twenty thousand dollars in addition to the funds accruing from the nominal fee of two dollars a student, which was waived in many cases. When the rival corporations of Memphis and South Memphis were united in 1849 the public voted to continue the free schools, and by 1852 thirteen schools were being operated with a total enrollment of 584. To meet the increased expenses a special municipal tax was levied in that year, and a county tax was instituted for the same purpose two years later, but no buildings were erected until after the war.

The failure of the aldermanic committee on education to provide for the opening of schools in the early fifties so aroused the public that a Board of School Visitors was appointed which, though possessing no legal authority, became a constant spur to the officials and prevented further attempts at allowing the enterprise to die of neglect. The permanence of the institution was guaranteed in 1856 when an act of incorporation required the city council to select one citizen from each ward to serve on a board which would have complete control of public education. By 1860 the salary of the superintendent had been raised to $2,500, and twenty-one schools with an enrollment of 1,682 and an average daily attendance of 798 were being conducted at an annual cost of $23,896.[53]

Like all America in that age, Memphians enthusiastically joined such secret societies as the Masons, Odd Fellows, Sons of Malta, and the Druids.[54] Glancing at random through the directory for 1860 one notices among other local organizations the Leath Orphanage, St. Peter's Orphanage, the Jockey Club, the Medical Association, and the Pioneer Boat Club. With the exception of the Memphis Typographical Union Number 11, labor was unorganized, though the employees of the Memphis and Charleston forced the railroad to reduce its working day from eleven to ten hours.[55] National movements like the Young Men's Christian Association and Bible and Temperance Societies resulted in the formation of local chapters, but the real fight against drunkenness was led by Father Matthews, a devout Catholic priest, whose mission in the slums fulfilled the function of the then unheard-of social settlement.[56] The organization of an historical society in 1857, the Old Folks of Shelby County, is unmistakable evidence that the community was acquiring a certain sophistication.[57]

A peculiar characteristic of frontier life which never faded in this river town but which grew stronger in spite of urbanization was its martial spirit. Citizens followed with enthusiasm the events of the Texan War of Independence, the Mexican War, the filibustering escapades of Walker and Lopez in Central America, and civil strife in Kansas. Nor was this interest without reverberations, for the militia muster of early days was succeeded by more formal companies which were social as well as military organizations. The Guards and the Blues preserved order during the flatboat disturbance in 1842, and the Rifle Guards, the Gaines Guards, and the Eagle Guards served in the Mexican War.[58] The events occurring in Cuba and

Kansas stimulated the formation of new companies in the fifties: the City Guards in 1852, the George Washington Riflemen and the Washington Rifle Company in 1853; the Young American Invincibles in 1854, the Steuben Artillery in 1858, and the Memphis Light Guards, the Jackson Guards, and the Memphis Southern Guards in 1859.[59] Yet with Irish as privates and the large number of Germans who appear in the roster of officers, this phenomenon cannot be considered purely indigenous in origin.

The sad experience of Memphis throughout the nineteenth century with what may be called municipal problems reveals that in spite of prosperity Americans failed completely in the task of adapting themselves to the complexities of urban life. Not until the end of the century did the cities of the United States achieve any appreciable success in this process of adjustment, and the amazing progress in this direction that has occurred since 1900 makes it difficult for us to realize the squalor, the dangers, the discomforts, and the impositions to which our urban grandfathers were exposed.

The rise of Memphis to a position of importance began in the early forties with the victory over Randolph and the conquest of the flatboatmen, but it was almost a decade later that the several projects on the lower Chickasaw bluff were unified and incorporated as a single municipality. McLemore's scheme of linking the fortune of Fort Pickering to the LaGrange railroad has already been mentioned.[60] In January, 1842, McLemore made his last attempt to organize a separate town, and for the next few years Fort Pickering possessed a newspaper, the *American Eagle*, and a school of "art, law, and medicine" under the direction of Rev. B. F. Farnsworth of New Hampshire.[61] "Visit sunny Italy," proclaimed the *Eagle,* "vine-clad France, romantic Switzerland, or traverse our own country from Bangor to

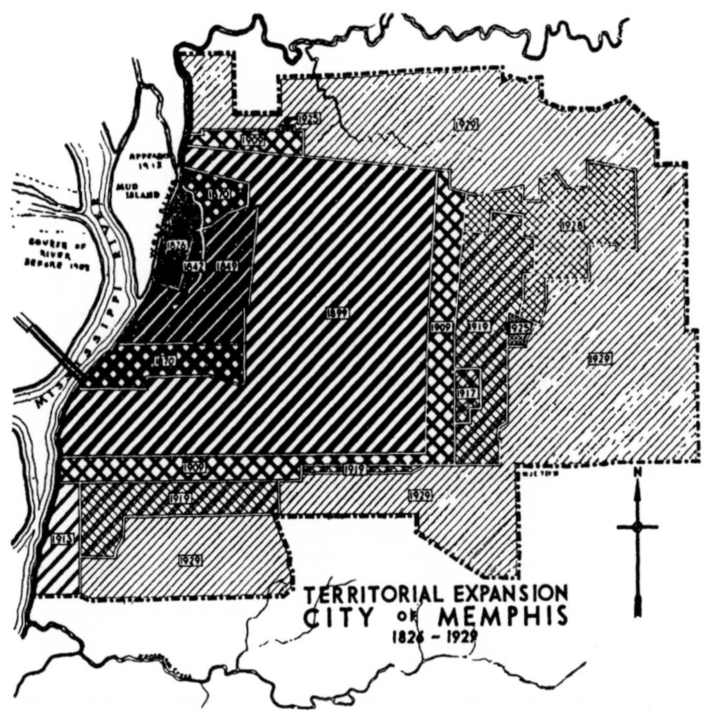

U. S. Census			City Estimate			
Year	Pop.	% Increase	Year	Pop. City	Pop. Suburbs	Total
1830	663		1820	53		
1840	1,799	171	1825	308		
1850	8,841	391	1828	500		
1860	22,623	155	1832	906		1,000
1870	40,226	77	1835	1,239		1,500
1880	33,592	—16	1846	3,500	500	4,000
1890	64,495	92	1854	12,687	2,000	14,687
1900	102,320	58	1865	27,703	10,000	37,703
1910	131,105	28	1869	39,401	7,000	46,401
1920	162,351	24	1875	41,500	8,500	50,000
1930	253,153	56	1885			59,875
			1890			85,290

the farthest extremity bordering on the Pacific, and you will not find a prettier site for a town than our own infant village."[62] But optimism alone was not sufficient, and Fort Pickering soon collapsed with the bankruptcy of the LaGrange road.

The town of South Memphis, incorporated by the Tennessee legislature in January, 1846,[63] was a far more serious threat to the larger city on the bluff. Upon the granting of a charter to the new town Judge Sylvester Bailey was elected mayor, and soon its boundaries were enlarged to include Fort Pickering.[64] After three years of separate corporate existence, citizens of both towns called a public meeting at the city hall in Memphis to consider union. Colonel J. T. Trezevant, mayor of the southern town, and Robertson Topp, who had long been interested in the project because of the extensive real estate he owned there, both spoke strongly in favor of unification.[65] In spite of opposition from a group of irreconcilables led by Judge Bailey, the public voted to send a recommendation for union to the legislature, and in December, 1849, an act was passed to that effect.[66] Several months of confusion ensued, during which newly elected officials of the enlarged town were afraid to assume office because of hostile public sentiment, but a second election in February, 1850, gave them such a large majority that their fears were overcome.[67]

Such was the final disposition of the rivalry between Memphis, South Memphis, and Fort Pickering, but irreparable damage had already been done to the welfare of the bluff community. Embers of the bitter discord continued to spark for many years; when an alderman from Pinch proposed an ordinance to limit the speed of horses, his colleagues from Sodom indignantly declared that the motion was a vindictive attempt to handicap the southern wards where distances were greater.[68] The struggle to draw business southward had destroyed the flatboat market, which once extended from Adams Street north along the bluff to the corporation line, and a severe increase in the price of provisions resulted.[69] Worst of all, it left the town's business district, which should have been less than half a mile long, spread out over a mile of river front, and this situation greatly increased the cost of municipal upkeep. Thus in spite of high taxes the city found its revenue inadequate to foster many projects necessary to urban health and the general convenience of citizens.

Memphis, consequently, intoxicated by the prosperity of its boom decades, rushed headlong into a debt which later contributed to its undoing. The epidemic of railroad construction and street improvement was universal in mid-nineteenth-century America, and the young town was for the first time experiencing growing pains. Yet the splurge of spending which ensued need not necessarily have proved disastrous except for inexcusable blundering on the part of the aldermen.

The first improvement of city streets was ordered by the council in 1845, and during the next four years $130,000 was spent for grading and graveling.[70] Superimposed on a clay soil, this gravel, within a year after its application, lay buried deep beneath a surface of mud as bad as ever, thanks to the constant pounding of heavy drays laden with cotton. One experiment of this kind should have convinced the council of the inadequacy of gravel, but the same process was repeated not once but half a dozen times in the next fifteen years. In 1850 the major part of a $150,000 bond issue was spent for more gravel, and most of the million dollars added to the bonded indebtedness by the Taylor administration between 1852 and 1855 was expended for the same purpose.[71] In the spring of 1858 public thoroughfares were worse than ever; drays were often inextricably stuck in the mire and cotton had to be hauled away a bale at a time. Only after half an hour of strenuous effort did a Negro succeed in rescuing a young boy caught in a mudhole at the corner of Main and Monroe.[72]

Engineers who were consulted recommended granite boulders, a macadam pavement of limestone and gravel, or cedar blocks, but regardless of this expert advice the aldermen in September decided upon another layer of gravel. "Memphis has just reached the age of Gravel," exploded the *Appeal*. "Sleep on, venerable Rip Van Winkle! No rattling of vehicles over solid pavement shall disturb thy slumbers. Thou shalt snooze in undisturbed tranquility with ooze, mud, and pure gravel for the bed of thy Sleepy Hollow."[73] When almost a million dollars had been literally poured into the mud, the council at last lost confidence in gravel and induced the legislature in 1860 to authorize an expenditure of $300,000, provided the consent of citizens was given at the polls, for paving streets and wharves with cobblestones.[74] In view of this whole performance it is difficult to avoid the suspicion that for years the officials had been in league with local gravel contractors.

If much money was wasted on streets, an equal amount was lost in subscriptions to railroad companies. Swayed by the eloquence of ex-Governor J. C. Jones and Colonel J. T. Trezevant, on several occasions aldermen voted subscriptions to the stock of various roads which totaled more than one million dollars by 1860. The $500,000 invested in the Memphis and Charleston was later recovered upon the sale of the stock at its par value, but on the $100,000 subscribed to the Memphis and Ohio, the $250,000 to the Mississippi and Tennessee, and the $350,000 to the Memphis and Little Rock, the city suffered a loss of $582,000.[75]

Between 1847 and 1860 the municipal debt increased from eighty thousand to more than a million dollars.[76] Since the latter amount was less than 2 per cent of the value of annual trade and only 5 per cent of the value of taxable property, it was not necessarily excessive for a growing metropolis. Yet local officials were guilty of criminal negligence, for with the exception of the railroads, on which no loss should have been sustained, the city had nothing to show for its enormous expenditure. This deplorable situation was due to a combination of indifference, graft, and downright ignorance on the part of aldermen. There were, moreover, other instances of the mishandling of public funds. In Tammany fashion $43,000 was spent on a wharf which should have cost only $17,000. The chain gang, in most cities a financial asset, actually cost the city $20,000 annually for upkeep; in June, 1858, one captain and two overseers were being employed to guard and direct the labor of two prisoners. Neither a new fire engine nor a town clock could be purchased because of municipal penury; yet the city attorney was readily granted an increase in salary of $1,500. It was quite customary for officials to buy poor horses, fatten them at municipal expense, and sell them at a large profit. Thousands of dollars were lost, furthermore, in stupid if not dishonest disposal of railroad stock and the navy yard property.[77]

During the nineteenth century the valley was never free from pestilence of one sort or another. Smallpox and cholera were perennial and yellow fever appeared frequently. A board of health was appointed in Memphis as early as 1838,[78] but throughout the ante-bellum period it remained a body which functioned only after an epidemic had become so threatening that the public was frightened into action. It is true that this was the prescientific age of medicine, as the germ theory of disease did not reach America until the seventies; yet Memphis can be rightly held somewhat responsible for its high death rate, since it did not even attempt to enforce the precautions considered efficacious by contemporaries. In 1849 Asiatic cholera swept New Orleans and Nashville, taking the lives of ex-President Polk and General Gaines in the latter city, but in Memphis it proved fatal only to the "flatboat people, the dissolute, and those who were enervated by dissipation.[79] In 1851 it returned to take a toll of ninety-three lives.[80] From 1852 to 1855 yellow fever raged in the valley, causing twelve thousand deaths in New Orleans alone, and in the latter year Memphis suffered 220 deaths in 1,250 cases.[81]

In the early fifties the newspapers sponsored a health campaign, and doctors advocated a sewerage system, water works, and education in hygienic practices, but all talk ended merely in the continuance of the powerless board of health. This board was ineffectual, for it served only in an advisory capacity to the aldermen, by whom all measures had to be initiated. The only sanitary ordinance passed was the authorization of the purchase of some property on Bray's Island in the river to serve as a quarantine station. When this question of quarantine to safeguard the city from a dangerous epidemic of yellow fever raging along the river in 1858 was being discussed officially, Alderman Finnie expressed the attitude of a large group of citizens. He "never knew any good to come from quarantine," he asserted. "If Providence intended the fever to come here, it will come in spite of all we can do."[82]

The public apathy which permitted this bungling was natural in view of the tempo of contemporary life in the valley. Men who were building roads, pioneering in commerce and industry, pushing back wilderness and river, and piling up personal fortunes were too busy to supervise the activity of public servants for whom they probably had only contempt. What little time the individuals of this bustling society had for governmental matters they gave to state and national politics, which were fast drifting into the maelstrom of civil strife. Not inclination but time was lacking, for public spirit and civic pride are as much the product of leisure as of enlightenment. Thus even before the war, death and disease, those twin spectres of the seventies, stalked in Memphis, proving that the catastrophe which was nearly to destroy it later was the inevitable result of conditions almost as old as the settlement itself.

It would be a mistake to infer from this failure of Memphis to cope with problems of finance, sanitation, and paving of streets—an experience common to most contemporary American cities—that there were not numerous signs of civic progress during the boom decades. In 1849 appeared the first city directory;[83] in the next decade gas lamps were installed on the streets to make less dangerous the way of those who were bold enough to venture out by night, and in 1860 a street railway company applied for a franchise for a mule-car system.[84] Though Front Row along the river was the principal business street of the town, Main Street one block east was beginning to rival it. In 1852 Adams Street was the southern boundary of the commercial district, which thereafter, to the joy of Sodom, spread swiftly southward.[85]

To the New Memphis Theatre, a far cry from the old Blue Ruin, now came Jenny Lind and Edwin Booth, English and Italian opera companies, Shakespearean troupes, and numerous other artists.[86] The large population of foreigners, particularly the Germans, were no doubt responsible for the intense interest in music and drama, similar to that existing at the same time in San Francisco, another young town; and to them should also go the credit for the organization in 1860 of a Philharmonic Society under Carlo Patti. Newspapers in the fifties constantly advocated such necessary municipal institutions as a public library and a chamber of commerce.[87] After a decade of wrangling an appropriation for the water works was voted in 1860.[88] That year also saw the organization of the first paid fire department, since recent conflagrations had resulted in the destruction of several hundred thousand dollars worth of property, and in March, despite misgivings on the part of certain older merchants, a chamber of commerce was formed.[89]

A city that grew in population and area as did Memphis in these prosperous years had little time for consideration of style and beauty in its architecture. The instability of life in a region where population followed rich soil produced a pragmatic philosophy and a practical attitude which saw virtue only in utility. As wealth increased, one-story cabins with clapboard roofs, puncheon floors, and stick chimneys had been replaced by one-and-a-half story structures with brick chimneys, board roofs, and walls of logs to which the adze had been applied in a rough manner. With the advent of sawmills came two-story frame buildings and shingle roofs fastened by nails instead of weight-boards. During the forties, however, bricks replaced lumber in the edifices of the well-to-do, and in the next decade commercial buildings reached the dizzy height of five stories,[90] but the criterion of construction continued to be size rather than design. Only in the residential section on Beale, Vance, and Linden streets did one find an occasional mansion, like that of Robertson Topp,[91] done in the classic style which architects still consider the crowning glory of the Old South.

Memphis was proud of the hotels which its position on the crossroads made necessary, particularly of the Gayoso House, reputed to be one of the most attractive in the South. Travel in that age, like medicine, was an ordeal which the public accepted as necessary but unpleasant. Frederick Law Olmsted, an observant northerner who "toured" the back country in the winter of 1853-54, stopped in Memphis at the Commercial Hotel, whose somewhat imposing bill of fare he includes in the account of his experiences. Unused to the fast eating which was customary in a western town, Olmsted found the choice dishes on the menu exhausted when he finally got service and he was forced to make a meal of grimy bacon, greasy cabbage, and Irish pudding. The coach service from the hotel to the railroad station a mile or so out of town was equally trying, as chivalry demanded that the male passengers push the "ladies and baggage" over all such obstructions as creeks and fallen timber, and one gathers that Olmsted was not entirely pleased with the facilities offered the tourist in the city.[92]

In spite of the metamorphosis which had taken place during these twenty years, the old Memphis of the flatboat era had not disappeared nor had its intensity diminished. Upon the flatboat town had been superimposed a stratum of society which suffered little from a superficial comparison with the upper class elsewhere in the South, but beneath that stratum surged the old life in all its pristine viciousness. In the numerous dives, gambling dens, and bawdy houses the scum of the river still congregated, and life there was cheap and murder commonplace. Natchez aristocracy and Natchez-under-the-hill, famous in literature as well as in history, were completely segregated and therefore each an entity to itself—but in Memphis the élite and the underworld existed on the same plane. Though they did not rub elbows in the ballroom or at the theater, they did meet in the market place, and each managed to leave its imprint on the other. Culture, consequently, was occasionally discovered to be only skin-deep and vice sometimes displayed finesse. With its two worlds and the no-man's land between, society as a whole presented a confused appearance, and Memphis of the fifties must have seemed to the stranger a city of contrasts.

The planter aristocracy of the interior of West Tennessee and the associated commercial groups in the towns of Brownsville and Jackson saw only the worst side of Memphis. Free though they were from religious bigotry, these country gentlemen regarded the neighboring metropolis as a modern Babylon. They despised the odors which arose from its streets, and they had only contempt for its inhabitants whom they chose to regard as "flatboat folk," refusing to differentiate between the respectable elements and the riffraff who congregated on the bluff. When forced to do so they visited it to transact business, but their antipathy for the city and its alien population became more intense as its prosperity increased. Their attitude was to a large extent colored by their jealousy of a successful rival, but it undoubtedly had a sound esthetic basis, for it is hard to imagine a greater contrast than that existing between a beautiful, homogeneous little town like Brownsville, arcadian in its simplicity, and the dirty, misshapen, heterogeneous, and vicious young giant on the bluff.[93]

Yet it should be stated emphatically that the Memphis of 1860, with its cotton trade, rail and river traffic, wholesale houses, and professional men, its six newspapers, twenty-one churches, three female seminaries, two medical schools, twenty-one public schools, and glamorous theater, was for its day a real city and no scrawny town. Though much of its prosperity was the result of its position as a cotton market, cotton accounted for only one third of the value of its annual trade. On the eve of the war it was the sixth largest city in the South, a rank it again occupied in 1930. West of the Appalachians only New Orleans, Louisville, and Mobile surpassed it, while most of its twentieth-century southern rivals were little more than villages, if not unheard of.

CHAPTER VI

MARS AND THE MARKET PLACE

To HIM WHO seeks to explain secession and the war which followed largely in terms of economic facts and political creeds, the Civil War must ever remain a mystery. True it is that only against the economic and political background does the play of emotions on the eve of the conflict appear intelligible; yet the clash of 1861, transcending a fight for mere pelf and spoil of office, became a crusade on the part of both North and South. Passion ruled, and though motives varied with individual and locality the course of events was determined, not by the few who reasoned sanely, but by the many who hated and feared, frequently because of the personal interests involved but also out of devotion to what was to them fatherland.

The South of 1861 was not the South of 1860. With the fall of Sumter and its reverberations, men like Bell and his group of ex-Whigs found themselves caught in a maelstrom. When the middle ground upon which they had stood had been dug away beneath them by the events of that fateful spring and they were faced squarely with the alternative of fighting for or against the South, almost without exception they chose the former course. Had the matter been purely one of protection of slave property, the major issue on which southern and northern civilizations had clashed, the vast majority of southerners could never have been induced to risk their lives in its defense, for four out of five owned no Negroes. The enthusiastic support which the southern cause received outside of the isolated upland regions reveals that men were fighting for more than property—for a way of living which they considered the best way and for their right to live it without interference. Disillusionment and return of reason came with the war; yet in many cases this conviction was so strong that for four years Kentucky bluebloods and small farmers from Tennessee continued to die on the field of battle rather than betray it. And though they bowed to a superior force and accepted the decision of arms in 1865, their ideal remained unshattered even in defeat.

Until men were swept off their feet by the hysteria of the mob, economic considerations were not disregarded. If the planters of West Tennessee were one in economic interest with those of the Deep South, the ties of Memphis, on the contrary, were to a considerable extent with the upper valley. Much of its prosperity, to be sure, was dependent upon the purchasing power of the surrounding district; yet that area it did not consider endangered. In an article prior to the election of 1860, entitled "How Lincoln's Election Will Affect Memphis—The Extent of Our Danger," the *Appeal* pointed out that "we who are the near neighbors of the Illinoisians and the Indianians" stood to gain if secession occurred to the southward.[1] Such a movement, it opined, if ignored by the federal government would peter out and the wayward states would soon "secede again backward into the Union." Should the secession of the lower South prove of more than a temporary nature, however, Memphis would gain all that Charleston lost.

"There is nothing of injury to this city to be apprehended from the election of Lincoln," it concluded. ". . . The apprehension of danger so far as it exists here is groundless. Memphis will gain both wealth and population from any civil commotion arising south of us, and we are satisfied that there never was a time when investments here will prove more profitable than those of today."

In the autumn of 1860 the sentiment of Memphis was overwhelmingly in favor of the Union. Douglas, whom the *Appeal* did all within its power to elect, spoke there on October 24 to a crowd of thirty thousand;[2] the Democratic organ was scathing in its incessant attacks upon the *Avalanche,* the states-rights organ which supported Breckinridge. In regard to the Yancey bolt at Charleston in the summer the *Appeal* had not minced words; though it considered Breckinridge a "moderate man . . . and a friend of the constitutional union" against whom it had "never breathed a word," it stated frankly that, "obscure the issue as they may, Messrs. Breckinridge and Lane this day represent a party virtually as sectional as Messrs. Lincoln and Hamlin."[3] With the *Bulletin* and the *Enquirer* equally vehement in support of Bell, the Yancey group had little chance and the vote in November went eight-to-one in favor of Union, Douglas receiving 2,319 votes and Bell 2,250 to Breckinridge's 572.[4] The contrast of the returns in Memphis with those for West Tennessee and the state at large indicates that the city was unique in its support of Douglas.[5] Though this strong pro-Douglas sentiment was partly due to his popularity with the Irish, is it not also further evidence of the consciousness of the city's interdependence with the upper valley?

That Memphis six months later was exerting every effort to secure the immediate secession of Tennessee is almost unbelievable; yet such was the case. To understand this sudden change in public sentiment, one must recall the political developments of the previous decade. In the early fifties the city had been excited, as had the rest of the South, by what it considered insults from northern Abolitionists and politicians in Congress. As early as 1849 one of its delegates to a Democratic convention in Nashville had suggested severance of economic relations with the North, and during the same year an Arkansas correspondent of the

Eagle had been dismayed to hear disunion spoken of in Memphis as a matter of small concern.[6] In the excitement over the compromise bill of 1850 the *Appeal* had asserted boldly, "If in the struggle to preserve our constitutional rights in the union dissolution should come, we say let it come!"[7]

Such instances could be repeated without end. Strengthened by the shift of Whigs like Jones to its standard when the Republican party appeared as a threat in 1856, the state Democratic machine under Harris received a small but consistent majority in Memphis for the next four years.[8] This conversion of Whigs, a reaction to the party of Frémont, which gave promise of uniting the South against the Black Republicans, was checked in the late fifties, probably by the economic rapprochement with the upper West, which became stronger after 1858.[9] Whatever the cause, in 1860 the conservatives, still powerful, voted for Bell and the Union, while the Democrats, no longer the fire-eaters of ten years before, voted for Douglas and the Union. To understand the striking metamorphosis which followed the election of 1860, it must be emphasized that this display of Union sentiment was no treason to the South, but merely an indication of confidence in the ability of a united Democracy under Douglas to safeguard southern interests within the Union at least as well as Pierce and Buchanan had guarded them. Memphis merchants had no desire to swap horses in the midst of prosperity.

From Lincoln's election in November until the state referendum on secession in February, unionists and secessionists fought for control of the city. Even before the election, "Minute Men," encouraged by the *Avalanche,* had been organized to arouse separatist sentiment in case of a Republican victory. At first thin, their ranks gradually swelled with recruits as events unfolded—the election of Lincoln, the secession of South Carolina in December, the failure of the Crittenden Compromise, and the action of those southern states which followed Rhett's "Sovereign" out of the Union in January. The eve of the new year found one group of Memphis citizens holding a huge Union rally one night and a second group a secession demonstration the next.[10] In his message of January 7, Governor Harris, pronouncing the Union beyond salvation and declaring the choice before Tennessee one of allegiance to a northern or a southern confederacy, called a special session of the legislature to "consider the present condition of the country."[11]

Yet the Republican success in November had produced no immediate change in public sentiment in the city. "Let every man put his foot on disunion," urged the *Enquirer*. "It is no remedy for southern wrong, or [rather] it is only the madman's remedy."[12] Criticizing the *Bulletin's* suggestion of "masterful inactivity" as the wisest course for Tennessee, the *Appeal* proposed that Harris call a convention of slave states to save the Union by agreeing on some concerted plan of action. At a public meeting on November 30, where there was much dissension, a series of resolutions was passed incorporating this proposal and stating that Memphis would abide by the decision of the convention.[13]

The course of the *Appeal* is so typical of the sudden and insidious transformation which occurred that it is worth following in detail. In November it published editorial after editorial with such captions as "The Federal Union, It Must and Shall Be Preserved," "No Dissolution Without Civil War," and "Our Rights in the Union, a Proposition for Tennessee." Its suggestion of a slave-state convention after Lincoln's election, though perfectly sincere, was the beginning of its reversal of position. When South Carolina seceded, the *Appeal* said that the destiny of the border and the slave states was the same, and it approved the burning of Andrew Johnson in effigy at Memphis because he had denounced the right of secession.[14] When the Crittenden

Compromise ended in failure soon afterwards, it lost all hope of saving the Union; early in the new year it was referring to its erstwhile enemy as "our friends of the *Avalanche*."[15] On the tenth of January it advocated the withdrawal of the border states as a last resort to prevent coercion and war, and on the following day it urged immediate action. Paradoxical as this swing around the circle seems, the *Appeal* was consistent in that it never wavered in its devotion to what it considered the best interest of the South, and its shifting course, which followed rather than led public opinion, was in direct harmony with the kaleidoscopic changes on the national stage.

Though Breckinridge Democrats were elected to the offices of both houses, the new legislature which met in January refused to assume the responsibility of calling a convention. Instead, it submitted the question to the people, who, by voting for delegates at the same time, revealed their true sentiment on secession. In February Tennessee defeated the proposal of a convention by a vote of 68,282 to 59,449, and according to the ballot for delegates secession was rejected 91,803 to 24,749.[16] Memphis voted almost unanimously for the convention, but in spite of the efforts of the *Appeal* and the *Avalanche* the Union candidates received a majority of 722.[17] Robertson Topp and his Whig Old Guard, who put their faith in the Washington Peace Conference then in session, still supported the Union, but so many of their number had become secessionists that they would not have emerged victorious without the vote of the foreigners. "From 1600 to 1800 foreign suffragens," charged the *Appeal*, ". . . voted in a solid phalanx for the Union ticket." It later admitted, however, that perhaps 15 per cent of the foreigners had favored secession, since it was a matter of record that a large group of Irish citizens had resolved in public meeting a few days before to "buckle on our armor and do battle in defense of our Southern homes and Southern institutions."[18]

This defeat merely whetted the purpose of the seven hundred Minute Men in Memphis.[19] Fate was with them, for the events of the next three months forced the conservatives into their ranks. The inauguration, the fall of Sumter, and the call of Lincoln for troops in April, coming as it did on the heels of the failure of the peace conference, ended all opposition. On April 2, Memphis merchants had resolved unanimously that, regardless of the action of the state, West Tennessee should join the Confederacy.[20] Two weeks later, in the largest mass meeting ever held within the city's precincts, three thousand citizens answered Lincoln's call for troops by voting without a single negative for immediate secession. A committee of safety was organized, new military companies began to appear daily, and it was asserted that the city could furnish one thousand troops to the Confederacy within seven days. "West Tennessee is now almost one military camp," wrote a Memphian. "The people are in earnest, . . . excitement giving away to cool determination and preparation for the contest."[21] When the secession ordinance, already approved by the legislature in May, was submitted to the electorate for ratification in June, only five votes were cast against it in the whole of Shelby County.[22]

Facts and figures alone cannot explain the road to war which Memphis followed in 1860 and 1861. In November the city voted eight-to-one against secession; in February it still voted four-to-three for Union, though most of the native Americans had already been won over to secession; and by April separatist sentiment, even before the firing on Sumter, had become so rabid that it swept all opposition before it. The economic man spoke in November, but as the events of the new year unfolded he gradually lost more and more of the veneer of civilization, until by April he was reduced to the primitive state and became the victim of his unchained passion.

It has often been stated that Harris and West Tennessee finally succeeded in leading the state out of the Union, as they had conspired to do from the first.[23] Both charges are untrue, for Harris did not commit himself to secession until after Lincoln's election, and Middle and West Tennessee alike went through the same process in change of sentiment. The determining factor was actually the course of the middle section of the state, for it held the balance of power between the valley in the West and the mountains in the East. The Nashville region had defeated secession in February by its strong Union vote, but Lincoln's call for troops resulted in the desertion of its leading Whigs, N. S. Brown, Felix Zollicoffer, Bishop Otey, and John Bell. Middle Tennessee followed their example in June by voting overwhelmingly in favor of secession. Without the aid of his Whig enemies, Harris would never have won the state for the Confederacy, and the experience of Tennessee in the war would have been similar to that of Kentucky.[24]

Long before Tennessee seceded, then, Memphis was part of the Confederacy in all but name. Even as early as April, 1861, every consideration was secondary to that of immediate preparation for war. As names like the Garibaldi Guards and the Emerald Guards indicate, the enthusiasm for military organizations became so universal that the Irish, Germans, French, Swiss, and Italians formed their own companies. These foreigners, however, did not continue to support the southern cause, as is evident from the large Irish vote in Memphis during the reconstruction era when former Confederates were disfranchised,[25] and their action in 1861 may have been due to terrorism or to a real fear of invasion.

When the news was received of a hostile force forming

at Cairo, the municipal council voted $59,000 for defense, and the river front was barricaded with a wall of cotton bales.[26] In response to a general appeal for armament, Little Rock sent four cannon and New Orleans contributed a battery of thirty-two-pound guns, three thousand Mississippi rifles, and half a million cartridges. The Quimby and Robinson foundry and that of the Memphis and Charleston Railroad converted their plants into armories for the casting of cannon and the manufacture of munitions, the necessary saltpeter being obtained from the upper White River region in Arkansas.[27] Replacing the large number of northern mechanics who had returned home, in many cases not of their own volition, upon the outbreak of hostilities,[28] hundreds of eager but unskilled citizens labored in the new factories to turn out sufficient arms and ammunition for the men in the field. Women encouraged enlistment by an irresistible adoration of the uniform, and creditors offered volunteers respite from debts while they fought beneath the Stars and Bars. The press sponsored "Save-Your-Powder" and "Plant-Corn" campaigns—with only partial success, however, until the reverses of the spring of 1862 forced the realization that war was not to be as brief as had first been anticipated.

This spontaneous activity was ignored neither by the state of Tennessee nor by Confederate authorities. Governor Harris in April sent General Anderson to organize and drill the militia, and the Davis government early established recruiting headquarters in the city. In May, Memphis answered Chase's embargo on trade south from Cairo, made official by Lincoln in August, with a similar embargo on up-river traffic.[29] Thereafter every boat which passed the bluff on a northward journey was searched by municipal officials and many were detained, though similar interference with passenger traffic on land was not attempted until later. Forts Pillow, Harris, and Randolph, built by slave labor, were constructed on the eastern bank of the Mississippi above Memphis, but forces were concentrated farther north at Columbus, Kentucky, which the Confederates occupied early in the summer. On July 13, General Leonidas Polk, an Episcopal bishop who had laid aside the cassock for the sword, arrived in the city to set up headquarters as commander of the Confederate left wing.[30] This honor and the previous election of a western man as president encouraged Memphis in its desire to become the southern capital,[31] and to lessen the sting of its disappointment at the selection of Richmond, the Rebel Congress in August voted the construction of two gunboats for its defense.

For months after the fall of Sumter a holiday spirit and a delusion of a brief and glorious war against a none too ardent enemy gripped the populace. The races were held as usual in the spring and autumn of 1861. The rout of the Federals at Bull Run created, if that were possible, an even greater overconfidence. This first victory produced such an exuberant celebration that the name of a street on the eastern boundary was changed to Manassas. To be sure, the skirmishing in Missouri and Kentucky, which concerned the lower valley more closely, was not entirely favorable to the South, but no one expected it to continue. The arrival of the popular Texan, Albert Sidney Johnston, to succeed Polk in September and the repulse of Grant at Belmont (Columbus) two months later kept enthusiasm at a high pitch.

Memphis had its first taste of war in the raw when trains laden with the wounded began to pour in from Belmont. The city became overnight a vast hospital, and its women, organized for that purpose since April, nursed the injured—in many instances their husbands, sons, and brothers. When, after the reverses of the second spring, civilians began to suffer from the shortage of necessaries and the rise in prices which resulted from the blockade, patriotism was no longer rampant. Though the families of the men in the army rationalized defeat and bore without a murmur the sacrifices that became increasingly necessary,[32] a growing indifference to the southern cause became noticeable in 1862.

Even in the midst of the enthusiasm of the autumn there were occasional instances of a lag in patriotism. In September, 1861, the council after long debate refused the request of military authorities to impress women for nursing services in the city's hospitals. The *Argus* raised its voice in January, 1862, in complaint against hard times and the "selfishness and idiocy" of Confederate generals. Appeals for more volunteers and preparation against Federal attack from the north, which even the most sanguine must have admitted to themselves might come, evoked little response from the public.[33]

The *Appeal* considered it necessary in April to defend the city against the charge of shirking its duty, though at the same time it reported with indignation that certain citizens had refused Confederate currency in payment for goods.[34] The presence of an able-bodied man in the city when the army was in such sore straits often indicated that he was lukewarm to the cause for which many of his fellow citizens were dying. Those few individuals who retained any devotion to the Union had long since realized the expediency of hiding their true sentiments. During the first five months of 1862, the darkest days Memphis knew in the course of the whole war, self-preservation became the first concern of all who were not sincerely devoted to the South.

It must be remembered that those residents who remained in 1862, with the exception of the older men and women, were by no means the cream of the populace. Young, himself a member of Forrest's brigade, states that Memphis contributed fifty companies of from eighty-three to one hundred and three men each, while the *Argus* asserted in June, 1862, that seventy-two companies of citizens had already enlisted.[35] In answer to the charge, which was constantly made in 1862, that the city allowed other sections to do its fighting, the *Appeal* observed that many of the men in civilian clothes on the streets were Confederate officials, refugees, teamsters, factory workers, and non-uniformed employees of the war department.[36] It was as natural as it was undeserved, therefore, that the stigma of infidelity to the South should have been placed upon Memphis by those unacquainted with the facts. Its better element supported the southern cause without stint of life or property, and that the majority of those who did not join the army were concerned only that their persons and possessions be unmolested, regardless of the fortunes of either side, was no reflection upon its whole citizenry.

The ultimate effect of war, which is a boom to some industries and anathema to others, is often detrimental to commerce and manufacturing. During 1861 the movement of people into and out of Memphis was greater than in any previous year of its existence, and its hotels, restaurants, and shops were constantly crowded.[37] Factories for military supplies other than armament alone employed between thirteen and fifteen hundred workers, many of them girls and women, but by September most peacetime industries were producing but half their normal output.[38] Flour mills, born of necessity when trade with the upper valley was cut off, were turning out four thousand barrels weekly in the autumn of 1861, an amount never before equaled in a southern city.[39] The towns of Virginia had taken the place of St. Louis and Cincinnati in the economic world, but the traffic with them introduced so many "shinplasters" into circulation that only by the greatest exertion were local bankers able to prevent a complete disruption of the monetary system.[40]

As long as it remained in Confederate possession, Memphis suffered most in the loss of its cotton trade. In spite of a law forbidding exportation of cotton except through southern ports and in spite of the request of the Confederate government that planters store their crop to keep it out of the market until famine forced European intervention, it trickled into the city during the fall of 1861 at a rate of one hundred bales a day.[41] Most of it was probably transferred for Confederate bonds which were offered in exchange for produce or specie. When capture became imminent, cotton which had not been shipped south was forcibly burned by cavalry detachments to prevent its falling into Federal hands, a practice continued by the Confederates in the vicinity for several years.[42]

Disaster followed disaster in the early months of the second year of war. After six months of desultory fighting in Missouri and Kentucky, the Confederate left wing had begun to fall back. Grant's thrust up the Tennessee in the spring of 1862 forced the evacuation of Middle Tennessee and subjected the forts on the Mississippi between Cairo and Memphis, hitherto impregnable, to an attack from the rear. Thus the surrender of Forts Henry and Donelson on the Tennessee and the Cumberland in February was quickly followed by that of New Madrid on the Mississippi in March, and on the second day of the battle of Shiloh in April, Island Number Ten fell. When at the end of May Beauregard evacuated Corinth, to which he had retreated after Shiloh, the Confederates at once withdrew from Fort Pillow and Memphis on the river. Meanwhile New Orleans had fallen before a Federal force moving up the Mississippi, and Farragut had run the batteries at Vicksburg.

Memphis followed these events with dismay. Governor Harris and his legislature, having deserted Nashville in February, had made the bluff city the wartime capital of the state, but after a brief interval they were forced to continue their hegira. In contrast to the feverish activity of the previous autumn, trade was now dull and confined chiefly to traffic in sugar and molasses. Prices were soaring, luxuries had disappeared, and the shortage of necessaries was becoming serious. The juice of parched rye had taken the place of coffee, and the mint julep was a fond memory. Grog shops were suppressed and stores closed at two in the afternoon. Prices were dictated by a provost marshal, and days passed without the receipt of a pound of freight. Cotton, selling at twenty-eight cents in Liverpool, was neglected on the plantation where corn and potatoes were now grown, hogs fattened, and vegetables cultivated. Clothes were a year behind the current fashion of the world outside, politics were nonexistent, and medicine was a luxury of the rich. The opera and the drama were no more, and erstwhile habitués of the theater patronized performances by home talent to raise funds for the purchase of soldiers' shoes.[43]

Aroused by the threats of the more ardent to burn the town rather than permit its surrender, General Bragg suspended the municipal government in March and inaugurated martial law, a move that increased his unpopularity with the citizens.[44] Those most closely identified with the southern cause departed after the fall of New Orleans at the end of April, though the *Appeal* remained until the day of the battle and made a successful escape to Grenada, Mississippi, with press and staff intact.[45] Upon the evacuation of Corinth, garrisons were hastily and perhaps foolishly withdrawn from the redoubts at Pillow and Randolph, and on June 5 the Federal fleet anchored just above Memphis. Jeff Thompson, the Confederate general stationed in the city with a small force, declared that he could hold the enemy back for a month if given the proper co-operation, but the meager response he received in his attempts to organize citizens into militia rendered him powerless.[46]

Early on the morning of the 6th the Federals steamed down upon the Confederate gunboats waiting before the bluff. Much to the disappointment of the large group of spectators who had assembled on the bank to see the Yankees destroyed, within an hour and ten minutes seven out of the eight Confederate vessels were captured, sunk, or burned. The Union fleet possessed an inestimable advantage in having the current with it, but Ellet's steel rams, inspired by the *Merrimac* and used here by the Federals for the first time, were the real cause of the devastation. After some difficulty Colonel Ellet, who lay wounded on his flagship, succeeded in getting from Mayor Park an admission that the town had been captured.[47]

Thus fell the "Charleston of the West," whose inhabitants four days before had publicly sworn never to surrender.[48] Not only was it captured without the immediate aid of any land force, but the single attempt at resistance on the part of its craven citizens was the firing of a pistol at a small detail from the fleet who bravely replaced the Confederate flag over the post office with that of the United States.[49] The majority were content to express their displeasure by profuse profanity and idle threats. After witnessing the battle, Jeff Thompson, either out of cowardice or disgust, left hastily "to pay a note in Holly Springs, Mississippi."[50] "As civil authorities have no means of defense," replied Mayor Park to the demand for surrender, "by the force of circumstance the city is in your hands."[51] At noon Colonel Fitch and his Indiana brigade arrived by land from Randolph and took complete possession. Unfortunately for Memphis, in its hour of need its manhood was fighting on other fields.

At the outbreak of war, in spite of the greater wealth and man power of the North, it was generally thought in the South and in England that the Confederacy would succeed. In the South the opinion was universal that one battle would end the conflict and that recognition by Europe would force the United States to acquiesce in the disruption of the Union. "The people of the Southern States may be wrong," declared the London *Times* in October, 1861, "but they are ten millions"; Gladstone asserted in his Newcastle speech a year later that "there is no doubt that Jefferson Davis and other leaders of the South have made an army; . . . and . . . what is more . . . they have made a nation."[52] The task confronting the Confederates was merely to repel invasion until the will to coerce was exhausted, a task in which they would probably have succeeded, thanks to the ardent peace group which existed in the North throughout the war, but for the personality of Lincoln. The military problem before the Federal government was immeasurably more difficult—it must invade a country fighting in defense not only of principle but also of its homes.

As war converted two more or less armed mobs into excellent fighting machines, so necessity converted opportunism into farsighted strategy, but only on the part of the Federals. Davis made the contest a struggle to defend Richmond and paid for his error with defeat. Had he withdrawn his defenses to North Carolina, where the mountains would have served as a barrier, and concentrated the larger part of his forces in the West, where the rivers flowing into the heart of the Confederacy made him exceedingly vulnerable, the issue might have been different.[53] Only the early victories in the West, made possible by Davis's neglect, which the layman, as easily as the military expert, can recognize as a major blunder, kept alive in the North a martial spirit that was never robust. Viewing the war as a whole, Federal tactics on land, supplemented by a blockade from the sea, consisted of three moves. A succession of Union generals after four years of effort finally bottled Lee up in southern Virginia; the army and navy, in the meantime, had cut the

COLONEL ELLET'S RAM APPROACHING THE CITY OF MEMPHIS, TENNESSEE, TO DEMAND SURRENDER
Sketched by Mr. A. Simplot for *Harper's Weekly*.

CLOSING SCENE OF THE NAVAL ENGAGEMENT BEFORE MEMPHIS, TENNESSEE
From left to right, "Van Dorn escaping; Federal fleet in pursuit; captured rebel Sumter; Beauregard sinking; Jeff Thompson blowing up."—From *Harper's Weekly*.

THE LEVEE AT MEMPHIS

Hauling sugar and cotton from their hiding-places for shipment north. Sketched by Mr. Alex. Simplot for *Harper's Weekly.*

HOISTING THE STARS AND STRIPES OVER THE POST OFFICE AT MEMPHIS

Sketched by Mr. Alexander Simplot for *Harper's Weekly.*

Confederacy in half by securing control of the Mississippi; and Sherman, marching from Chattanooga to Savannah and then north through the Carolinas, destroyed the bases in Lee's rear.

The conquest of the valley resulted as much from bungling and poor generalship on the part of the Confederates as from the ability of Grant, Sherman, Porter, and Farragut. The thrust down the valley stopped at Memphis when Halleck, who took charge in the field after Donelson, foolishly divided his large force over a three-hundred-mile front by sending Buell east toward Chattanooga.[54] Halleck's right wing, composed of Sherman at Memphis and Grant in northern Mississippi, was given Vicksburg as its objective; yet thanks to the skill of Van Dorn and Price, who had come over from Arkansas, and to the peculiar topography of the Yazoo-Mississippi delta, these Union generals spent an entire year in the effort to surmount the last obstacle to complete control of the river. After half a dozen ingenious schemes had failed, Grant in desperation cast caution to the winds. Cutting himself off from his base of supplies and from communication with headquarters, he marched into the interior from Grand Gulf, a short distance below Vicksburg. The Confederates outnumbered his forces, but they were handicapped by receiving orders from three different commanders, Pemberton, Joseph E. Johnston, and President Davis. Attacked thus by land and river, Vicksburg fell on the 4th of July after a siege of forty-eight days.

Concentrating their attention on Chattanooga and Atlanta, the Federals thereafter were content to hold the river by means of strong garrisons at strategic points. The interior on neither side was ever actually subjugated, and for two years it was the scene of constant guerrilla warfare, made famous by the lightning maneuvers of the ubiquitous Forrest. Skirmishing continued in Mississippi and Arkansas until the very end of the war, and Memphis, where the Federal fortifications at Fort Pickering were reputed to be the strongest in the valley, was attacked in a brilliant but impossible raid by Forrest in August, 1864.[55] While the city escaped the destruction that fell to the lot of other southern towns, until hostilities ceased it was always within a short distance of these irregular operations.[56]

The significant role of Memphis in the war was its position as the depot for most of the contraband trade between North and South. In spite of its capture early in the contest, Confederate forces managed to keep its communications with the Deep South open until 1865. Between June, 1862, and June, 1864, according to Senator Zachariah Chandler, from twenty to thirty million dollars worth of supplies reached the Confederacy through Memphis alone.[57] Always anxious about the upper West, Lincoln dared not cut off completely that section's valuable trade with the lower valley, and even during the brief period of a nominal policy of absolute nonintercourse, the system of permits provided the favored few with a ready and accessible loophole. The popularity of Grant's victories along the Tennessee was due largely to the fact that they heralded a revival of trade and a voracious market for the glutted warehouses of the upper valley.[58]

Grant and Sherman both realized the absurdity of fighting the enemy with one hand and feeding him with the other, but politicians like Sherman's brother, the honorable senator from Ohio, kept them from forcing the government to cease its vacillating policy. On one occasion Grant in anger ordered all Jews in his department to leave within forty-eight hours, and later he forbade cotton speculators to operate south of Helena.[59] Sherman with characteristic directness described the situation exactly. "If trade be opened," he wrote in August, 1862, "Memphis is better to our enemy than before it was taken."[60]

When the city fell, the treasury department appointed treasury officials, who immediately opened offices. Loyalty was at a premium, for permits were granted only to those who had taken an oath of allegiance, but bribery and corruption were evident from the start.[61] Favoritism was rife, and large quantities of shoes, cloth, percussion caps, and other supplies necessary to war were rushed into the hands of the waiting Confederates. Determined to keep gold, salt, arms, silver, and treasury notes from passing through the lines, Sherman organized a board of trade, but it proved only as efficient as the man behind it and after his departure it became ineffective.[62]

The Federal government was anxious to secure cotton which it could ship abroad to relieve the shortage that was likely to cause European intervention; yet, if gold were paid in exchange, it could be used to purchase guns in the West Indies.[63] Confederate money was under a ban, but Sherman solved the dilemma by allowing buyers to pay with Tennessee and southern bank notes or to give obligation to pay at the end of the war, payment in gold and silver being forbidden.[64] When the war department declared trading in cotton free toward the end of the summer, this arrangement was set aside, though Sherman obeyed the order with much misgiving.[65] During the season of 1863-64, fifty thousand bales were handled in Memphis.[66]

The army of the West was paralyzed by hordes of speculators who followed on its heels to reap the harvest that awaited in its wake.[67] The pressure became tremendous when cotton reached the undreamed-of price of one dollar a pound early in 1863.[68] "The mania for sudden fortunes in cotton," observed Charles A. Dana on a special mission in Memphis, "raging in a vast population of . . . Yankees scattered throughout the country and in this town has to a large extent corrupted and demoralized the army. Every colonel, captain, and quartermaster is in secret partnership with some operator in cotton; while every soldier dreams of adding a bale of cotton to his pay. I had no conception of the extent of the evil until I came and saw for myself. No private purchase of cotton should be allowed in any part of the occupied region."[69] Generals were even more vehement in regard to the harpies who "follow in the track of the army, and barter the cause for which it is fighting with all the baseness of Judas Iscariot, but without his remorse."[70] Senator Collamer suggested that the government withdraw its army and enlist a force of "Yankee pedlars . . . to go down there and trade them all out."[71]

Officers were powerless in face of the glaring fraud in the permit system.[72] Doubtless many of them felt that, since corruption was universal, they should derive their share of the spoil. Strict enforcement of the regulations of the war department would have been impossible; besides, the Confederates devised ingenious methods of smuggling. In a barn in northern Mississippi Sherman found the carriages of a funeral cortege which had escorted a coffin full of medicine out of Memphis to Van Dorn's suffering army.[73] For months after the capture of the city, dead animals with bellies stuffed with gold and other contraband were carried beyond the lines, ostensibly to the dump heap.[74] The guerrillas who were always prowling around captured shipments of goods almost at will, and officials amenable to bribery could easily be found.

By its lax policy in allowing contraband to pass into the hands of the enemy, the Federal government undoubtedly prolonged the struggle, and the advantage derived from the early capture of Memphis was to a large extent nullified. The Confederate army may have been fed from the granaries of Georgia and Alabama, but its martial necessaries were smuggled through the lines from the cities of the upper West no less than from the Bahamas. Had Sherman's policy of strict regulation of trade been enforced in Memphis and other captured cities, it is conceivable that the South would have been forced to submit long before Appomattox.

For three years after its capture Memphis remained in Federal hands, but not without challenge. Strangely enough, only during the last year of the war was municipal government replaced by martial law. Insofar as the civil aspects of their task were concerned—the restoration of normal conditions and the encouragement of Union sentiment—the Federals achieved little, and in their more important objective, the prohibition of trade with the enemy, they failed completely, as has been shown. General Washburne, in command of the post in 1864, was not exaggerating when he declared that "Memphis has been of more value to the southern Confederacy since it fell into our hands than Nassau [Bahama Islands]."[75]

The scene in June, 1862, was one of unbroken confusion, aggravated by the danger of a return attack by the Confederates. Commander succeeded commander in rapid order, Fitch, Slack, Wallace, Grant, Hovey, and Sherman, and in spite of the efforts of the thousand merchants who immediately rushed in from the North, stores remained closed and trade meager.[76] Scores of conflicting orders were issued by the local commanders and by the war and the treasury departments, varying in quality from criminal leniency to unwise severity without any attempt at consistency. Municipal officials and editors were required to take an oath of allegiance, and the citizens were also encouraged to do so, but the large number reported to have taken it proved upon investigation to be, in almost every case, the new arrivals.[77] Proclamations ordering the stores to open were disregarded by the residents, who, to compensate for their disgraceful surrender, were trying to salve their troubled consciences by nonintercourse with the victors.

A few of the poor, probably out of hunger, welcomed the invaders with an avidity which some Yankees mistook for genuine loyalty to the Union, but more critical observers admitted that few acquiesced in such sentiment.[78] "Affairs in this city seem to be in bad order," wrote Grant in disgust upon his arrival late in June, "secessionists governing much in their own way."[79] What was needed was not consideration for the conquered but the mailed fist, and Grant was the man to apply it.

Such was apparently his intention, for he required all of the seven hundred voters in the municipal election of June 26 to take the oath of allegiance.[80] Yet he had hardly embarked on his program when military necessity demanded his departure, and he intrusted its execution to Hovey, his successor. Early in July persons connected with the Confederacy in a civil or a military capacity were ordered to leave within five days, and General Order No. 1, issued on the 18th, gave men between the ages of eighteen and forty-five the choice of taking the oath or leaving the city.[81] This measure by no means insured a loyal population, and it drove hundreds into the southern army.[82] To the many, who had taken the oath purely for the commercial privileges attached to being on the winning side,[83] were thereby added numerous others who, willing to pay lip service to the United States rather than lose their property, became Confederate sympathizers out of spite for the Federal military.

Because of Halleck's folly, throughout the summer the Union forces on the bluff remained inadequate,[84] and the danger of a Confederate counterattack was serious. Since fortification of the entire six miles of the city's boundary was out of the question, Grant erected emergency defenses south of the town.[85] For the next five months Sherman devoted most of his attention to their completion, and by November the huge depot, for it was that rather than a fort, was finished.[86] In spite of Grant's victory at Corinth in the fall, the Confederates threatened Memphis seriously in December to relieve the pressure on Vicksburg. "I hold city by virtue of heavy guns bearing upon it," wrote Hurlburt on the 24th, "and the belief that an attack would cause its destruction."[87]

When Sherman reached Memphis on July 19 he found its stores, schools, and churches still closed in spite of all attempts of his predecessors to prime trade and to restore the usual social activity.[88] The 8,227 bales of cotton, 9,702 hogsheads of sugar, and the 8,624 barrels of molasses received by northern merchants within the month after the battle undoubtedly aroused the envy of many of the inhabitants, who by this time were beginning to feel that they had atoned for their earlier conduct.[89] Consequently, when the new commander issued an order allowing trade without passes over the five roads leading into the city from the surrounding region, a brisk business sprang up.[90]

In view of the reputation of this *bête noire* of the South, it should be emphasized that in Sherman's occupation of Memphis, his first experience with a conquered population, he displayed as much regard for the rights of citizens and sincere concern for the welfare of the city as the demands of a precarious position allowed.[91] It is difficult to see how his sense of justice could have been keener, and his actions reveal a consideration for ethics and an intelligence rare in a military commander.

Not only was Sherman eager to meet the civilian population halfway, but he was willing to make the first move, as his order opening trade proved. He punished pillaging severely, and for the houses destroyed in building the fort, which he might have confiscated without regard for the owners, he carefully made fair compensation.[92] He revived the defunct civil government of Mayor Park and refused to assume its functions,[93] as local officials suggested that he do, for he considered himself educator and not war lord. While he had no intention of permitting hostile acts, he did expect to meet and to tolerate unfriendliness which he considered quite natural under the circumstances. "If all who are not our friends are expelled from Memphis," he commented, "but few will be left."[94] Yet his actions give one the impression that he was optimistic enough to hope that by a policy of justice tempered with intelligent mercy he might nurse back into health a loyalty to the Union of which only a vestige remained.

He did not hesitate, however, to use severe measures when the occasion demanded them. Following Grant's instruction, Sherman sent south all families whose fathers were already there, and he took possession of vacant stores and residences belonging to disloyal persons, the rents from which produced considerable income.[95] The bands of guerrillas, which preyed upon loyal and disloyal alike and even occasionally raided the city's suburbs, felt the full force of his wrath. When these so-called "partisans" continued to fire at transports on the river and later at trains on the Memphis and Charleston, he burned Randolph in retaliation and issued an order that for every similar attack, ten persons who had not taken the oath should be ejected from Memphis.[96] Twenty people were ordered to leave on October 18 for this offense, but he suspended sentence for a fortnight to allow Confederate authorities to explain the matter.[97] The task of rehabilitation, to which he gave a tireless energy, included such diverse matters as sponsoring Union clubs and militia organizations, aiding municipal police in suppressing the crime then so rampant, advising merchants against the use of "shinplasters," and caring for the large number of poor and destitute throughout the winter.[98]

His policy regarding the fugitive slaves who were flocking to the city was particularly fair. At first Negroes had been so carefully excluded from the lines that Grant found few upon his arrival in June; yet in August Sherman had thirteen hundred at work on the fort, and by the last of October their number had increased to six thousand.[99] Until the courts should determine the status of slaves, Sherman refused either to encourage runaways or to aid their masters in recovering them.[100] If Negroes remained in Memphis they had to work on the fort, and in return they received food, clothing, and a pound of chewing tobacco a month. For this service wages were to be paid to loyal masters later. Black women were a novelty to most Yankees; —according to one naïve cavalryman they "felt loving towards us because they thought we were bringing them freedom, and they wouldn't charge us a cent."[101]

Had Sherman been dealing with any but a mongrel population it would have responded to his treatment. The *Bulletin,* suppressed later by another commander for refusing to co-operate in one of Andrew Johnson's futile attempts at a congressional election, was outspoken in praise of his work, and on the eve of his departure the leading citizens gathered at a banquet in his honor.[102] Though he could not inculcate an honest allegiance in the hearts of the people, he had the satisfaction of knowing that he had brought economic activity and public order into being where neither had existed before his arrival. "I traverse the city every day and night," he boasted with pardonable pride, "and assert that Memphis is and has been as orderly a city as St. Louis, Cincinnati, or New York."[103] This extended and intimate experience with noncombatants, furthermore, was vital to the evolution of his famous philosophy of war. "We cannot change the hearts of these people of the South," he admitted in defeat to Grant, "but we can make war so terrible that they will realize that . . . they are mortal and should exhaust all peaceful remedies before they fly to war."[104]

Hurlburt and Washburne, his successors, displayed little of his indefatigable energy or his keen insight. The very nature of military occupation was hostile to sound economic and social rehabilitation, and the frequent change of commanders,[105] coupled with an inexpedient leniency, rendered the task even more difficult. During the first three years of war the population of the city had doubled and its character was more promiscuous than ever. Among its bustling forty thousands were speculators and soldiers, Negroes and prostitutes, deserters and spies, whom the materialistic philosophy that results from an appeal to arms had converted into a mob with instincts little above those of animals.[106] Numerous attempts to limit the consumption of liquor proved futile, and venereal disease became so prevalent that houses of prostitution were ordered to close their doors.[107]

The *Bulletin* cleverly described the native population after the capture as consisting of three groups: the "original" Union men (everyone who took the oath voluntarily protested that he had been loyal from the first), "law-and-order" men, and those "who never discovered until too late how ardently they loved the southern cause."[108] Fifteen thousand had taken the oath of allegiance by January, 1863;[109] yet interest in civil affairs was so slight that scarcely five hundred voted in the congressional election of that spring. Though within six months after the capture the original population had been largely replaced by a horde of northern speculators and camp-followers, the few ardent secessionists who contrived to remain played so skillfully upon the antipathy which military occupation always creates that Federal authorities received the impression that the sentiment of the majority was pro-southern.

The re-election of Mayor Park in 1864 convinced General Washburne that the city was still disloyal, and he considered it sufficient reason to proclaim martial law until the cessation of hostilities.[110] In spite of the various militia organizations and Union clubs, men had to be impressed by the Federals for service in the army during 1863.[111] Northerners in Memphis were interested only in opportunities for personal gain,[112] and a handful of determined and unregenerate "Secesh," who perjured themselves, were able to embarrass the military officials. After the capture, both loyal and disloyal sentiment was practically nonexistent in Memphis, but public opinion was bitter against any regulations which interfered with business and pleasure, war or no war.

CHAPTER VII

RETURN TO NORMALITY

FEW SOUTHERN TOWNS suffered as little from the four years of the war as did Memphis. Though many of its individual citizens were ruined, the city enjoyed an almost continuous trade, which, abnormal and spasmodic as it was, nevertheless sustained the ordinary business institutions that otherwise would have gone out of existence. In 1865 the valuation of taxable property was set at eighteen million dollars, roughly what it had been in 1860, nor had it fallen much below that figure in any of the intervening years.[1] In view of the high prices which prevailed in 1865, these statistics represent an actual loss, but a much smaller one than might be anticipated. Within five years after 1860 wharfage receipts had doubled, and the public schools, which had never ceased to operate, were caring for an enrollment of 2,418 at a per capita expenditure of $52.44 at the close of the war, in contrast to an enrollment of 2,073 at a per capita expenditure of $28.41 five years before.[2]

Many of the northerners whom war had attracted to Memphis chose to remain as citizens upon the cessation of hostilities. This new blood was stimulating, and those who returned home advertised the city's commercial advantages in the world above the Mason and Dixon line. Intangible though such publicity was, it proved no mean asset when northern capital and northern firms began to turn their gaze southward, as they were soon to do.

In an absolute sense the Civil War was by no means an unmixed evil for Memphis, for its growth in the sixties was much greater than that of its sister cities. While much of the South was a generation in recovering from the ravages of war, the bluff city was on its feet within five years. Twice as large in 1870 as Atlanta, its future rival, it needed an increase in population of only a few thousand to pass Charleston and Richmond and take its place beside New Orleans and Louisville as one of the leading commercial centers south of the Potomac and the Ohio.[3]

Though war proved economically a mere interlude during which the city almost held its own, some of the consequences, nevertheless, were directly detrimental. Its hinterland in Mississippi, Arkansas, and Tennessee had been sacked and millions of dollars had been lost through emancipation of slaves. Levees and railroads had been destroyed, and this prostrate region was forced at the darkest moment in its existence to adjust itself to an entirely new and untried system of labor. Until this tri-state area recovered, there was a definite limit to the prosperity possible for its metropolis.

Socially the war was catastrophic, for it accentuated all of the vicious characteristics of Memphis. By converting the Negro into a free man it brought him into the city in vast numbers, to become a perennial burden as well as a disrupting force in the community. In the ten years between 1860 and 1870 the Negro population increased from three thousand to fifteen thousand, as shown in Table IX, and the race problem, which had hardly existed in 1860, became more serious after the war with the passing of time.

Society in the sixties underwent many changes of a permanent nature. The close of the war found four distinct groups in the city which seemed to defy amalgamation—the Negroes, the Federal soldiers, the northern merchants, and the natives.

Dismayed at the new Memphis, the returning Confederates nevertheless seem to have accepted the passing of the

TABLE IX

NEGROES IN MEMPHIS AND SHELBY COUNTY

Year	Negroes	Whites	Total	Per cent Negroes
	Memphis			
1850	2,486	6,355	8,841	28
1860	3,882	18,741	22,623	17
1870	15,741	24,485	40,221	39
1880	14,896	18,696	33,592	44
1890	28,706	35,789	64,495	44
1900	49,910	52,410	102,320	48
1910	52,441	78,764	131,105	40
1920	61,181	101,170	162,351	37
1930	93,550	156,603	253,153	39
	Shelby County			
1820	113	251	364	31
1830	2,111	3,537	5,648	37
1840	7,116	7,605	14,721	48
1850	14,578	16,579	31,157	46
1860	17,229	31,861	48,090	35
1870	36,640	39,737	76,377	48
1880	43,903	34,527	78,430	55
1890	61,613	51,027	112,740	54
1900	84,773	68,784	153,557	55
1910	91,719	99,720	191,439	47
1920	98,962	124,254	223,216	44
1930	127,324	179,158	306,482	31

old order and quietly to have taken their places in a strange world. Upon its return in the autumn of 1865 the *Appeal* sincerely but somewhat dramatically expressed their attitude. Without "unmanly excuses" or "stultifying recantation of opinions and sentiments once honestly entertained" it admitted that the "stern logic of events" had compelled their renunciation. "We frankly accept," it concluded, "the indestructibility of that Union of States and people which makes us for all time a mighty and indivisible Republic; we recognize and abide by the logical sequence of the late unhappy Civil War, in the destruction, now and forever, of the institution of African slavery. Between the veteran Federal soldier and the unflinching Confederate soldier, who have so often met each other in the raging conflict of battle, there is a feeling of respect that affords the sure foundation upon which the restored union will rest."[5]

Unfortunately for sectional relations, it was not the veteran Federal soldier but the speculator who had followed him at a safe distance who "helped" the South recuperate.

The reconstruction of Tennessee was unique in being the product of a legislature elected by its own citizens, which contained no Negroes and few carpetbaggers.[6] Omitted by Lincoln from the provisions of the Emancipation Proclamation, this state freed its own slaves and of its own volition ratified the Thirteenth, Fourteenth, and Fifteenth amendments. Unaffected by the congressional reconstruction acts and the other punitive measures of that body, it had, however, a tragic era all its own; for it lay at the mercy of a group of Radicals from the eastern section of the state led by Governor Brownlow, who surpassed Thad Stevens and the Joint Committee of Thirteen in vindictiveness.

Topographically Tennessee is one of the most heterogeneous states in the Union. The mountain region in the east, often referred to as the "Switzerland of America," is in an economic and cultural sense a second West Virginia. The central section around Nashville, where tobacco and wheat, as well as cotton, are staples, is similar to the basin of Kentucky one hundred miles to the north. The low plateau in the west between the Tennessee and Mississippi rivers, where cotton is king, resembles the hill country of northern Mississippi. Each of these divisions in turn possesses a prosperous urban center in a fertile valley, Knoxville and Chattanooga on the Tennessee, Nashville on the Cumberland, and Memphis on the Mississippi. The interests of these cities conflict with those of a back country, which varies in size from the vast uncultivated tracts in the mountains to a small area along the western watershed of the Tennessee.

The alignment of piedmont and valley in 1861 thrust secession upon loyal mountaineers. So bitter was their resentment that they immediately made a strenuous but unsuccessful effort to form a separate state, a movement which they revived upon two other occasions.[7] Thus an ironical situation existed during the early years of the war, for that part of the state where the secessionists had prevailed fell into Federal hands, while the Confederates continued to hold the only section where loyalists were in the majority. The troops who crushed the mountaineers by brutal methods came largely from Middle and West Tennessee, though much of the devastation suffered by East Tennessee was the work of its own guerrillas and the Federal armies that later occupied it.[8] The intense hatred which these mountain folk displayed when fate gave them an opportunity for vengeance was to their minds only just compensation for the wrongs which they had suffered for half a century at the hands of slaveholders. Reconstruction in Tennessee, therefore, was more than a political contest; it was a sectional and a class struggle which had been brewing as long as the state had existed.[9]

In the spring of 1861 Andrew Johnson became military governor in the state where he had formerly been civil executive. With the exception of Hood's raid in the last year of the contest, the Confederate army ceased to be a menace after Bragg's evacuation of Chattanooga in the fall of 1863; yet Johnson was never able to hold a satisfactory election until the very end of the war. Considering Lincoln's policy too lenient he succeeded in crippling the strong peace party among the unionists of the state by his "damnasty oath," which was far more severe than that required by the president for amnesty.[10] In January, 1865, a Radical Unionist convention in Nashville, assuming constituent powers, passed an amendment to the state constitution abolishing slavery, repudiated the secession ordinance, and nominated candidates for the coming state election. With practically all but East Tennesseans disfranchised, these measures and the entire radical ticket were approved in February by a vote of 25,293 to 48.[11] Since the total vote was more than 10 per cent of that in 1860, the state had complied with the requirements of Lincoln's proclamation of December, 1863. The process of restoration was apparently complete, but Stevens, eager to embarrass the new president, was able by adroit obstructionist tactics to delay readmission until the summer of 1866.[12]

The leader of these Tennessee Radicals, who instigated and executed a revenge which without his personality would probably have never materialized, was Johnson's successor as governor, "Parson" William G. Brownlow, one of the most striking figures in American history. An ex-Methodist circuit rider and former editor of the *Tennessee Whig* (the title varies), he once had been ferocious in his defense of slavery. Already when he became governor, his unrestrained tongue and crusading spirit had made his life a series of attacks and slander suits. The war converted him into as staunch an enemy of secession as he had formerly been a champion of the "peculiar institution," and the subjugation of East Tennessee engendered in him such hatred of the Confederates that he spoke from the heart when he said, "intelligent, influential men of wealth who instigated this rebellion have forfeited all rights to protection and life, and merit the vigorous and undying opposition of loyal men."[13] A John Randolph of the backwoods, he used the bludgeon instead of the rapier, but he wielded his cruder weapon with all the effectiveness of that earlier master of invective. Though he was in his sixtieth year when he became governor, the Memphis *Ledger* was scarcely guilty of hyperbole when it stated that Brownlow was still able to "express more vituperativeness and scorching hate than any half a dozen men that ever appeared in American Politics."[14]

With the aid of the Radical majority in the legislature Brownlow securely established his oligarchy in control of the state during his first administration. By two drastic acts he denied the franchise forever to all who had supported the Confederacy at any time by overt action or secret influence, and he put teeth into the law by personally appointing his own commissioners to examine the qualifications of each voter in every county. When the Conservatives supported Johnson, who contrary to expectations had made Lincoln's lenient program his own, Brownlow threw his lot in with the Stevens-Sumner faction and became a bitter foe of the President.

Much as the Governor and the Radicals hated the Negro,[15] to please their new allies they gave the blacks certain civil rights in 1866 and granted them the franchise the following year. This act had the additional virtue of providing the Radicals with sufficient votes to win every election, besides serving as the bitterest punitive measure to which ex-Confederates could have been subjected. These decrees Brownlow enforced with the aid of a hand-picked militia, Federal troops, and a muzzled judiciary. His crowning bit of legislation was the Metropolitan Police Act of May, 1866, which gave him the power of appointment and complete control over the police in Memphis, Nashville, and Chattanooga.[16] So smoothly did his organization function that he was re-elected in 1867 over Emerson Etheridge, the candidate of the aroused Conservatives, by a vote of 74,484 to 22,584.[17]

This victory was achieved, however, by tactics which drove thousands of loyal unionists into the ranks of the opposition. The franchise acts had reduced the electorate until the vote of East Tennessee, formerly a third, now amounted to three fourths of the state's total.[18] The *Republican Banner* of Nashville estimated that 80 per cent of the moneyed and landed interests of Tennessee had been disfranchised.[19] In the congressional election of 1865, which was held while the enforcement of the disfranchisement act remained in the hands of county clerks, the Conservatives elected five out of the eight successful candidates. Brownlow immediately threw out the votes of twenty-nine counties on the grounds of fraud and proceeded to pass a second act more stringent than the first. The Conservatives constantly sought to defeat obnoxious legislation by absenting themselves from the meetings of the legislature to prevent a quorum, but their efforts were in vain. In 1867, in spite of opposition within their own party, they made a spirited but unsuccessful bid for the Negro vote.

With Radical ascendancy at its height, the disfranchised Confederates lent their moral support to the Conservatives, and as they possessed no resort to the ballot box, they turned to extra-legal methods. The Ku-Klux Klan, originally a social organization, became a vigilantes' association and joined battle with Brownlow's militia and the Union League for victory in the presidential election of 1868. Though Grant defeated Seymour in Tennessee by a thirty thousand majority, it is apparent from a comparison of the returns with those of the gubernatorial contest of 1867 that within a year the Radicals were shorn of eighteen thousand votes while the Conservatives gained four thousand.[20] When in January, 1868, Negroes were given the right to hold office and to serve on juries, and a severe Ku-Klux act was passed the following autumn, civil war seemed imminent. Only the unified efforts of thirteen ex-Confederate generals of the state prevented bloodshed at this crisis; yet they made it clear that restoration of the franchise alone could insure peace.

"Brownlow, himself, is the real cause of the trouble in Tennessee," commented the New York *Herald,* "the only state that is in the hands of a born swaggerer and bully. . . . It is a pity that the country should hear the murmur of war, even though faintly, simply because an irritable, ill-natured, narrow-minded, and pugnacious man happens to be governor of Tennessee."[21]

When Brownlow resigned in February, 1869, to take the seat in the Senate to which he had been previously elected, D. C. Senter, speaker of the state Senate, succeeded him as governor. Senter at once took steps to conciliate the Confederates by mustering out the state troops assembled to suppress the Klan. In June he became a candidate for re-election on a platform of restoration of suffrage to all who had been disfranchised. Thereupon the Radical party split, and Senter used his control of the electorate, which Brownlow's machinery made possible, to permit many ex-Rebels to vote. Supported as well by the Conservatives and a large number of Negroes and Radicals, he received 120,333 votes to his opponent's 55,036. Immediately the legislature proceeded to nullify the work of its predecessor, and the constitutional convention of 1870 restored the franchise to all male citizens twenty-one years of age and over, who had been residents of the state for six months and who had paid their poll tax. In spite of an appeal from East Tennesseans, Grant refused to interfere, and in November the Democrats, having absorbed the Conservatives, elected their candidate for governor with ease.[22]

Until the enfranchisement of the Negro in 1867, the Radicals in Memphis were constantly defeated at the polls by large majorities. No influential Memphians participated in the state election of February, 1865, only 879 votes being cast in the whole county. In the congressional contest of the following summer, though Brownlow's first disfranchisement act had been passed, the conservatives received 1,100 of the 1,300 votes while the leaders of the local carpetbaggers, Hunter and Beaumont, had but 50 votes between them. In December the Radical candidates for the legislature fared little better, as they received about one third of a total vote of more than 1,800. When the successful Conservative candidates from Memphis resigned some months later in protest against the governor's arbitrary conduct, no Radicals could be induced to oppose them and they were flung back in Brownlow's face with a larger majority than formerly. Public meetings and political clubs, meanwhile, had enthusiastically endorsed the program of President Johnson.[23]

This Conservative strength in Memphis is surprising but significant. The electorate, composed as it was of northern immigrants and southern renegades with whom the disfranchised had as little intercourse as possible, was surely not motivated by altruism in opposing the proscription of ex-Rebels. Its antipathy for Brownlow is difficult to explain except on the theory that it desired the restoration of normal trading conditions. These merchants wanted a policy of *laissez faire* on the part of the state, but being a commercial group like the ante-bellum Whigs, they could expect no sympathy from an East Tennessee governor and a legislature representing the interests of yeoman farmers. They objected to the disfranchisement of the majority of white citizens and the enfranchisement of Negroes not merely because they saw that business would suffer, but because they also realized what a weapon they would be placing in the hands of the agrarians. How could immigrants be expected to come to a city, asked a correspondent of the *Avalanche,* where they would be forced to live under a Negro government?[24]

The smaller group of Yankees who formed the local Radical party had been attracted to Memphis by the prospect of spoil which the political situation promised, not by opportunities for commercial profit. Their ranks, at first thin, swelled steadily as the Brownlow program began to assume its full proportions. Through their newspaper, the *Post,* they carried on a constant agitation among the Negroes, which was later to pay them well.

In spite of their victories in local elections prior to the admission of the Negro to the electorate, Memphis Conservatives were not immune to Brownlow's ire—as they discovered to their sorrow. Though the Chamber of Commerce gave the Radical legislature a banquet in Nashville,[25] for four years Memphis, as the largest city in the state, suffered severely from ruinous state taxes and trade restrictions. The Metropolitan Police Bill of 1866 placed its public order in the control of three commissioners, appointed by Brownlow, who discharged the existing force and hired a new one.[26] S. B. Beaumont, the local Radical who had been several times defeated for various municipal offices, became superintendent of the Memphis District. In spite of all attempts to oust him he retained this position until the Radicals fell from power, though the *Appeal* declared that the efficiency of the force under his supervision was such that the city would have been "better off without any."[27]

Other measures were passed to increase patronage and facilitate Radical control of the municipality. The courts were reorganized and made subservient. When Judge Hunter, a carpetbagger from Cairo, fined the editors of the *Avalanche* for contempt of court because they criticized him, excitement ran high until a higher court reversed the decision.[28] The seat of the county government was transferred from Raleigh to Memphis to provide a greater harvest and facilitate centralization.[29] The powers of the municipality were enlarged by several amendments to its charter, and two new wards consisting of territory to the south of the corporation limits, where the freedmen had congregated, were added in 1867 to increase the Negro vote.[30]

These measures put Radicals in a position to distribute offices and favors, but they remained a minority group among the electorate until the enfranchisement of the Negroes in 1867. After the passage of the franchise act, decks were at once cleared for the gubernatorial campaign in the summer, which it was apparent would be decided by the black vote. General Albert Pike, editor of the *Appeal,* declared that the ballot "might just as safely be given to so many South American monkeys. . . . We do not want their votes and never shall."[31] But the Memphis conservatives and their candidate, Emerson Etheridge, were of a different mind, for they extended themselves in a strenuous effort to win the support of the freedmen, though in the end the Union League and the Freedmen's Bureau proved more successful. In the election early in August, in which both parties co-operated with Federal troops to preserve order, hundreds of Negroes were fraudulently voted to give the Radicals their first victory in Memphis by a majority of thirteen hundred (Table X). Thirty-six hundred Negroes and twenty-eight hundred whites took part in the voting.[32]

The Conservative advances to the Negroes were rewarded in the municipal election of the following January, for J. W. Leftwich, their nominee for mayor, received three hundred more votes than his two Radical opponents together. A large group of the blacks broke with the carpetbaggers and formed an independent organization.[33] The fact that the number of voters, however, was only two thirds that of the previous August points suspiciously to intimidation, particularly since the *Ledger* gave the Irish full credit for the victory.

The presidential campaign of 1868 kept passions aroused, and Federal troops were again requested to preserve order at the polls.[34] To avoid investigation by national authorities the Klan and the Conservatives had to be so circumspect that Grant received more than 99 per cent of the Negro vote of over forty-three hundred. Yet this proved the last Radical triumph, for Senter split the party in 1869, and the

TABLE X

MEMPHIS ELECTION RETURNS, 1865-1870[35]

Date	Election	Conservatives	Radicals	Total
1865				
February	State		879	879
August	Congress	1,090	295	1,385
	Legislature	1,114	236	1,350
December	Legislature	1,285	566	1,851
1866				
October	Municipal (no factions)			1,809
		(Ethridge)	(Brownlow)	
1867		white, 1,963	868	2,831
August	Governor	black, 628	3,000	3,628
	Total	2,591	3,868	6,459
			(Beecher)	
1868		(J. W. Leftwich)	(Fitch)	
January	Municipal	2,306	1,995	4,301
		(Seymour)	(Grant)	
November	President	white, 2,436	535	2,971
		black, 86	4,283	4,369
	Total	2,522	4,818	7,340
November	Congress	white, 2,431	291	2,722
		black, 85	4,212	4,297
	Total	2,516	4,503	7,019
1869		(Senter)	(Stokes)	
August	Governor	5,133	2,922	8,055
1870		(Brown)	(Wisener)	
November	Governor	4,919	1,805	6,724

following year, with Confederates largely replacing the Negroes in the electorate, the Democrats won a majority of more than three thousand in Memphis.

The rather voluminous research regarding the Negro in the South during the reconstruction period has treated the problem as a rural one. It is true, as this research has assumed, that the labor of the black man, free or in bondage, was indispensable to the production of cotton, and that cotton alone could restore prosperity in the conquered region. Whatever the political and social consequences of emancipation, the economic status of the freedman was the basis of reconstruction. Sound though this approach is, however, it leaves out of consideration the thousands of Negroes who, apparently untempted by the prospect of forty acres and a mule, flocked to southern cities during the war and remained in them.

When one recalls that from 1860 to 1900 the number of Negroes in Memphis increased from three to fifty thousand while the number of whites was increasing from nineteen to only fifty-two thousand, the momentous nature of this movement becomes obvious. Unsuited to urban existence and debarred as a race from competing with white men in the professions, in clerical work, or in skilled manual trades, these descendants of slaves, scarcely two centuries removed from the African jungle, are still an undigested body in the city's craw—even after seventy-five years of participation in free society. If they have greatly aggravated the problem of municipal crime and poverty, it is not so much that they are vicious or shiftless by nature as that they are the victims of an economic maladjustment which their number and their temperament, as well as their social and economic status, make inevitable.

At the close of the war the various military organizations which had been caring for the Negro since 1862 were consolidated into the Freedmen's Bureau, and Memphis immediately became one of the five sub-districts in Tennessee. Though rations were not issued after August, 1867, $34,000 was distributed to Negroes in the city as a bounty during February, 1868, alone.[36] While in many sections the Bureau proved as beneficial to the starving whites as to the blacks, in Tennessee it found its services monopolized by the emancipated slaves.[37] Its primary function was to provide food and shelter for its protégés, but it also had jurisdiction in all civil and criminal cases involving freedmen until their testimony was allowed in state courts (May, 1866), and it established schools to provide for their education.

In 1865 Memphis found itself faced with the task not merely of putting its own thirty-five hundred ex-slaves back to work but, in addition, of finding employment for five to ten thousand new ones who had descended upon it. A few of these Negroes, who formed a colony south of town just outside the corporation limits, managed to pick up odd jobs, but the vast majority subsisted on rations distributed by the Bureau and on what they secured by the use of their wits.[38] Indistinguishable among the shadows that swallowed it, nightly a huge black army crept into the city, the women to walk the streets and the men to steal and murder if necessary. Though the loaves and fishes they garnered were numerous in the aggregate, such spoil proved little when divided among so many; and the majority, poorly fed and half-clothed, were forced to live a wretched existence—fifteen or twenty of them often occupying the same room.[39] Fields were lying fallow a short distance away for lack of laborers, but as long as the Bureau continued to provide the barest subsistence the freedman would enjoy his new freedom in the city.

Thus in spite of the work of the Bureau the Negroes, nominally wards of the nation, actually lived off the community by "spilin' the Egyptians." Regardless of the impartiality of higher officials, the minor agents who came into contact with the blacks frequently used their position for political purposes.[40] These agents, in most cases carpetbaggers or former Federal soldiers, were often prejudiced against southerners and ignorant of the Negro's temperament. Consequently the universal antipathy with which the Bureau was regarded in the South is understandable, for by its charity it inevitably encouraged its wards in idleness and crime.[41] Having postponed rehabilitation several years and having made the final solution of the labor problem immeasurably more difficult, it withdrew in 1867 and left the South to work out its own salvation.

Harper's Weekly

CITY OF MEMPHIS, TENNESSEE, AFTER THE WAR

SCENE IN MEMPHIS DURING THE RIOT
Shooting down Negroes on the morning of May 2, 1866. Sketched by A. R. W. for *Harper's Weekly.*

SCENE IN MEMPHIS DURING THE RIOT
Burning a Freedmen's school-house. Sketched by A. R. W. for *Harper's Weekly.*

In response to a military order of December, 1864, Memphis undertook to provide for the education of its Negroes, continuing the work started two years earlier by a nurse in one of the hospitals who had opened a night school for colored attendants.[42] Supported jointly by the Bureau, the city, northern philanthropy, and the Negroes themselves, during 1865 a system of schools was organized that attracted almost two thousand pupils. Within a year after the close of the war there had been established for the welfare of the colored urban population an orphan asylum, numerous churches, and a dozen secular schools taught by white as well as black teachers.[43]

Racial relations reached a boiling point in 1866. Between the workingmen of Memphis, chiefly the Irish, and their new black competitors had long existed an intense hatred.[44] Encouraged by Radical agitators, upon occasion the Negroes attempted to attain social equality, and both parties were in an ugly mood. The spark which started the actual conflagration was the discharge in the spring of four thousand black troops whom the Federals had stationed in the city to preserve order in 1865.[45] During the few days of idleness before their formal withdrawal, these soldiers, emboldened by whisky, persecuted the poor whites in Fort Pickering. Naturally the police force, over 90 per cent Irish in composition, waited impatiently for an opportunity to revenge this treatment of their brethren.

Fate was in their favor, for on the afternoon of May 1 a group of black troops attempted to prevent several policemen from making an arrest in South Memphis.[46] At once the rest of the force, the firemen, the politicians, and the rabble all rushed to the scene. In their frenzy they slaughtered Negroes and burned dwellings indiscriminately, not confining punishment to the discharged soldiers who had started the trouble. At midnight a company of Federal troops restored order temporarily, but rioting broke out afresh on the following morning and continued intermittently for two days. When the fury of the Irish had spent itself, forty-six persons had been killed, two of whom were whites, and seventy-five wounded. Property damage included the destruction by fire of ninety-one Negro houses, four Negro churches, and twelve Negro schools at an estimated loss of $130,000.[47]

Memphis immediately gained unfair but unavoidable notoriety. Though its newspapers had deplored the riots and had constantly counseled moderation, and though few paroled Confederates had taken any part in the proceedings, the northern press represented the affair as a brutal retaliation upon the Negroes by ex-Rebels who were still anti-Union in sentiment.[48] To the Radicals in Congress the incident was a godsend, for it gave them propaganda invaluable at the moment.[49] Brownlow profited as well, for as a direct result of the riots he succeeded in getting his Metropolitan Police Bill passed without opposition.

The enfranchised Negro was of paramount political significance during the period of Radical supremacy. Thanks to a copious distribution of silver dollars and cheap whisky, the minority party among the whites were able by their control of the black vote to obtain majorities for Brownlow and Grant when otherwise they would have been defeated. The Klan, which did not become militant in Tennessee until 1867, was apparently unable to intimidate the Negroes in elections because of the close scrutiny exercised over the city by Federal authorities after the riots of 1866, but the small vote in the municipal election of 1868 suggests that this organization was able to control both Negroes and Radicals if unhampered by external interference.[50]

Because of its nature as a secret and extra-legal society the truth about the Klan will never be known. Outside the columns of the Radical *Post* there was little reference to its local activity. The Metropolitan Police discovered a Ku-Klux oath in the city, but it was later proved to be spurious.[51] Though fifty Negroes were driven from their homes for supporting the Radicals in the election of 1867, there was no indication that such persecution was the work of the Klan.[52] Judge Hunter adjourned his court reputedly out of fear of the order; yet here again the evidence was vague.[53] General Forrest, Grand Wizard of the organization, undoubtedly received the support of his fellow citizens, for according to the testimony of several members every ex-Confederate in Memphis was a Klansman.[54] Composed as it was of the better element among the citizenry, and not the rabble responsible for the earlier riots, the Klan was careful to create no scenes. To it belongs most of the credit for the little social order that existed in the city during the late sixties, and its lack of publicity is a sign of efficiency rather than inactivity.

Toward the end of the reconstruction period the condition of Negroes in Memphis gradually improved. Schools were re-established, and when they became completely free the attendance in them increased from 307 to 1,190.[55] As a result of the efforts of the Congregationalists of the American Missionary Society, which had operated smaller colored schools in the city for several years, a donation from a Pennsylvania doctor was used to found LeMoyne Institute, a secondary school for Negroes which later became a reputable college.[56]

In the elections of 1869 and 1870 the blacks were kept from the polls by moral suasion and economic pressure rather than by open violence,[57] but once their Radical "friends" had disappeared they lost all interest in voting—which after all had attracted them only as a source of money and whisky. Bourbon Democracy bore the ex-slave no malice; the Ku-Klux disbanded upon the demise of the Brownlow régime, and in 1871 Negroes were actually invited to hold office in Shelby County.[58] During the disorder which followed the enactment of the Civil Rights Bill of 1875 a Memphis mass meeting protested against the killing of Negroes in Somerville and Gibson County, and Mayor Loague (1873-75) appointed a number of black policemen.[59] Despite this improvement in social and political relations, the size of the black element prevented its assimilation by urban trade and industry. Only by public and private charity was the continued existence of many of the Negroes, precarious even with such assistance, possible in the postwar city.

War can destroy the bad as well as the good, but in the late sixties the seamy side of Memphis with its mud, filth, political corruption, municipal debt, disease, and crime stood out in bolder relief than ever before. W. H. Russell, an English press correspondent who toured the South in 1862, thus recorded his impressions in verse:

"I wonder why they gave it such a name of old renown
This dreary, dismal, muddy, melancholy town?"[60]

Streets were in such wretched condition in 1867 that almost all of the travelers coming north from New Orleans, who would have to transfer from station to station in Memphis by coach because of the lack of a central depot, chose to follow the route from Grenada to Jackson, Tennessee, rather than subject themselves to the discomfort and danger of the thoroughfares on the bluff.[61] After much discussion and bickering between citizens, officials, and contractors, the Nicholson Pavement, composed of specially treated wooden blocks, was put down in the business district during the fall of 1867. Though this material was more satisfactory than gravel, it began to decay in a few years, and the expense entailed was no small factor in the city's ultimate bankruptcy.

Both before and after the war Memphis was notorious

for the corruption and inefficiency of its municipal government.[62] The advent of the Radicals to power meant merely that two bands of thieves instead of one would pillage the public. During the riots of 1866 Mayor Park had been almost constantly intoxicated, and on a later occasion he was fined in the police court for drunkenness and disorderly conduct.[63] Local officials and office seekers, instead of curbing the May Day mob, had urged it on; City Recorder Creighton even exhorted the crowd to "clean every Negro son-of-a-bitch out of town."[64] Among the aldermen existed a "ring" which grew rich off the taxpayers by requiring a fat commission on every contract. There were repeated charges of bribery in regard to the Nicholson Pavement, and it was a matter of record that a new policeman who accidentally wounded himself in the heel was allowed a compensation of $900 in addition to his usual salary.[65]

The *Argus* led such a vigorous attack upon the administration during 1866 that Park, who was a sot but not connected with the inner circle of the city council which profited from the graft, challenged its editors to a duel.[66] W. O. Lofland, the reform candidate for mayor, was successful in the October election, but he found himself unable to remedy the situation. J. W. Leftwich, the leader of the Conservatives who succeeded Lofland, denounced his aldermen as "with few exceptions, a parcel of thieves and scoundrels."[67] "This town is a political cess-pool," wrote a reputable local attorney to a Nashville friend, "and the leading spirits won't let a decent man raise his head. If you won't follow mildly in their lead, you are at once forced to the other side."[68]

The abnormal expenditures which reconstruction made necessary, coupled with wholesale corruption on the part of the aldermen and the failure of many citizens to pay taxes, produced a staggering debt by 1870. In that year the scrip which the city had been issuing for some time was at such a discount that one hundred dollars was being borrowed to discharge sixty-five dollars of indebtedness, and the municipality was paying double for its supplies.[69] As a result of the investigation of the "Citizens' Union" several aldermen were indicted by the grand jury, but they retained their seats, apparently without being subjected to prosecution. John Johnson, an able Irish merchant who became mayor in 1870, cut expenses to a minimum, created a sinking fund, and attempted to collect back taxes. A capable accountant himself, he made the first thorough analysis of the city's finances, as shown in Table XI. During his tenure of office much real estate was sold by forfeiture for taxes, and in spite of persecution from ward politicians and the fatal unpopularity which his sane course aroused, he reduced the debt from $3,902,512 to $3,352,077.[70]

TABLE XI

MAYOR'S REPORT FOR 1872: "EXPLANATORY STATEMENT OF HOW MEMPHIS COMES TO HAVE SO LARGE A BONDED DEBT AND SO LITTLE TO SHOW FOR IT"

	Amount Issued	Amount Realized by City	Loss
Subscription to M. &. C. RR....	$ 500,000	$ 500,000.00	$............
" M. & O. RR....	100,000	17,450.00	82,550.00
" M. & T. RR....	250,000	40,000.00	210,000.00
" M. & L. R. RR..	350,000	60,000.00	290,000.00
Funding, Currency, 1866.......	187,000	156,427.92	30,572.08
Paving, Currency, 1867........	900,000	759,521.95	140,478.05
Funding, Currency, 1868.......	1,135,000	686,777.67	448,222.33
Funding, Currency, 1869.......	67,000	17,789.17	49,210.83
Funding, Gold, 1870...........	308,000	308,000.00	....
School Purposes..............	220,000	....	220,000.00
Total..............	$4,017,000	$2,545,966.71	$1,471,033.29

Analyzed loss:

RR. subscription.............	$582,550.00
Funding process..............	251,767.08
Sales to meet expenses........	416,716.21
School purposes..............	220,000.00

In 1867 came a severe attack of cholera, followed by the town's third epidemic of yellow fever with a death rate, during October and November alone, of 550 out of the 2,500 stricken.[71] The Howard Association, reorganized to care for the sick, became a permanent organization in that year. The medical profession was aware of the danger before the arrival of the fever, but the reorganized board of health was denied any real authority by the council, which was jealous of the board because it consisted of the mayor's appointees.[72]

If Memphis was the toughest town on the river even before it was overrun by Negroes, one can imagine the deplorable effect of four years of war and the influx of ten thousand freedmen. No day passed without one and often several murders; yet the culprit was rarely convicted.[73] The metropolitan police were helpless, and burglary became so common that citizens formed the habit of protecting their own property without the assistance of the law, a custom which lingered on in a modified form during the early twentieth century. In addition to adult criminals, the community was terrorized by a group of youthful robbers known as the "Mackerels."[74] It was estimated in 1867 that there were between two and three thousand dope addicts in the city and that a thousand men and boys gambled nightly in its numerous saloons.[75] Five years later, when this postwar lawlessness had subsided a bit, eighteen houses of prostitution still remained, which employed one hundred and fifty women.[76]

With its wholesale trade gone, its railroad lines broken, and war prices still prevailing, Memphis in 1865 energetically devoted its efforts to a restoration of prewar prosperity. The municipal government resumed control in June, under military surveillance to be sure, and in the same month the Chamber of Commerce was reorganized.[77] The street railway company which had received a charter on the eve of the conflict now laid its tracks and began operation.

"Memphis astounds me with its rush and roar of business," commented a Kentuckian who visited it in the fall. "So soon after the war it is wonderful. I predict that it will be the greatest city in the Mississippi Valley, St. Louis not excepted."[78]

Judging by the commercial activity of the following spring, these remarks were not as superficial as they sound. Five thousand spindles at the cotton mills on Wolf River were requiring the services of ninety operatives.[79] Local foundries were working overtime and wholesale hardware houses were doing a tremendous volume of business to supply a section that had sheathed its sword and was again following the plow.[80] In response to high rents fifteen hundred buildings were in process of construction, and in March the German merchants organized a National Bank with a capital of $175,000.[81] The increase in trade between Memphis and St. Louis which had occurred during the war had produced a constant agitation for a railroad to that point, and a contract was signed with the engineers in the fall of 1867.[82]

Just when recovery seemed assured the full effect of the Brownlow program fell upon the city and its hinterland, and for three years it suffered a lull in trade. Violent fluctuations in the value of goods made both consumer and producer conservative.[83] In 1868 three banks failed and five thousand people were reported to have left the town because of the depression and high rents.[84] "I don't get ten dollars in money," complained one lawyer, "although my usual fees are generally $200 to $300 a week."[85]

Besides the political and social turmoil which hardly attracted purchasers or new firms, there were definite economic factors responsible for this stagnation of trade. At the very time that it was forced to compete with northern cities which cut prices to obtain the southern market, Memphis was burdened with a 4 per cent tax on real estate in addition to state merchants' taxes and a federal levy of three cents a pound on cotton.[86] During 1867 the tri-state region, as a result of the punitive measures of the Radicals in Congress and a short cotton crop, was in the throes of famine;[87] immediately trade in its metropolis declined.

Three years later, however, signs of recovery were numerous. Indeed, the new Memphis forgot the tragic era when it compared the statistics for 1870 with those of 1860. (See Table XII.) During these ten years, though its white inhabitants increased only five thousand, its population doubled. When the Democrats returned to power in the state the city had rebuilt its four railroads; two new lines were under construction, one along the Mississippi to Paducah, Kentucky, and the other to Selma, Alabama; and roads to St. Louis, Kansas City, and El Paso were projected. Cotton, still 80,000 bales short of its 1860 peak, was much greater in value because of the high postwar price.[89] Banking capital was short of the 1860 total by $300,000, but increased insurance funds more than made up the difference.[90] From its harbor were operated eleven steamboat lines employing forty boats averaging 16,306 tons each, and it led the United States in the manufacture of cottonseed oil with an annual output of 7,400 barrels.[91] The city was sufficiently modern to possess five daily newspapers and three suburbs (Fort Pickering, Chelsea, and Scotland); and its central location and accommodations were already making it popular as a

TABLE XII

RECEIPTS OF SEVEN REPRESENTATIVE ARTICLES AT MEMPHIS, 1860-1870[88]

	1859–60	1860–61	1866–67	1869–70
Cotton (bales)	369,603	112,952	217,626	290,737
Agricultural implements	11,030	26,630	35,584	128,006
Dry goods (pkg.)	25,064	3,919	11,717	39,366
Hardware (pkg.)	10,611	12,645	22,056	42,708
Hogs	5,552	4,987	11,911	27,475
Whisky (bbls.)	30,471	9,201	10,071	9,625
White lead (kegs)	3,089	668	3,901	8,611

convention town, for no less a body than the National Typographical Union held its annual meeting there in 1867. The great increase in wholesale trade at the end of the sixties foreshadowed its future as a distributing point and dispelled forever its reputation as a "six-months-cotton-town," if indeed the commerce of the fifties had not already removed that stigma.[92]

By 1870 the lusty young river town was back in stride, and in blissful ignorance of the dark days just ahead it prepared to enjoy a commercial utopia which war had only postponed.

CHAPTER VIII

THE STING OF THE YELLOWJACK

MAN, PREHISTORIC and modern, has ever regarded plagues with superstition and awe. Since the classic description of the plague in Athens by Thucydides many epidemics have had their chroniclers, but only the last half century has possessed the medical knowledge necessary for a scientific study of these catastrophes. Pestilence will probably continue to possess dramatic interest for the layman and scientific interest for the doctor; but the student of economic and social history has an entirely different approach to it, one which is highly pertinent to a study of Memphis. What effect do epidemics have upon the character and the growth of a city, and what part do they play in competition between urban centers?

The health of Memphians, situated as they were in the midst of a swampy region inundated annually by the Mississippi, was wretched throughout the nineteenth century; not until 1900 was it known that the mosquito was the cause of much of its perennial sickness. Germs of exotic diseases brought to New Orleans from Asia, Africa, South America, and the West Indies, soon found their way up the river. In an age when bacteriology did not exist, no distinction was made between cholera and smallpox, which were contagious, and dengue and yellow fever, which were not transmitted directly. Not only were all of these diseases common in the valley, but also dysentery, pneumonia, and that chronic ailment of all lowlands, chills and fever.[1] Preventive steps were never taken until pestilence was upon the community, and then quarantine and disinfectant were resorted to regardless of the nature of the disease. Since the cause of sickness was unknown, and the diagnosis therefore unreliable, it is not surprising that the wise sought safety from epidemics in flight rather than in nostrums and medical care.

The sanitary conditions in Memphis during the seventies were perhaps no better than those of the poorest medieval borough. The water supply, which in ante-bellum days had been the Wolf and the Mississippi, consisted of defective wells and cisterns, supplemented in 1873 by a plant reputed to purify river water.[2] Subject to no inspection of any kind, milk was both diluted and polluted; the *Ledger* reports an instance of a live minnow found swimming in one pail.[3] According to the same paper, streets were "huge depots of filth, cavernous Augean stables, with no Tiber to flow through and cleanse them." Front yards, back yards, avenues, alleys, and gutters were full of garbage, refuse, dead animals, and stagnant water, all producing a stench which, but for the adaptation peculiar to the olfactory sense, would have driven human life from the town. The whole corporate area, with its thousands of "privy vaults," drained into Gayoso Bayou, a stream which had once been several miles in length, but which in the seventies had for many years been merely a series of stagnant pools, separated by dams of decaying organic matter and human excrement. Travelers pronounced the city the dirtiest in the country; "I've been to Cairo," facetiously exclaimed one Radical, "and there's dirt for you. . . . I've been to Cologne where it's pure smell—but they all back down before Memphis."[4]

In the absence of reports from an organized board of health before 1879 one can only imagine the high annual toll of endemic diseases before that date, but of those which were epidemic there exists the record shown in Table XIII.

TABLE XIII

EPIDEMICS IN MEMPHIS PRIOR TO 1880[5]

Year	Disease	Results	
1740	Fever	Bienville's army decimated	
1827	Dengue	.....	
1828	Smallpox	.....	
	Yellow fever	53 deaths in 150 cases	
1832-33	Cholera	Severe	
		Cases	Deaths
1835	Cholera	350	55%
1842	Smallpox	.....	.....
1845	Dysentery	400	50
1849	Cholera	1,200	33%
1855	Yellow fever	1,250	220
1860	Dengue	.....	.....
1867	Yellow fever	2,500	.....
	Cholera	600	.....
1873	Yellow fever	5,000	2,000
	Cholera	1,500	276
	Smallpox	.....	.....
1878	Yellow fever	17,600	5,150
1879	Yellow fever	2,000	600

The lower valley as a whole was sickly, but its few crowded cities were far more vulnerable than the thinly populated and less exposed districts of the interior. Memphis had suffered almost as much from pestilence before 1870 as had New Orleans, the worst plague-ridden town in the country; yet the press and the loyal citizens on the bluff would never admit that it was abnormally unhealthy. One boast in particular was full of tragic irony: "I honestly believe Memphis," wrote its first historian in 1872, becoming for the moment an apologist, "to be the healthiest place on the river from the mouth of the Missouri down."[6]

"Vomito negro," as it is vividly termed in Spanish, ravaged the equatorial and Caribbean regions of the western hemisphere during the four centuries prior to 1900 with an average mortality of more than 50 per cent.[7] Carried by ships along both shores of the Atlantic from Africa to New England, it caused epidemics in cities as far east as Marseilles and as far north as Boston. The West Indies con-

sistently suffered the highest mortality, but Philadelphia, New Orleans, and Memphis experienced severe attacks on several occasions. Endemic to the tropics, the disease has always been more prevalent in the warmer regions of the temperate zone than in those where the temperature is lower.

After the Philadelphia plague evoked the interest of Benjamin Rush in the 1790's, American physicians constantly sought to discover the cause of yellow fever and the means of its propagation. Not until 1900, however, did Major Walter Reed prove by a series of experiments in Cuba that the disease could be transmitted only by the bite of the female of that species of mosquito technically known as the *Aëdes aegypti*.[8] It was announced in 1918 that the bacteria which produced the fever had been isolated, but medical opinion at present rejects this theory in favor of a virus yet unidentified as the cause.

The pattern of American epidemics has been somewhat as follows: an individual, usually from the tropics, came into port with the germ in his blood stream. Yellow fever mosquitoes proceeded to bite him, and after an incubation period of twelve days the insects by their sting transmitted the germs to other people. This process was repeated wherever those who were thus infected happened to go, as long as the temperature permitted the continued existence of mosquitoes. The infection can apparently be contracted by no natural means other than the agency of this insect.[9]

Once the fever broke out in a person, it ran its course in a brief period which varied from twenty-four hours to four or five days. In the initial stages the victim suffered from chills, fever, and severe pains in the head and back. Soon these symptoms disappeared and they were followed by subnormal temperatures and pulse, which gave the patient an impression of convalescence. This was actually the critical stage, for after a brief interval he began to vomit a black substance composed of blood and the acids of the stomach, the only positive sign of the disease. Within a few days he was either dead or on the road to recovery.[10]

The average doctor of the seventies knew little of the symptoms or treatment of yellow fever, and the public was still more ignorant. Certain individuals made remarkably accurate observations,[11] but no one even remotely associated the disease with the mosquito. Though a student in medicine at the University of Pennsylvania in 1803 proved conclusively that yellow fever was not contagious in the usual sense of that word, quarantine and disinfectant were still religiously prescribed three quarters of a century later.[12] Some eminent authorities held that yellow fever was caused by a living organism, permeating the atmosphere under certain conditions, that this organism was received into the blood stream through the lungs, and that the disease could be contracted by direct contact.[13] The more popular theory, and one which many doctors endorsed, argued that the filth of the city and the decaying Nicholson Pavement had filled the air with noxious poisons, while the godly considered the plague a divine punishment for the celebration of the semi-pagan festival of Mardi Gras, inaugurated in Memphis in the early seventies.[14]

In a section where all varieties of fever were common, no malady could be positively identified as the yellow pestilence until the unmistakable symptom of black vomit occurred. Inasmuch as an official announcement that the fever was epidemic would create a panic and practically depopulate the town, health authorities were hesitant to take that step until they were certain that the plague was inevitable. By that time hundreds were already infected, and the wholesale flight which followed spread the virus through the surrounding area.[15] As a matter of fact, the medical profession was helpless in the face of the fever. According to the chairman of the New Orleans board of health, perhaps the leading authority, it "must run its course, and nothing that we know of can stop its progress."[16] Once the yellow-jack struck, the unfortunate community could only wait until the frosts of late autumn brought belated relief.

The season of 1872-73 was a calamitous one for Memphis. The fever scourge was but the last of five major mishaps that occurred within a period of seven months. December found the city in the throes of the "epizootic," an equine malady which paralyzed the horse-drawn transportation system and business in general quite as severely as a failure of the supply of gasoline and electricity would tie up a twentieth-century metropolis. In midwinter also came a severe freeze, which suspended traffic on land and river for more than a month and destroyed property worth several million dollars. During the cold weather appeared a violent form of smallpox, followed in the spring by a milder attack of the cholera. This latter infection was so severe in the rest of West Tennessee that well-to-do Memphians, anxious to secure the services of their own physicians should they be stricken, postponed their annual departure to watering places until July. At last confident that no further misfortune could arise, citizens settled down to the lazy existence of the dull midsummer season, awaiting the fall with optimism.[17]

Their troubles were by no means over, however, for a worse fate lay in store for them. Early in August a steamer from New Orleans stopped for provisions at the bluff alongside Happy Hollow, an under-the-hill community exclusively Irish in composition.[18] When the boat departed several hours later, it left behind two sick men who died within several days. Fever immediately broke out in the hollow with an average mortality of two deaths a day, and by the first of September it had reached the top of the bluff.[19] Thence it spread through Pinch, also largely Irish,[20] but it was not until the ninth that the public had any inkling of its danger. When the board of health, uncertain for several weeks as to an exact diagnosis, announced on the fourteenth that yellow fever was epidemic, an exodus ensued until only fifteen thousand out of a total population of forty thousand were left in the city at the end of the month.[21]

Those remaining, the majority of them Negroes who seem to have been immune until 1878,[22] had no alternative but to let the fever spend itself, wondering all the while which of their number would be the next victims. The climax came early in October with seventy-one deaths on the fifth and sixty-two on the tenth.[23] Every organization, creed, and nationality secured donations, largely from outside, and ministered to their sick brethren, spending a total of $332,288 in two months.[24] The Howards, under Dr. L. P. Blackburn of Louisville and Major W. T. Walthall of Mobile, erected a hospital and alone spent $124,000 in relief work, but the Catholic priests and sisters bore the brunt of the burden, for it was their communicants who suffered most.[25] Frosts of late October brought welcome respite, and before Thanksgiving the yellowjack had disappeared.

Of the fifteen thousand who braved the peril of the fever, five thousand were stricken and two thousand died.[26] At least half of the victims were Irish Catholics.[27] Few influential citizens were lost since few had exposed themselves to the virus for any length of time. By Christmas most of the merchants had returned and trade was brisk as usual, but in the future they would never be free from the fear that in the late summer the plague would strike, swift and deadly, before they could flee.

This first siege of fever in the seventies produced a cautious attitude among inhabitants which was definitely detrimental to the city's welfare. Men would continue to profit from the economic advantages which Memphis offered, but they lived in a temporary world which they must be ready to desert upon a moment's notice. Thus, while the value of annual trade reached seventy-five million dollars in 1875, the value of taxable property dropped from thirty million in 1874 to twenty million in 1878, and in the latter year one third of this property had been confiscated by the state in forfeit for taxes.[28] Population should have increased ten or fifteen thousand between 1870 and 1875, but actually it showed no appreciable gain during those years. The Panic of 1873 and the mounting municipal debt contributed to this economic stagnation, but the fever was without question the primary cause.

Before the ordeal of 1873 had become but a remembered nightmare, the scourge again prevailed in what is, relatively, one of the most severe fever epidemics in American urban history. In May, 1878, upon a report that the disease was epidemic in the West Indies, merchants unsuccessfully petitioned the authorities to establish quarantine. On July 26 the newspapers announced that the fever had been on the increase in New Orleans for two weeks. Immediately quarantine stations were set up at Germantown on the Memphis and Charleston Railroad, at Whitehaven on the Mississippi and Tennessee, and at the lower end of President's Island in the river.[29] Rumors of a frightful outbreak in Grenada, Mississippi, arrived on August 10, and when they were confirmed three days later the bluff community became acutely apprehensive.[30] Little did it suspect that the yellowjack had already entered the city by the usual route from the river, but its sense of security was abruptly shattered by the announcement of the board of health that a Mrs. Bionda, the wife of an Italian snack-house keeper who catered to rivermen, had died of yellow fever on August 13.[31] Sixty-five new cases were reported during the next two days, and before officials pronounced the plague epidemic on August 23, hundreds of deaths had occurred.[32]

The panic-stricken populace did not wait for an official

announcement before acting. On the day of Mrs. Bionda's death began a mad exodus, by rail, by river, by wagon, and on foot, which carried from the town within a fortnight twenty-five thousand of its inhabitants, among them several of its doctors and most of its Protestant ministers.[33] There may have been some excuse for the latter since it was largely the poor Catholics who, because of penury, remained to die in the inferno, but for months the papers denounced the Protestant clergy for their desertion in no uncertain terms.

In the frenzied rush to safety all semblance of courtesy disappeared, nor could police and railroad officials enforce the slightest degree of order. Regardless of age or sex everyone took care of himself, and in numerous instances fathers deserted wives and families. In self-defense many of the neighboring towns established shotgun quarantines and refused to allow trains to stop, even compelling some of the refugees to camp in the forest without food or shelter.[34] Out of fear of infection the residents of Jackson not only destroyed every animal which came from Memphis, but in their panic they even broke to pieces a stove which had recently arrived from the bluff.[35] In spite of his cassock Father Quinn was denied admission to numerous towns in West Tennessee because he was known to have been in Memphis.[36]

About five thousand of the inhabitants, lacking the means of their more fortunate fellows, entered the several camps which had been established at a safe distance in the vicinity.[37] By the middle of September only 19,600 people remained in the city, 14,000 of whom were Negroes, and most of the whites were Irish.[38] At first the disease had been confined to Pinch, but soon it spread throughout the town in every direction at a rate of several hundred new cases each day. Five weeks after the existence of the plague had been formally announced, the infection had penetrated the suburbs and the surrounding territory within a twelve-mile radius.[39]

"Deaths to date 2,250," read a telegram from the relief committee to Booth's Theater in New York on September 20. "Number now sick about 3,000, average deaths 60 per cent of the sick. We are feeding some 10,000 persons, sick and destitute. . . . 15 volunteer physicians have died, 20 others are sick, and a great many nurses have died. Fever abating a little today, for want of material, perhaps. . . . We are praying for frost—it is our only hope."[40]

Soon after the death of Mrs. Bionda Memphis was converted into one vast hospital that was daily becoming more and more of a charnel house. All business ceased, and of the many social and economic institutions only the press, telegraph, railroads, steamboats, druggists, undertakers, doctors, and Catholic clergy made any attempt to continue functioning.[41] Every type of organization participated in relief work, but the Howard Association, the Citizens' Relief Committee, and the Catholic Church carried most of the burden. It was as imperative to feed the well as to nurse the sick and bury the dead. Though contributions and volunteers had poured in since quarantine had been lifted on August 16, hundreds died of neglect. The Howards alone furnished twenty-nine hundred nurses and one hundred and eleven doctors, and spent over half a million dollars in caring for fifteen thousand victims.[42]

The large number of Negroes, susceptible to the virus for the first time in 1878, could not be persuaded to leave as long as they were assured free rations.[43] In many cases they were left to care for vacant houses by the owners who had fled to safer regions. Considerable petty thievery went on, and there were numerous unfounded tales of rape of white women by Negro men.[44] It was estimated at one time that two hundred tramps were scouring the city in search of spoil.[45] As on all occasions when life is cheap and highly uncertain, debauchery was conspicuous. Yet on the whole public order was as well preserved as could be expected, thanks to the efforts of the Relief Committee and to the loyalty of the two military companies, composed of Negroes, that were stationed opposite Court Square to preserve order.[46]

The horrors of the epidemic defy description. Bodies were constantly found in an advanced state of decomposition. In one instance workers discovered half a cadaver of a Negro woman covered with hundreds of dead rats which had eaten the flesh. The county undertaker had four furniture wagons in service all day long; yet at the peak of the pestilence victims succumbed so fast that scores lay unburied. Hundreds of corpses were interred in shallow gullies with no marks of identification. One party of workers came upon a live infant, coated with black vomit, suckling the breasts of its dead mother. During the duration of the epidemic all babies, with few exceptions, were stillborn. Strange anomalies occurred in the presence of death—strong men turned cowards and lewd women saints.[47]

In the midst of awful tragedy appeared the miraculous and the comic. One little girl in her eleventh year, who had been dumb and paralyzed for some time, recovered complete possession of her faculties after a long siege of the fever. To ward off the disease people drenched themselves with cologne and rosewater, or wore on their persons onions and little bags of asafœtida, that evil-smelling stuff which superstitious folk in the South still use to insure immunity.[48] Men could be seen everywhere wearing sponges on their noses, and streets were covered with lime for the purpose of disinfection. As the last rites were being said over one Irishman in St. Patrick's Cathedral, the mourners were terrified to see the shrouded figure in the coffin open its eyes and ejaculate, "What the hell are you doing?"[49]

The unprecedented severity of the epidemic was due to its early appearance and to the unusually hot weather, which lasted throughout early fall.[50] The wild scattering of people, which began in August, produced a high mortality in the whole valley; refugees from the city carried the infection as far as Bowling Green, Kentucky, and Chattanooga, Tennessee, though neighboring towns along railroads were hardest hit. Brownsville reported 844 cases, LaGrange 152, Martin 126, Collierville 121, and Paris 118.[51] Only those towns escaped which, like Jackson, refused to admit anyone who had been exposed. As the plague declined in the city, more through lack of subjects than for any other reason, the local committee began caring for the sick and destitute in the county, and the Howards administered to the entire tri-state region.[52]

When frost fell in the middle of October and a freeze occurred soon afterwards, the end of the epidemic was announced. According to the medical estimate, which is probably an understatement, in Memphis alone the total mortality was 5,150 out of a population that never exceeded 20,000 during the epidemic.[53] Roughly 17,600 of both races were stricken, and of the 7,000 whites who remained not more than 200 escaped the fever. Of these whites 75 per cent died in contrast to only 7 per cent of the Negroes.[54] Again the toll was heaviest among the Irish, as is evident from the fact that the Catholic Church lost two thousand of its parishioners, as well as thirteen priests and thirty nuns.[55]

Immediate signs of recovery were not apparent in the season of 1878-79, as they were following the plague of 1873. Thousands of refugees failed to return, and debt became so pressing that the municipality surrendered its charter and became a mere taxing district of the state. In spite of an energetic sanitary campaign during the winter, sporadic cases of fever appeared during the spring in different parts of town.[56] The outbreak which came with the heat of July produced once more the inevitable exodus, and again over half the population fled to Nashville and St. Louis.[57] This attack of the scourge, milder than the last, endured until the middle of November, four long months, with a mortality of more than six hundred out of two thousand cases.[58] Only the immunity acquired in the previous year saved the town from complete devastation; never did the future seem so dark as in those December days of 1879, when even the most loyal inhabitants were leaving for healthier sites. After three epidemics of such intensity as these in a single decade, it is remarkable that Memphis did not become, like Randolph, a forgotten village on the banks of the Mississippi.

Though Memphis suffered more than most American cities, unsanitary conditions were general throughout the nation until the end of the century, and every port and river town was at one time or another stricken with devastating epidemics of smallpox, cholera, or yellow fever.[59] Some attempts were made to improve public health, for the Federal government established marine hospitals along the coast and the Mississippi River to confine sailors afflicted with exotic diseases, but as late as 1873 only thirty-two cities in the United States had local boards of health.[60] Yet these organizations were helpless as long as medical science was ignorant of the origin of disease, and the seeming apathy of the nation was due actually to a lack of knowledge rather than to a lack of energy or concern.

In the last half of the nineteenth century, as a result of the experiments of European scientists like Louis Pasteur and Robert Koch, preventive medicine made significant advances. The fruits of their research in bacteriology, particularly concerning the germ theory of disease, were introduced to America by young doctors like William Osler, William H. Welch, and Hermann Biggs, who had studied abroad. In the nineties a new public health program was launched under the direction of Biggs, who served as pathologist and director of the bacteriological laboratory of the New York City Health Department from 1892 to 1914,[61] and his methods were soon applied in other American cities, particularly in Memphis. In the last decade of the century the scope of the Marine Hospital Service was enlarged, and in 1902 it became the Public Health Service.[62]

The fever in Memphis was of more than local significance; it was an event of immense national importance, for it aroused the country to the ever-present threat of disease at the very time that the discoveries of Pasteur and Koch were being disseminated. In his bachelor's dissertation submitted at Cornell in 1882, young Biggs had commented specifically on the Memphis epidemic of 1878, observing that it was "proven to have been due to filthiness and unpaved streets, insufficient drainage, obstructed and offensive sewers, and the want of proper precautions during the prevalence of the epidemic."[63] The experience of the city was a warning to the nation, and the sanitary campaign upon which it immediately embarked proved an inspiring example.[64]

Though municipal indebtedness antedated the era of epidemics, the bankruptcy which engulfed Memphis in 1878 was largely the result of the fever. Disease, debt, and municipal corruption were kindred forces which had constantly threatened the city's welfare, and their menace was removed only when the long-insensitive community, at last aroused by the destruction for which these three factors were responsible, faced ruin unless they were speedily eliminated.

Few cities have continually possessed conditions so favorable to the demagogue as did Memphis prior to 1880. Its ignorant proletariat, too poor to pay taxes, was several times as strong at the polls as the rival commercial class;

and the presence of the Irish, who have excelled in the art of ward politics wherever they have appeared in the United States, gave the masses unusual power. To acquire and retain office, professional politicians had merely to keep the rabble amused and satisfied by a careful regard for its prejudices and an occasional distribution of favors where they would count for the most. Since neither of the groups which benefited from the system bore the expense, they were little worried by the increasing debt as long as further credit was not denied the municipality. Protests of merchants and owners of property could be safely disregarded, and it was not so much a tactical blunder on the part of the "Ring" as the unforeseen accident of the fever that killed the goose which laid the golden egg.

If Memphis merchants were so prosperous, it may be asked, why did they not use economic pressure upon the politicians? As a matter of fact, such was one of the purposes of the local Whig party in the fifties, but nativism and the events of 1860 and 1861 so fired the passions of its members that control of municipal affairs became a secondary issue. The chaos of war and reconstruction scattered the party, and before the new elements, introduced in the sixties, could be assimilated into a solid conservative bloc, the plague again disrupted society.

Mayor Johnson's program of financial reform was continued by his successors, Loague (1873-75) and Flippin (1876-79), both of whom realized that the increasing rate of taxation was driving business away from the bluff. The debt had been funded during the reconstruction régime at a tremendous loss, for many of the municipal bonds had been sold at a rate of twenty-one cents on the dollar. With population at a standstill, assessments constantly decreasing, and a million dollars of taxes in arrears,[65] interest on the indebtedness could not be met except by raising the tax rate. Federal courts were granting creditors judgments which federal marshals forcibly collected from the tills of merchants on Front Street. Flippin spent much time in New York during his administration haggling with bondholders and at last persuaded the majority of them to agree to a refunding on a basis of sixty cents on the dollar.[66] Yet in spite of these efforts municipal indebtedness had increased to six million dollars on the eve of the great epidemic.

When taxes reached four cents on the dollar in 1873, a determined and united commercial class began to fight for its very existence. The Memphis Cotton Exchange, organized after the fever in 1873, the Chamber of Commerce, and the People's Protective Association joined in a demand for the repeal of the city's charter and the creation of a new form of municipal government, consisting of three commissioners to be appointed by the governor with the consent of the Senate. The report of the lawyers who drew up the resolution is an accurate analysis of affairs.

"We believe that we may safely, within truth, affirm," it read, "that in a majority of cases the rents of real estate in this city do not pay the taxes, repairs, and insurance. But few are willing to buy or build; they prefer to rent. Much of our capital, even though an interest of 10 per cent is allowed, seeks investment abroad; scarcely any comes to our city and many of our people are seeking new homes because there can be no prosperity in a city governed and taxed as we are." Pointing out the waste and the expense of frequent elections and of numerous "local governments," the report concluded: "We have in our midst a large and controlling voting element which has but little at stake in the welfare of our city. Combined as it generally is with some other element more ambitious of office than of the good of the city, it has little difficulty in fixing upon us incompetent and corrupt officers, and as a consequence bad measures. The result of this is a constantly increasing indebtedness . . . indirectly created by a class of voters who pay little or no taxes. . . . We hesitate not to affirm that our purpose is to remove our city government and the business interests of the city away from the popular elections of the times and from all partisan influences."[67]

The electorate, the press, and the administration naturally refused to listen to such a drastic proposal, and no public meeting could be coaxed or badgered into what it considered municipal suicide. This popular opposition proved a real obstacle, but the minority found other means of achieving its ends. A competent city attorney was appointed to protect the city from the incessant barrage of mandamuses and injunctions, and the tax rate was somewhat reduced. The new charter of 1876, obscure in origin and unpopular with the masses, was the first step towards the merchants' "New Deal."[68] By this charter the council was forbidden to make cash donations or to subscribe for the stocks or bonds of any company or corporation. The maximum tax rate was set at $1.60, a budget for expenditures was required, the number of policemen was reduced, and a board of fire and police commissioners was created.[69]

The epidemic of 1878 left the demoralized and impoverished community no other alternative than to accede to the wishes of the conservative group. If the city was to survive, for several years all funds must be applied to measures necessary to fit it for human habitation, a course which would be impossible if interest on previous bond issues were to be paid. Consequently, recommendations were sent to the legislature, and in January, 1879, the charter of the corporation of Memphis was formally repealed.[70] In its place a unique taxing district was created, to serve merely as the agent of the state of Tennessee, and the state itself collected taxes and drew up an annual budget specifying for what purposes money should be spent.[71] Under this act the local council consisted of two boards, one of three fire and police commissioners, two of whom were appointed by the governor and one elected by the voters, and another of five commissioners of public works, three of whom were elected and two appointed. Judicial and executive authority was vested in the chairman of the first board, who was appointed by the governor, and provision was made for a permanent health body. The commissioners were not allowed to issue bonds or to contract debts unless such expenditure was specified in the annual budget, and they were required by law to make quarterly reports to the county court and biennial reports to the governor.[72]

This taxing-district charter, later declared constitutional by both state and federal supreme courts, is the basis of the present city government.[73] The conservatives did a thorough job, and for a dozen years the control of municipal affairs was removed "from the popular elections of the times." The attempts of creditors to bleed the town were successfully thwarted until the community, for the first time in its history, instituted certain sanitary and administrative reforms vital to its welfare.

If Memphis history were to be divided into two periods, and there is ample cause for such a division, then 1880 and not 1860 would be the critical date. The social and economic consequences of the fever epidemics were so far-reaching as to warrant the conclusion that there have been two cities on the lower Chickasaw bluff: one which existed prior to the pestilence, and a second metropolis which sprang up like some fungus growth on the ruins of the first. Both possessed certain common characteristics thrust upon them by identity of location—cotton, the Negro, and the river—but the eighties witnessed such a metamorphosis in urban personnel as well as in physiogomy that the Radicals who had departed upon the collapse of the reconstruction régime would hardly have recognized the town in 1890.

While other southern cities were in many cases experiencing a 100 per cent increase during the fever decade, population in Memphis declined from forty to thirty-three thousand. This decrease was confined largely to white inhabitants, for few men of means cared to remain in a town whose future was so perilous. Even the most loyal citizens admitted that by the close of the decade one third of the white population had disappeared through emigration.[74] Many refugees remained permanently in St. Louis, and most of those who returned were apparently transient. The amazing extent to which newcomers took the places of former residents in the years following 1880 is revealed in a census taken in 1918 by the National Bureau of Education. Of the 11,781 white parents residing in Memphis forty years after the great epidemic, only 183, less than 2 per cent, had been born there.[75]

The populace changed not merely in personnel but also in quality. Among the victims of the three epidemics were thirty-four hundred Catholics, including twenty-four priests and numbers of nuns; the plague, therefore, almost annihilated the Irish.[76] Many industrious Germans joined their brethren in St. Louis, and one of their leading clubs in Memphis, the *"Maennerchor,"* became virtually defunct for lack of members.[77] Of the once numerous German organizations on the bluff, only Germania Hall remains in the twentieth century. It is significant, too, that after the plague the proportion of Negroes increased, until by the turn of the century they constituted half of the total population.[78]

In the history of the city the year 1880 marks a distinct cultural break. It is no wonder, in view of the above statistics, that the modern Memphis possesses no aristocracy, no tradition, and little interest in its past. The names of only a few families, like the Topps, McGevneys, McLemores, Trezevants, Overtons, and Winchesters, have appeared consistently in its annals. As the war had disrupted a *petite noblesse* in the process of aging, so the fever destroyed a second embryonic aristocracy before it was born. If the loss of so many Irish was considered by some good riddance of undesirables, the diminished scope of the Catholic Church was regrettable, for it had served as a check on rural provincialism. The migration of the Germans was equally serious, since it took from the community an influential group which possessed taste in esthetic matters as well as sober commercial judgment. Thus the cost of the fever is not to be reckoned by the number of victims, but by the intelligent and solid citizens it drove elsewhere.

The old Memphis, with all its filth, was unique; the new city, with all its improvements, was typical and in time became a southern Middletown. In losing its filth and some of its notorious viciousness it also lost a certain quality for which paved streets and a sewerage system were by no means complete compensation—that unnamable quality which conspicuously differentiates Boston, Charleston, and New Orleans from Pittsburgh and Kansas City. Once heterogeneous, it became homogeneous and progressive; formerly cosmopolitan, it became hopelessly provincial. Gone were the minority groups so necessary to a healthy intellectual atmosphere; and in their places, during the eighties and the nineties, came farmers from Mississippi and Tennessee, a simple and virtuous country folk, but stubborn and often unlettered.

In 1900, consequently, Memphis presented a strange paradox—a city modern in physical aspect but rural in background, rural in prejudice, and rural in habit. From every man was demanded allegiance to four conventional ideals: to an unadulterated Protestant fundamentalism; to a fan-

VICTIMS OF THE FEVER AWAITING BURIAL IN ELMWOOD CEMETERY, MEMPHIS, 1878

Harper's Weekly

VIEW OF THE NAVY YARD, MEMPHIS, FROM THE ARKANSAS SHORE

"One ship of war, the *Allegheny,* was built at a cost of half a million dollars, but her speed was such that she was considerably annoyed on her maiden voyage in the river by little boys in skiffs, who paddled around and around her."

Harper's Weekly

THE GREAT MISSISSIPPI RIVER BRIDGE AT MEMPHIS, COMPLETED IN 1892

The first bridge across the Mississippi south of St. Louis. "The third largest in the world, from end to end. Cost, $3,000,000."—From a photograph by Coovert, Greenville, Mississippi.

tastic entity called the Old South; to the principle of white supremacy; and, rather paradoxically, to the Constitution of the United States.

Because of the prosperity which began in the eighties and which made Memphis the third largest city in the South by the end of the century, the theory that the fever may have had dire economic consequences has been generally dismissed. On the contrary, this prosperity came in spite of the pestilence, and but for the pestilence it must have been greater and more permanent. A careful comparison of the growth of Memphis with that of other southern cities during the last century justifies the hypothesis that the plague kept it from becoming a much larger city than it is at present.

On the eve of the Civil War Memphis was the thirty-eighth city in population in the United States. Within ten years it had risen to thirty-second, but during the fever decade it fell to fifty-fifth, and since then it has never been higher than thirty-sixth.[79] Instead of a population of 80,000 in 1880, which from the rate of increase during the past thirty years it had reason to expect, it actually found itself with 33,000. In ten fateful years it had lost its superiority over both Nashville and Atlanta, and its position was eventually challenged by those parvenus among southern cities, Birmingham and the Texas towns. The story is clearly told in Table XIV, which is taken from the federal census:

TABLE XIV

COMPARATIVE EFFECT OF YELLOW FEVER UPON THE GROWTH OF MEMPHIS

	1860	1870	1880	1890	1900	1930
Memphis	22,623	40,226	33,592	64,495	102,320	253,153
Atlanta	9,554	21,789	37,409	65,533	89,872	270,366
Nashville	16,988	25,865	43,350	76,168	80,865	153,866
Birmingham	......	......	3,086	26,178	38,415	259,678
Dallas	......	......	10,358	38,067	42,638	260,475

The New South was an offspring of the union of bountiful natural resources and northern capital. Here the deterrent effect of the fever is particularly obvious. In 1870 no southern town was more likely to become the first depot of northern capitalists than Memphis. Better located than either New Orleans or Louisville, the only cities of the trans-montane South that outranked it, the town on the bluff possessed commercial and industrial possibilities with which the North, as a result of the profits made by Yankees in the contraband trade of the sixties, was well acquainted.[80]

Within a decade the notoriety which accompanied the three epidemics completely altered this situation. It became known throughout the nation that life was extremely hazardous in Memphis, that its taxes were prohibitive, that its municipal bonds had been virtually repudiated and its municipal charter surrendered. Even in the Gilded Age capital was not unnecessarily reckless, and for a quarter of a century the double stigma of debt and disease kept northern investments in the city at a low figure. It is rather ironical that the largest inland cotton market in the world has not possessed a single cotton mill since 1893, and that the largest hardwood lumber market in the United States manufactured little furniture before 1900.

The industrial handicap has been overcome in the twentieth century, but much of the purely commercial damage arising from the fever remains. The misfortune of Memphis proved the opportunity of St. Louis and Atlanta. The scourge of 1878 drove several firms to St. Louis,[81] and undoubtedly many houses seeking the trade of the lower valley located their headquarters at the mouth of the Missouri, when but for the fever they would have preferred the mouth of the Wolf. The horizontal trade of Memphis suffered as well as the vertical; for northern concerns, in search of a location for a single branch office to serve a South that was still moving west, chose an inland town in Georgia in preference to a railroad center on the middle Mississippi. Predictions as to what might have been are but the opinion of an individual, whether he be historian or steamboat captain, but it can be suggested with some justification that Atlanta owes its present position as the "New York of the South" more to the work of the *Aëdes aegypti* in Memphis a half a century ago than to any other cause.

CHAPTER IX

THE NEW CITY

Much of the beauty of modern cities indirectly had its origin in urban calamity. The burning of Washington by the British in 1814 resulted in a new and carefully planned capital that is America's outstanding contribution to urban architecture. If Louis Napoleon is to be execrated for bringing on Paris the terrible siege of 1871, it should also be remembered that he is responsible for its spacious boulevards. The Great Fire of 1666 in London gave the genius of Christopher Wren a unique architectural opportunity of which he took full advantage. So, too, the fever in Memphis produced a new city which, if it could not be called beautiful, was at least sanitary.

Refugees of the plague of 1879, meeting in exile in St. Louis, decided that return to their former residence was out of the question unless immediate steps were taken to insure an improvement in public health.[1] At once committees of citizens set about the task of rehabilitation and reform. The National Board of Health, upon invitation, made an extensive survey of sanitary conditions and submitted numerous recommendations to local officials. Early in 1880 work was started on the installation of the untried but economical Waring sewerage system, and by 1900 one hundred and fifty-two miles of sewers were in operation.[2] During this same period most of the old Nicholson blocks were replaced by ninety-five miles of hard pavement, though the new century found streets still in a poor condition.[3] The water supply continued to be a source of trouble until an ice company in 1887 accidently discovered artesian water at a depth of four hundred feet beneath the surface of the bluff. Forty wells and three pumps were soon constructed which guaranteed a daily output of thirty million gallons, three times the amount necessary to satisfy the current demand.[4]

In this era the board of health, for the first time a permanent organization with power to act, made consistent progress in sanitation. Hampered by lack of funds, nevertheless it inaugurated garbage service, house-to-house inspection by sanitary police, plumbing regulation, meat and milk inspection, birth registration, and compulsory vaccination against smallpox. It was undoubtedly directly inspired in these efforts by the work of Hermann Biggs, who was at this very time giving New York its first lesson in public health. Crematories for the disposal of garbage replaced the dumpboat on the Mississippi, and an isolation hospital, as well as a bacteriological laboratory, was established. Health officers did what they could to reduce the danger of infection from Gayoso Bayou, but that stream remained a menace until it was covered over at a later date and converted into a sewer main. As a result of this pioneer activity the death rate per thousand dropped from an average of thirty-five for the non-epidemic years, 1875, 1876, and 1877, to twenty-two in 1898.[5] When yellow fever threatened upon several occasions, quarantine was strictly enforced.[6] The pestilence never again proved serious, however, for the breeding places of the mosquito, quite accidentally to be sure, had in many cases been destroyed.

The problem of debt, no less than that of disease, was handled with facility. Official protestation to the contrary notwithstanding,[7] the suspicion cannot be avoided that citizens had hoped by the taxing-district act to repudiate the municipal debt. In its decision of 1879 the state Supreme Court concerned itself only with the constitutionality of the measure. In 1880 the Circuit Court of West Tennessee granted creditors judgments against the city which amounted to $350,000, but the United States Supreme Court upon appeal reversed the decision, holding that recourse could be had through the Tennessee legislature alone.[8] In 1881 the state Supreme Court ruled that suits against the old corporation could be revived against the taxing district.[9] Consequently, over a period of years four liquidating boards were created by the legislature and authorized by it to settle at different rates.[10] In spite of the recommendation of a citizens' mass meeting that twenty-five cents on the dollar be offered, the first board, appointed in 1882, was instructed to settle at thirty-three and one-third cents. This rate met little response from the creditors and it was raised the following year to fifty cents. After two years of negotiations on this basis, only one million dollars of indebtedness remained unfunded, and it was disposed of by a third board in 1885 at approximately seventy cents on the dollar.[11] Thus New York capitalists who had bought the bonds at an average price of twenty-five cents made a profit of 100 per cent on their southern venture, but the unfair stigma of repudiation clung to Memphis until its bonds were reinstated as safe for investment by eastern states in the 1920's.

In these years the modern city began to emerge. Telephones and electric lights came in the eighties.[12] Along the river front arose huge compresses, grain elevators, railroad depots, and warehouses. Two Chicago capitalists, C. B. Holmes and A. M. Billings, consolidated and electrified an antiquated street railway system that was using, in the early nineties, much of the equipment with which it had started a quarter of a century before.[13] After three and a half years of work and an expenditure of more than three million dollars, in 1892 the Kansas City and Memphis Railroad and Bridge Company completed the only bridge across the Mississippi south of St. Louis.[14] Standing like sentinels above the levee appeared the Federal Building, of white Tennessee marble done in bastard Doric, and the Cossitt Library, of red sandstone in the Romanesque.[15] Back from the river, but still in the business district, numerous other public buildings were erected: the First Methodist and the Second Presbyterian churches, both Gothic; the Randolph Building, the Tennessee Club, the Grand Opera House, the Collier *(Appeal)* Building, the Athletic Club (Lyceum Theater), the Cotton Exchange, and the new Gayoso Hotel. Yet the ostentatious prosperity of the day was nowhere so evident as in the horrible but costly residences of brick and wood built in such numbers along the fashionable avenues Shelby, Waldran, Poplar, Union, Rayburn, and Vance.[16]

The new form of municipal government proved fairly efficient, economical, and generally free from corruption, but merchants were soon clamoring for a restoration of the autonomy which they had formerly been so eager to surrender.[17] A legislature, rural in composition and therefore unsympathetic if not hostile to the welfare of a growing metropolis, could hardly be expected to handle the finances or direct the public policy of Memphis in a satisfactory manner. Through its control over the budget the state was able to divert the larger portion of income from taxation into its own coffers, and the municipality was constantly embarrassed by lack of money.[18] The final *coup de grâce* of the taxing district came, however, not because of the intrinsic unsuitability of the form of government, but as a result of one of those petty incidents which in a democracy often change the course of history. The announcement by local officials in 1893 of a policy of toleration but control of gambling excited such a furore among righteous and God-fearing citizens that the state was compelled to restore popular election of officers and local control of taxation and expenditures.[19]

The primary motive behind the public works of this period was commercial, but toward the end of the century a few men were beginning to think of city beautification.[20] The value of the land designated by the early proprietors for parks and the penury from which the city had long suffered had resulted in the sale of most of the promenade and several of the public squares to private interests. After a decade of constant agitation by Judge L. B. McFarland, a park commission was created in the summer of 1900, which purchased eight hundred acres of land and converted it into the present Riverside and Overton parks.[21]

The growth of the city in the years following the fever culminated in a "Greater Memphis" movement. A 200 per cent increase in population had been unaccompanied by any addition of territory, and the extensive suburbs were much in need of conveniences. Several years of campaigning by enthusiastic citizens induced state officials to give their approval to the project, and in January, 1899, the municipal area was enlarged by legislative act from four and a half to sixteen square miles.[22]

The year 1880 is the critical date in Memphis history, not merely because of the disaster of the fever, but also because the new decade marks the emergence of the New South. In the eighties the Land of Cotton began to enjoy the commercial and industrial prosperity which the fifties had promised, a prosperity that sprang from sources both indigenous and external. A section rich in mineral deposits, water power, timber, and fertility of the soil, but lacking the capital necessary for their development, aroused the cupidity of enterprising Yankees, and the South became popular as a field for investment. Free from narrow G. A. R. prejudice, Jay Gould and the "Iron Buccaneers" gladly exploited the conquered region as they had been exploiting the North.

In the post-bellum era cotton continued to move west. In 1900 Texas—now the land of promise that Mississippi had been prior to the war—was producing one fourth of the nation's cotton and the Indian Territory was in the midst of a boom.[23] It was the development of the valley, however, that possessed real importance for Memphis. It has been said that Mississippi has two cities, Memphis and New Orleans; Arkansas as well, it might be added, had only two cities before 1900, Memphis and St. Louis. During the eighties and nineties the construction of railroads and levees and the drainage of land converted the Yazoo Delta and the St. Francis Basin from dense swamps into vast plantations that produced more cotton per acre than any other land in the country. Between 1880 and 1900 the value of this botton land in the Memphis area increased from forty-eight to two hundred and fifty million dollars.[24]

The progress of the lower valley and the new Southwest during these years considerably nullified what must otherwise have been the baleful effect of the recent epidemics upon Memphis. Prosperity was almost thrust upon the city from without, and even the menace of the yellowjack did not deter ambitious southerners from enjoying the numerous advantages of its location. St. Louis and New Orleans, three hundred miles to the north and four hundred miles to the south respectively, were its only competitors for the trade of this area, but neither was as favorably located as the Tennessee town.[25] The bridge across the Mississippi and the excellent railroad system constructed by its new merchants pushed back the limits of its hinterland until they reached from eastern Texas to northern Alabama, from southeastern Missouri to Louisiana.[26] By rail and river huge quantities of cotton, lumber, produce, grain, iron, coal, and mules poured into Memphis; out of it came groceries, dry goods, provisions, agricultural implements, cotton gins, and hundreds of other articles needed by the farmers who looked to it both as a market and as a purchasing center.

The growth and diversity of these economic interests require analysis, for the developments of this period de-

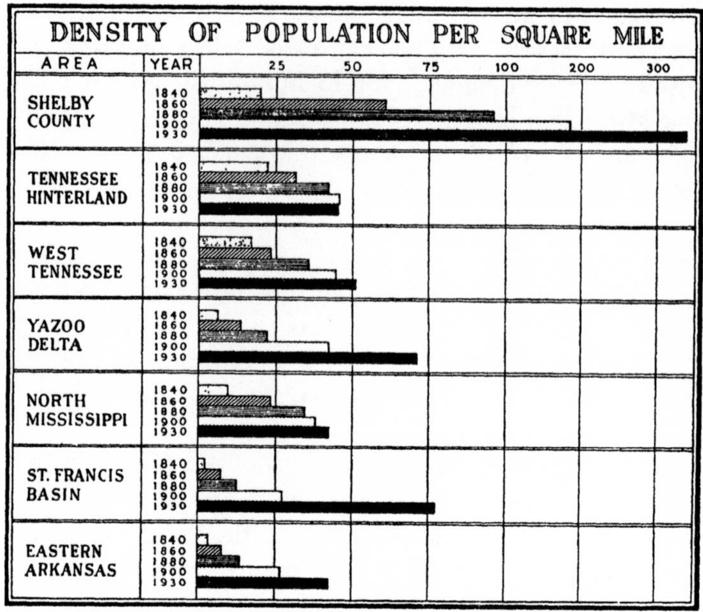

INCREASE OF POPULATION IN THE MEMPHIS HINTERLAND

To show this increase, the area has been divided into seven sections: (1) Shelby County including Memphis; (2) the immediate Tennessee hinterland, Tipton, Fayette, Lauderdale, Haywood, and Hardeman counties; (3) the rest of West Tennessee; (4) the Yazoo Delta; (5) North Mississippi; (6) the St. Francis Basin in Arkansas; (7) the rest of Eastern Arkansas.

In the chart above the population per square mile is shown for the years 1840, 1860, 1880, 1900, and 1930, in each of the seven sections. For instance, in 1840 Shelby County had fewer than 25 (18.4) persons per square mile; in 1860, 60; in 1880, 97.9; in 1900, 191.7; in 1930, 382.6. For statistical table, see note 26a, page 265.

termined the character of the twentieth-century metropolis. Between 1880 and 1900 the population of the city increased from thirty-three to one hundred and two thousand, and the value of annual trade, estimated at $72,000,000 in 1881,

THE PRESENT MEMPHIS HINTERLAND

The extent of this hinterland has been determined by two factors: transportation and the rivalry of other cities. Before the railroads of the fifties, it was confined to the banks of rivers. With the rail development of the eighties it reached its farthest limit, Texas, Alabama, Louisiana, and Missouri. Since the late nineties it has gradually shrunk to its present size and has been fairly permanent for fifteen years. For the density of its population see opposite page.

reached $200,000,000 early in the nineties.[27] According to the Memphis Clearing-House Reports, the most authentic index to business conditions, annual clearings and balances amounted to $58,000,000 in 1880, $160,000,000 in 1891, and $138,000,000 in 1898.[28] As these figures suggest, the low price of cotton in the last decade of the century and the poor financial conditions of Cleveland's second administration somewhat retarded progress, though only one bank failed during the crisis in 1893.[29] The following summary, which appeared at the end of the century, hardly indicates the existence of a depression:

FACTS ABOUT MEMPHIS[30]

Largest Inland Cotton Market in the World
Largest Hardwood Lumber Market in the World
Second Largest Lumber Market in the World
Largest Producer of Oil from Cottonseed in the World
Largest Snuff Market in the United States
Ninth Wholesale Grocery Market in the United States (Fifth in 1891)
Largest Boot and Shoe Market in the South
Estimated Value of Annual Trade $275,000,000

Railroads have been far more vital to western and central regions of the United States than to the extreme southern and eastern.[31] Memphis, because of its connection with the upper valley and the trans-Mississippi territory, has been more concerned with railroad construction on a large scale and in every direction than any other southern town. While St. Louis was building a great southwestern system during the score of years following secession, its southern rival had been prevented by war and pestilence from completing a single road except the one to Little Rock. In fact, Jackson had practically replaced it as the junction for railroads passing through West Tennessee.

With 1880, however, a new era began, for within the next twelve years seven new lines entered the city. In 1881 the Chesapeake, Ohio, and Southwestern took over and immediately completed the long-unfinished road to Paducah, thus providing another route to the East.[32] Three years later the Louisville, New Orleans, and Texas, a subsidiary of the Huntington system, was built along the river through the Yazoo Delta to Vicksburg, Baton Rouge, and New Orleans. Both of these lines, as well as the older Mississippi and Tennessee to Grenada, were purchased by Harriman's Illinois Central in the next decade and consolidated into a single system. The Tennessee Midland, begun in 1887 with southeastern Virginia as its destination, was soon absorbed by the Nashville, Chattanooga, and St. Louis. The Kansas City, Fort Scott, and Memphis, considered by many the most important of all local rail connections, reached its southern terminal in 1883.[33] Four years later this road bought the last of the several Birmingham projects and extended its tracks to that city.[34] The completion in 1888 of a spur of Jay Gould's Missouri Pacific from Bald Knob, Arkansas, to Memphis (known locally as the Iron Mountain route) afforded a much needed access to Louisiana and Texas as well as to points in Arkansas previously tributary to St. Louis.[35] In 1891 the Cotton Belt (St. Louis-Southwestern) leased the privilege of running its trains over the Bald Knob spur, and the bluff city, by virtue of these two roads to the Southwest, became a formidable competitor for the trade of that region.

The control of southwestern railroads enabled St. Louis to discriminate against Memphis. To some extent this discrimination was offset by the efforts of Chicago and Kansas City to divert traffic from the Missouri metropolis, but it was the steamboat, more than any other factor, that brought lower freight rates.[36] Prior to 1880 limited rail facilities had necessitated a continued dependence upon the river, but as a result of the construction of the eighties traffic on the Mississippi somewhat declined.[37] Yet bulky products like coal, cotton, and lumber were shipped by water in preference to rail, and the usefulness of the river had by no means passed.[38] There were still large tracts along the lower Mississippi whose only means of contact with the outside world was the steamboat. The Association for the Improvement of Western Waterways held conventions at Memphis in 1887 and 1899, and it continually petitioned Congress for federal aid in constructing a deep waterway from the Great Lakes to the Gulf and in building levees to protect the riparian land.[39]

The emancipation of slaves and the breakup of the large plantations after the war profoundly changed the system of cotton growing. Under the new dispensation the factor replaced the planter in control of production, for with most of its real property destroyed by war the South was forced to raise its crop on credit. In return for a mortgage on the planter's land or crop the factor advanced him, at a rate rarely less than 10 per cent and often more, the credit necessary to purchase seed, supplies, and labor. Though interest was charged on the full amount from the date of contract until the cotton was sold, little money was used in the transaction, for the factor merely advanced goods on account as they were needed. All cotton produced was turned over to him, and he arranged for its sale in consideration of a brokerage fee of 2½ per cent. Should a balance remain after interest charges and other fees were subtracted, it was returned to the planter, who in turn was forced to adopt this same method in dealing with his tenants. Brokerage was lucrative, for the factor was at the same time banker, broker, and usually wholesale grocer, who supplied the planter with the Bourbon he served his friends, the salt meat he fed his Negroes, the shoes his children wore, the petticoat that delighted his wife, and the gin which cleaned his cotton.[40]

Through the power and prestige that came from handling an annual crop of from four to seven hundred thousand bales, cotton factors ruled Memphis during the eighties and the nineties. As presidents and directors of the leading banks they had complete control of local finances.[41] Almost without exception the cotton firms conducted a wholesale grocery trade—a trade so large that in 1891 forty-one of these houses were doing an annual business in groceries alone of thirty-five million dollars.[42]

Factors, though most important, were but one of the many groups in the city whose livelihood came from cotton. Memphis was full of spinners' buyers, brokers, buyers for export, cotton classers, weighers, compress hands, and clerks. Large New York, Liverpool, and Continental firms kept representatives there to buy the strong short-staple "benders" produced only in the Mississippi bottoms, or the long-staple variety grown in Fayette County to the east.[43] Ample storage, compress, transport, and financial facilities, together with an active and experienced cotton exchange of one hundred and seventy-five members, gave the city's cotton such an excellent reputation that occasionally it sold for a higher price than that of New Orleans.[44] It was a picturesque sight during the rush season from October to January, when the cotton was brought to market, to see the white staple piled high along both sides of the streets for several miles, and there was a certain rhythm in the rumble of the heavily laden drays and the shouting of the Negroes at their mules. The scope of the Memphis cotton interests in this period is shown in Table XV.

If cotton was the woof of the economic cloth, it was by no means the whole cloth. Trade in wholesale groceries was a close second to it in value; shipments of lumber soon exceeded it in volume; and manufactures, still in their early

Table XV

A. Post-Bellum Cotton Statistics for Memphis*

Year	Bales Received at Memphis	Value	Bales Produced in U. S.
1860-61	360,653	$18,500,000	3,656,080
1861-65	....	....	....
1865-66	112,296	23,000,000	2,193,987
1866-67	218,226	29,000,000	2,019,774
1867-68	253,207	25,000,000	2,598,993
1868-69	247,698	31,000,000	2,439,039
1869-70	296,737	29,588,500	3,154,946
1870-71	511,432	39,552,356	4,352,317
1871-72	380,924	36,550,617	2,974,351
1872-73	415,255	37,500,000	3,930,508
1873-74	429,327	32,864,981	4,170,388
1874-75	322,004	22,540,080	3,827,845
1875-76	487,376	27,070,615	4,632,313
1876-77	384,358	20,040,426	4,474,069
1877-78	412,393	20,887,705	4,773,865
1878-79	386,129	17,456,892	5,074,155
1879-80	409,809	23,752,529	5,761,252
1880-81	470,267	23,090,109	6,605,750
1881-82	339,240	18,825,388	5,456,048
1882-83	510,789	25,069,524	6,949,756
1883-84	450,077	22,917,920	5,713,200
1884-85	430,127	21,441,831	5,706,165
1885-86	545,566	23,623,007	6,575,691
1886-87	663,277	30,099,510	6,505,087
1887-88	652,407	29,495,320	7,046,833
1888-89	704,142	33,981,892	6,938,290
1889-90	578,036	29,271,743	7,311,322
1890-91	723,120	31,144,778	8,652,597
1891-92	772,606	28,632,778	9,035,379
1892-93	427,370	18,492,299	6,700,365
1893-94	488,191	18,302,280	7,549,817
1894-95	587,654	16,125,225	9,901,251
1895-96	429,712	17,442,010	7,157,346
1896-97	561,747	20,500,382	8,757,964
1897-98	690,238	19,500,000	11,199,994
1898-99	785,850	28,982,195	11,274,840
1899-00	596,945	23,215,191	9,436,416

B. Transportation of Memphis Cotton, 1896-1897

	Bales Received	Bales Shipped	
Railroads	357,692	536,471	
Steamboats	131,553	39,188	(all to north)
Wagons	72,502	....	
Total	561,747	575,929	

*This information is taken from the *Memphis Cotton Exchange Directory, 1896-97*, and the *Commercial Appeal*, Oct. 31, 1900.

stages in the nineties, were eventually to become far more important. As the fifth wholesale grocery market of the United States in 1891, Memphis did a larger business in that line than St. Louis, a city several times its size.[45] Merchants on the bluff supplied planters annually with sixteen million dollars' worth of provisions, largely western in origin, such as hay, corn, bacon, pork, flour, and oats; and the yearly trade in dry goods, hardware, drugs, boots and shoes, coal, mules, and truck amounted to another sixteen million.[46] The Kansas City road converted the city into a grain market of no little importance and a leading distributing point for meat and livestock as well.[47] Out of a total yearly commerce estimated at two hundred million dollars, the jobbing trade, wholesale and retail, amounted to one hundred and ten million.

Cypress, cottonwood, and poplar had for many years been floated down to Memphis on the spring flood to the small mills in the northern outskirts along Wolf River. The hardwood interests of the country, finding their eastern and upper western forests exhausted in the eighties, began to look southward at the huge stands of virgin timber in the lower Mississippi Valley, which were as yet inaccessible because of insufficient transportation.[48] Stackhouse Brothers of St. Louis, the Darnells of Indianapolis, and Moore and McFerrin of Hoopeston, Illinois, were the first to realize the possibilities of Memphis in the timber field; after 1890 so many lumbermen followed their example that 425,000 tons of lumber were being shipped from that point annually at the end of the century in contrast to only 107,000 tons of cotton.[49] Capital invested in mills increased from $300,000 in 1883 to $3,400,000 in 1898, and the annual amount of lumber handled by Memphis dealers increased from 100,000,000 board feet in 1887 to 269,870,000 in 1898.[50]

The output of most mills within a two-hundred-mile radius, and of many mills as far away as East Tennessee and Texas, was sent to Memphis for distribution. Since lumbermen of the bluff city owned mills throughout the tri-state area, however, little more than half of the product was cut locally.[51] Into this market came huge quantities of white oak, walnut, gum, hickory, ash, cypress, poplar, cottonwood, and yellow pine, to be shipped to every part of the globe, and European firms as well as eastern factories constantly kept buyers in Memphis to watch the prices;[52] not carloads but whole trainloads of lumber were sold to single firms.

The distinction between sawmills and factories using lumber as their raw product must be kept clearly in mind. While there were in Memphis numerous small manufacturers of cooperage, doors, blinds, wagons, boxes, and other rough wooden articles, they consumed only 13 per cent of the timber handled by the dealers of the city.[53] Thus it is evident that the fear of the fever and the local reputation for high taxes and municipal debt kept large manufacturers of lumber products away until the twentieth century. Furthermore, the few bold northerners who developed the lumber business were forced to get their capital from the outside, since the cotton men in control of local finances had difficulty in supplying their own needs. Yet by the turn of the century the omnipotence of King Cotton was severely challenged by a rival sovereign.[54]

Industry in Memphis was retarded by the same conditions responsible for the delayed development of lumber, but in spite of that fact, between 1880 and 1900, the value of manufactured products increased from four and a half to eighteen million dollars. Though cottonseed and lumber easily led the list, diversity of output rather than concentration on a single product was the outstanding industrial characteristic. Trusts controlled the cottonseed-oil mills, but plants on the whole were owned by individuals or corporations that were little more than partnerships, and factories therefore operated on a small scale.[55] The most comprehensive description of industrial Memphis is the compilation from the federal census on manufactures shown in Table XVI.

TABLE XVI

A. MANUFACTURING IN MEMPHIS, 1880-1900[56]

Year	No. Est.	Capital	Wages	Value Material	Value Products
1880.....	138	$ 2,313,975	$ 845,672	$2,419,341	$ 4,413,422
1890.....	345	9,357,821	3,158,675	7,090,190	13,244,538
1900.....	659	11,189,249	3,641,435	9,656,969	17,923,059

B. VALUE OF PRINCIPAL PRODUCTS

	1880	1890	1900
Cottonseed oil and cake	$835,000	$1,924,004	$2,231,313
Carriages and wagons	176,500	386,203	333,238
Men's clothing	175,500	249,195	782,498
Foundry and machine-shop products	252,400	1,251,905	1,078,713
Lumber—sawed	300,660	815,915	3,051,181
Printing and publishing	165,714	738,870	775,697
Tinware, copperware, and sheetiron ware	203,000	103,569	271,665
Cars and general shop construction	....	312,377	757,046
Bread and bakery products	68,000	378,313	668,653
Flour and grist mills	....	975,250	....
Saddlery and harness	75,020	391,100	271,665
Lumber—planing mill products	....	757,663	245,000
Carpentering	64,500	386,203	697,500
Plumbing and gas fittings	73,000	399,850	384,910
Furniture	....	....	272,682

C. URBAN MANUFACTURING IN THE SOUTH, 1880, 1900, 1930

1880	
1. Louisville	$ 35,423,203
2. Richmond	20,790,106
3. New Orleans	18,808,096
4. Nashville	8,597,278
5. MEMPHIS (7)	4,413,422
1900	
1. Louisville	$ 78,746,390
2. New Orleans	63,514,505
3. Richmond	29,900,616
4. Nashville	18,469,823
5. MEMPHIS	17,923,059
1930	
1. Winston-Salem	$301,524,926
2. Louisville	270,925,614
3. Richmond	234,619,094
4. MEMPHIS	169,702,182
5. New Orleans	148,388,315

A few observations are necessary to clarify the information in this table. Since Kentucky coal, shipped to Memphis by river, sold for two dollars per ton, citizens held great hopes for the future of iron and steel works,[57] but by 1900 the superiority of Birmingham in this field was obvious. After struggling along for a dozen years, the Bluff City Cotton Mills failed in 1893 because of unskilled management and the use of second-hand machinery. In view of the success of similar steam mills in New Orleans,[58] it is an unexplained mystery that forty years have passed without any local attempt to resume such an enterprise. The Kansas City grain trade brought several flour and grist mills, but after a few years they apparently failed or moved elsewhere.[59] Regardless of all vicissitudes, however, at the end of the century Memphis ranked fifth among southern cities in the value of its industrial products, as shown in Table XVI, C.[60]

By 1880 the inhabitants of ante-bellum Memphis, whom the opportunities of the West had lured to the bluff from older sections of Tennessee, from the states along the Atlantic coast, and from Europe, had been scattered by war and pestilence. The 68,000 newcomers who arrived during the two decades following the fever were, in contrast to their predecessors, drawn largely from adjacent regions in the tri-states, predominantly from the east bank of the river. The influx from northern states was to increase sharply after 1900, but in the nineties the nation still vividly remembered the fever. An objective critic of the present Memphis inevitably comes to the conclusion that for half a century every town in North Mississippi and West Tennessee has been sending a steady stream of its sons and daughters to the neighboring city. Table XVII presents statistics for the year 1918 which relate to this aspect of the city's population.

TABLE XVII

PLACE OF BIRTH OF WHITE PARENTS IN MEMPHIS, 1918[61]

Place of Birth	Per Cent	Place of Birth	Per Cent
Tri-States		Other Southern States	16
Tennessee	34	North and West	15
Mississippi	18	Foreign countries	11
Arkansas	4	Memphis	2

In these years many Memphians amassed great wealth, as wealth was measured in the South; yet they did not lose the self-reliance and the genuineness which arise from intimate contact with the soil. They were a solid and self-made generation whose roots had wrested nourishment from the hard earth of adversity. Some were older men who, returning from the battlefield in 1865 to find their estates destroyed and lacking the means of restoring them, had moved to town, where by years of incessant endeavor they had built up a second fortune; others of this post-fever generation, like Horatio Alger's heroes, had left the farm as lads and found riches in the city. Almost without exception the large wholesale houses arose within a single decade, and their builders were bound to possess a large share of the self-confidence and the optimism generally prevalent among Americans of that period.

"America is the center of the universe, anyway," wrote one Memphis enthusiast in 1899. "Diagonals drawn from the four corners of creation intersect in the United States, and there is no doubt, no doubt whatever, in the mind of a western man that the point of crossing lies somewhere in the Mississippi Valley—that region of splendid prospects . . . whose ultimate destiny is being worked out by the descendants of the self-same race that . . . carved out an empire of the free from the untamed wilderness; of the men who first discovered that a breath of America's free air was worth more to a man than a sip of Old England's Ale."[62]

These Bourbon Democrats, as they and their sons came

to be called, retained many bucolic traits. They clung to the emotional religion of the backwoods that smelt of brimstone; they extended a lavish hospitality to stranger and friend alike; and they believed in the goodness and honesty of their fellows. In daily transactions that frequently amounted to half a million dollars it was rare that anyone requested a written contract.[63] Yet the younger members of this plutocracy, who lacked the pre-war background and grace of their fathers, displayed numerous characteristics of the *nouveau riche*. They had made money, and they proceeded to spend it in gaudy fashion.

"Those princely mansions!" exulted a contemporary in describing the monstrosities which the élite had recently erected as residences. "The late architectural ideas, Gothic, Byzantine, Norman, English Castellated, French Renaissance. . . . Here certainly, you will say when you behold them, here there is wealth and taste exemplified . . . in such homes as these of Memphis business men—the banker Porter's in the order of the French Renaissance, which cost him $65,000; the Warriner residence, patterned after the style of the English Renaissance, the outlay for which was $50,000; the Mallory residence, Norman, $45,000; the residence of the great factor, Napoleon Hill, French Renaissance, $45,000 also; the castellated stone domicile of Gilbert D. Raine, $40,000; and each a model of its kind."[64]

There were other ways, of course, of spending money ostentatiously. One could belong to the New Jockey Club and attend the races at Montgomery Park which attracted turfmen from the entire nation, or he could breed fast horses and fine cattle at near-by country estates.[65] He could hunt and fish with friends from New York, Liverpool, and Chicago at any of the half a dozen sporting lodges located within a radius of a hundred miles.[66] Those who preferred ostentation without exercise could join the Tennessee Club and attend the theater, which offered opera, concerts, and drama at prices that in some instances exceeded fifty dollars a seat. Furthermore, there were vicarious means of advertising opulence. One's children attended the private educational institutions, then more numerous than the inferior public schools,[67] while one's wife joined the Nineteenth Century Club where she became a "New Woman" by studying village life in India and Egyptology.[68]

Members of a leisure and moneyed class have often become superficial patrons of the arts, but such patronage does not necessarily indicate genuine esthetic interest, and such conspicuous artistic activity of a passive nature is always subject to question. Memphis had its Mozart, Mendelssohn, Apollo, and Beethoven societies, which frequently sponsored "music festivals" by professional talent and upon several occasions produced oratorios like the "Messiah" or brought the St. Louis Symphony Orchestra down for a concert.[69] Miss Mary Solari, a Memphian who had studied in Florence, opened a school of fine arts in 1894, and the following year a music conservatory was founded. Other individuals, mostly women, dabbled in literature and even published volumes of verse. Joseph Jefferson, DeWolf Hopper, Sarah Bernhardt, Frederick Ward, Richard Mansfield, Otis Skinner, and other idols of the contemporary stage played frequently before packed houses.

Yet this supposedly cultured society produced no artists of national reputation and few amateurs of any promise. To the musical world it gave Marie Greenwood, one of the lesser southern prima donnas.[70] Its best painter, Carl Gutherz, of Swiss parentage, came to Memphis as a boy from Ohio, and left it a few years later to study at the École des Beaux-Arts in Paris. Gutherz spent most of his later life abroad or in the East, and his reputation rests upon certain murals in the Congressional Library. Local literati, though legion, were rather poor. Perhaps the best of them were Mrs. Virginia Frazer Boyle, who became poetess laureate of the United Confederate Veterans, and Walter Malone, whose chef-d'œuvre is his poem, "Opportunity," from which Edgar Guest may have received his initial inspiration. It is fair to say that this society of the nineties patronized art exuberantly, not for art's own sake, but for the legitimate purpose of entertainment and in many cases for ostentation. The best people without exception religiously attended the concert and the drama; yet it cannot be gainsaid that in creative art Memphis throughout the nineteenth century stood far below other southern cities, such as Nashville and New Orleans.

Of the white clerks and laborers employed by factors, lumbermen, and manufacturers less is known, but undoubtedly their lack of means did not prevent them from enjoying life. If their income did not permit membership in exclusive hunting lodges, it was an easy matter to find all the game they wanted within a few miles of the city. Their social needs, according to their different temperaments, were satisfied by the church, the secret society, the saloon, and the gambling hall. Their children, if they obtained an education, attended public school,[71] and their wives could belong to less fashionable clubs, secular as well as ecclesiastical, without undue expense. Labor unions became common in the eighties, but apparently they wielded little influence.[72] Nor does any serious class consciousness seem to have existed, probably because the wage-earners, imbued with the current optimism, saw no reason why they could not become rich like their employers.

It is regrettable that so little is known of the fifty thousand blacks who formed the inarticulate third estate of this society. They kept no diaries, and their actions, other than those of a criminal nature, received scant notice in the newspapers except on election day. No files have been preserved of the first Negro paper, the Memphis *Free Speech,* started by a woman in 1890, for its tone grew so militant that a mob burned its press.[73] One small riot in 1892 seems to have been the only violent outburst of race prejudice after the reconstruction era, and the lynchings common in the surrounding rural districts occurred in Memphis at surprisingly infrequent intervals. Until 1905 a dozen blacks held lesser positions in the city hall, and several of them served as policemen.[74] Southerners have always been somewhat sentimental about their "darkies," as the epithets "uncle" and "auntie" usually applied to the Negro suggest; and before the town grew too large many a black man was the protégé of "Marse" Somebody-or-other, who usually assisted him when he fell sick, lost his job, stumbled into paternity, or ran afoul of the law.

The Negroes, as long as they observed a certain unwritten code regarding their relations with the whites, were allowed to live their own lives without interference. The majority of those who earned an honest living were employed as draymen, servants, and helpers in the building trades then so prosperous, and every concern which could use rough manual labor had a crew of "buck niggers" on its premises. Though the blacks were largely responsible for the unusual number of homicides and burglaries committed in the city, they were, nevertheless, essentially religious; as early as 1875 there were more Negro Protestant churches in Memphis than white.[75] To satisfy further their gregarious instincts, they formed scores of secret societies with such fanciful names as the "Daughters of the Maccabees," the "Ancient Knights of the Crusades of America," the "Seven Star Grand Assemblage of the U. S. A.," and the "Wisdom of Wisemen of America."[76]

During these years Beale Street, the Main Street of Negro America, "owned by the Jews, policed by the whites, and enjoyed by the Negroes,"[77] began to possess much of the color which was later to be publicized throughout the world. Already its pool rooms, barber shops, saloons, the aters, pawnshops, and dance halls teemed with prostitutes, murderers, dope peddlers, "voodoo doctors," crap-shooters, and card sharps. Music, good or bad, found there an appreciative audience, and West Dukes, Jim Turner, and Charlie Bynum with their brass bands and orchestras were already creating the atmosphere which would give the twentieth century the "blues" of W. C. Handy. Without question, its leading figure in the nineties was Robert R. Church, Sr., who had made a million dollars in real estate since the Civil War. Church was liked and respected by the whites, and his civic pride was demonstrated in his purchase of the first municipal bonds ($1,000) issued by the new city to discharge its previous indebtedness.[78] Only a small minority of urban Negroes actually lived on Beale, but it was the street where all blacks, from town or country, went to strut when the gods were good and to forget when they were otherwise.[79]

The Negro was not the only holdover from pre-fever days. Military companies were still popular, though fewer and more exclusive.[80] In every block of the business district there were at least one and often several saloons; in spite of the pleas of Susan B. Anthony, Carrie Chapman Catt, and Sam Jones, the evangelist, and in spite of the crusade waged by the many local temperance associations, Memphis continued to have whisky until a state-wide prohibition statute was enacted in 1909.[81] Occasional attempts were made by Law and Order leagues to suppress vice, but gamblers and prostitutes still served a large clientele—no longer, however, as openly and honestly as in earlier days. This was a sporting town, and farmers who came to the big city only twice a year considered their visit an event which called for thorough celebration. Even among good church members there remained a vestige of that antebellum catholicity of taste which considered a discreet sowing of wild oats by youth not only natural but desirable.

In Memphis, as elsewhere in the South after reconstruction, the Democratic party became sacred. Ex-Governor Isham G. Harris and his successor, T. B. Turley, representatives of the local Bourbons, were elected to the United States Senate from Tennessee. Because of the support of the Negroes, during the eighties the Republicans polled a considerable minority in federal elections.[82] The blacks were to a large extent disfranchised by a series of state election laws in 1889,[83] but those who were still qualified to cast a ballot soon realized that it was a privilege which white men regarded as peculiar to their race, and the Negroes gradually ceased to exercise their franchise. The several hundred Republicans in the city were mostly newcomers from the North, but among them were a few southerners like W. R. Moore, the leading wholesale dry-goods merchant, who had given allegiance to the party of Lincoln since the war.[84] These dissenters, for so they were considered, participated as a group only in federal elections, and in state and municipal politics they acted as individuals. With the small local coterie who possessed great influence in the Republican primaries they did not associate.[85]

Nowhere does the contrast of the commercial town to the surrounding agrarian area appear so clearly as in the election of 1896. Populism found the conservative merchants of Memphis cold. Violating their faith in the Democratic party when they felt the financial security of the nation at stake, they gave McKinley a majority of two hundred, the only instance between 1870 and 1928 in which the city went Republican.[86] Once the threat of bimetalism was dispersed, however, they ceased their apostacy and lent Bryan their overwhelming support in 1900.[87]

By 1900 the heroic age of Memphis was over and the city had at last acquired security and respectability. Prior to 1890 every decade brought new scenes and cataclysmic changes; after that date life began to lose its dynamic and dangerous quality, and citizens could look to the future with a greater degree of certainty. This new security brought economic greatness and a safer and saner way of living, but it destroyed much of the protean and virile personality the town had always possessed. In the nineties men had not dueled for a generation;[88] soon the magnificent steamboats on the Mississippi would be no more; and the time was not far off when it would be illegal to possess whisky.

Indeed, the bluff had witnessed a grand panorama in its time: the French, the Spaniards, the Chickasaws, the Indian factors, the land speculators, the flatboatmen, the slave-traders, the Whig merchants, the Federal soldiers, the carpetbaggers, the doctors and priests who had died fighting the yellowjack—but like the buffalo and the wild pigeon they were forgotten. In their places were a new people who knew not their fathers; who built bridges, paved streets, laid sewers, erected tall buildings, and made more money than Isaac Rawlings had ever dreamed of.

In 1890 America's last frontier was passing; and in Memphis the spirit of the frontier, which had lingered on long after the Indian trading post had become a city, was almost dead.

NOTES

NOTES

Chapter I

1. Thomas Jefferson, *Writings*, ed. Paul Leicester Ford (10 vols. New York, 1892-99), VIII, 144-45.

2. The classic illustration of this changing of the Mississippi is the case of Delta, Mississippi. Once three miles below Vicksburg, this village suddenly found itself two miles above, when the river took a cutoff in the 1870's.—Mark Twain, *Life on the Mississippi*, p. 5.

3. Because of this formation the itinerary of early settlers in the Southwest, dependent almost entirely upon navigable streams for transportation, was quite circuitous. Pioneers from North Carolina and Virginia usually reached the lower Mississippi via the Tennessee and the Ohio.

4. "Relation of the Gentleman of Elvas," Samuel C. Williams, ed., *Early Travels in the Tennessee Country*, p. 6 n. Hereafter cited as *Early Travels*.

5. As to De Soto's exact point of crossing there has in recent years been a heated controversy between local historians of Tennessee and Mississippi, chiefly between J. P. Young of Memphis and Dunbar Rowland of the Mississippi State Archives.—See Dunbar Rowland, ed., *Symposium on the Place of Discovery of the Mississippi River*. I consider the problem insoluble for the following reasons: (1) The only source material, consisting of brief accounts of De Soto's expedition by three of its members, the Gentleman of Elvas, Luis Hernandez de Biedma, and Rodrigo Ranjel, and a fourth account written fifty years later by Garcilasso de la Vega (the Inca), is unreliable because these memoirs are contradictory and are lacking in detail. Sections of these accounts pertaining to the crossing of the river are reprinted in Williams, *Early Travels*, pp. 5-14. (2) The maps used by the contestants to support their respective theses were roughly drawn two centuries after De Soto's march by men who probably knew less about his actual route than do present historians. (3) The topographical approach, the only sure one, is impossible because of the numerous changes of the river during four centuries, and particularly because of the New Madrid earthquakes of 1811 and 1812, which affected the whole middle valley.

The statement that De Soto discovered the Mississippi is, in its strict interpretation, an error which is often repeated. A stream which is unquestionably that river appeared on a map of North America in an edition of Ptolemy's *Guide to Geography* printed in Venice in 1511.—J. G. Shea, *Discovery and Exploration of the Mississippi River*, p. 2. De Soto himself knew of its existence, for soon after leaving Florida in 1539 he sent a small party back to Havana with instructions to meet him at its mouth in six months.—B. F. French, *Historical Collections of Louisiana* (5 vols. New York, 1846-53), II, 99.

6. Reuben Gold Thwaites, *France in America, 1497-1763* (Vol. VII of "The American Nation: A History" Series. 31 vols. ed. A. B. Hart. New York, 1904—), p. 56.

7. Williams, *Early Travels*, p. 44 n.

8. *Ibid.*, p. 45 n.

9. Marquette's Journal, Williams, *Early Travels*, pp. 44-45.

10. J. P. Young, "Fort Prudhomme," *Tennessee Historical Magazine*, II, 244 n.

11. "Relation of Henri de Tonty," Williams, *Early Travels*, pp. 50-53.

12. Journals of Father Gravier (1700) and Diron d'Artaguette (1723), Williams, *Early Travels*, pp. 68, 74, 80.

13. Journal of John Jennings (1768), Williams, *Early Travels*, p. 220.

14. Verner W. Crane, *The Southern Frontier, 1670-1732* (Durham, N. C., 1928), pp. 45-46.

15. B. F. French, *Historical Collections of Louisiana and Florida* (New York, 1869, 1875), p. 63.

16. Justin Winsor, *The Mississippi Basin: The Struggle in America between England and France, 1697-1763*, p. 54.

17. Thwaites, *op. cit.*, p. 74, map.

18. Adair traded with the Indians from 1735, the date of his arrival in Charleston, until 1769. For twelve years, 1744-1749, 1761-1768, he lived among the Chickasaws, by whom he was highly regarded, and there he wrote much of his *History of the American Indians* (London, 1775), the best source on the Chickasaws and the other southern tribes. From his book it is apparent that he was anxious to establish an Anglo-Chickasaw alliance, and his presence among the Chickasaws created a real English sphere of influence. Hereafter cited as *American Indians*.

19. The present Pontotoc and Union counties in Mississippi.

20. About 1760 Adair estimated their number as 450 warriors, which would imply a total of perhaps 2,000 persons (*American Indians*, p. 353), but he specifically states that they were formerly more numerous. The commissioners of the United States who arranged the Treaty of Hopewell in 1786 gave the following estimate of the relative fighting strength of the southern tribes: Choctaws, 6,000; Creeks, 5,400; Cherokees, 2,000; Chickasaws, 800.—J. H. Malone, *The Chickasaw Nation*, p. 242.

21. C. Thomas, *The Indian in Historic Times* (Philadelphia, 1903), p. 319.

22. J. B. Bossu, *Travels through that part of America formerly called Louisiana* (tr. J. R. Forster, 2 vols. London, 1771), I, 309; Adair, *American Indians*, p. 355; S. C. Williams, *Beginnings of West Tennessee*, 1541-1841, pp. 20, 21. Hereafter cited as *West Tennessee*.

23. P. Hamilton, *Colonization of the South* (Philadelphia, 1904), p. 327.

24. Williams, *West Tennessee*, p. 12. Prudhomme was either the first or the second Chickasaw bluff, not the lower.

25. F. X. Martin, *The History of Louisiana from the Earliest Period* (2 vols. New Orleans, 1827), I, 301.

26. *Ibid.*, p. 77.

27. So named because it was completed on Assumption Day, August 15.—"Journal of the Chickasaw War, 1739-40," J. F. H. Claiborne, *History of Mississippi*, pp. 72 ff. This twenty-page diary, kept by a soldier under Chevalier de Nouaille, is a detailed account of the whole campaign.

28. *Ibid.*, p. 77.

29. *Colonial Records of the State of Georgia* (ed. A. D. Candler. 22 vols. Atlanta, 1904-1913), VI, 448-50.

30. South Carolina State Archives (Office of the Historical Commission of South Carolina, Columbia, S. C.), 5 Indian Book, p. 123.

31. Malone, *op. cit.*, p. 270.

32. Williams, *West Tennessee*, p. 33.

33. Donelson and Martin Treaty, *American State Papers: Indian Affairs*, I, 326-432; III, 548.

34. J. A. James, "Spanish Influence in the West during the American Revolution," *Mississippi Valley Historical Review*, IV, 193-208.

35. Williams, *West Tennessee*, p. 37 n.

36. *Ibid.*, p. 35.

37. The account of Madame Crozat, *ibid.*, p. 36.

38. *Ibid.*, p. 37. A trading post had been established there about 1780 by Captain Richard Brashears, one of Clark's officers, in an effort to placate the Chickasaws. See John Pope, *A Tour through the Southern and Western Territories of the United States of North America* (Richmond, 1792), p. 24, and Williams, *West Tennessee*, p. 49 n.

39. A. P. Whitaker, *The Spanish-American Frontier*, pp. 84-85.

40. S. F. Bemis, *Pinckney's Treaty* (Baltimore, 1926), pp. 306, 333.

41. Whitaker, *op. cit.*, p. 54.

42. Malone, *op. cit.*, p. 348.

43. American Historical Association, *Report, 1896*, pp. 1081-82; Carondelet to Robertson, May 21, 1793, *American Historical Magazine*, II, 365.

44. Draper Collection, 40 Clark MSS, p. 18, cited in Williams, *West Tennessee*, p. 50.

45. Henley to Robertson, July 9, 1794; Henley to Gordon, Sept. 26, 1795, *American Historical Magazine*, II, 376, 358-59. Williams, *West Tennessee*, p. 53 n., suggests that Gayoso, who undoubtedly knew of this transaction, may have come into possession of some documents confirming his suspicions. Godoy told Pinckney that the bluff had been seized to prevent Americans from occupying Muscle Shoals, and General James Wilkinson seems to have suggested such a step to Gayoso.—Bemis, *op. cit.*, pp. 323-24, 345.

46. E. Merton Coulter, *A Short History of Georgia* (Chapel Hill, N. C., 1933), p. 189, map.

47. Williams, *West Tennessee*, p. 53.

48. Letter of Gayoso to his wife, quoted in Williams, *West Tennessee*, pp. 54 n., 55; Whitaker, *op. cit.*, p. 215.

49. *American Historical Magazine*, III, 393-94.

50. Williams, *West Tennessee*, p. 56.

51. Ostensibly for war against the Creeks.—John Haywood, *The Civil and Political History of the State of Tennessee*, p. 451.

52. Carondelet's instructions, quoted in Williams, *West Tennessee*, p. 58.

53. Whitaker, *op. cit.*, pp. 215-16.

54. Guion to Wilkinson, Aug. 14, 1797; Guion to the Secretary of War, July 24 and Oct. 22, 1797, Claiborne, *op. cit.*, pp. 182-83; Williams, *Early Travels*, pp. 376, 380.

55. James Wilkinson, *Memoirs* (3 vols. Philadelphia, 1816), II, 449; Williams, *West Tennessee*, p. 60. Fort Pickering stood near the present mound in De Soto Park, while Forts San Fernando, Assumption, Adams, and Pike were all built on the northern extremity of the bluff near Wolf River. Williams has corrected Memphis historians on the date of Fort Pickering.

56. W. C. C. Claiborne to Madison, Nov. 24, 1801, *Mississippi Territorial Records,* I, 346.

57. Francis Baily, *Journal of a Tour in the Unsettled Parts of North America,* quoted in Williams, *West Tennessee,* p. 389; Thomas Ashe, *Travels in America, performed in 1806,* I, 297; Christian Schultz, *Travels on an Inland Voyage . . . ,* I, 112.

58. Fortesque Cuming, *Sketches of a Tour to the Western Country,* p. 268.

59. James D. Davis, *History of Memphis and the Old Times Papers,* p. 194. Hereafter cited as *Memphis.*

60. Thomas Jefferson, *Writings* (Ford ed.), VIII, 269-70, 330.

61. Ashe, *op. cit.,* p. 298.

62. R. B. J. Twyman, *Memphis City Directory, 1849,* p. 101. Hereafter cited as *Twyman's Directory.*

63. Davis, *Memphis,* p. 162; Cuming, *op. cit.,* p. 266. This refutes J. M. Keating's account of Foy in his *History of Memphis.* Keating, writing in the 1870's, must be taken with considerable reservation on early Memphis history.

64. Davis, *Memphis,* p. 162; J. H. Shinn, *Makers and Pioneers of Arkansas* (Little Rock, 1908), pp. 41, 117-18. After the Judge's death in 1823, his sons refused an extravagant price for their land from John Overton, one of the proprietors of infant Memphis.

65. Guion to the Secretary of War, Oct. 22, 1797, quoted in Williams, *Early Travels,* p. 380. Francis Baily in May, 1797, counted five or six families on the bluff.—Williams, *Early Travels,* p. 100.

66. Guion stated that there were four white families on the site in 1797. Ashe (1806) estimated a dozen families, and Schultz (1808) saw a dozen houses. Bradbury in 1811, during the New Madrid earthquakes, found twenty whites there who told him that the larger part of the inhabitants had fled.

67. Ashe, *op. cit.,* p. 297.

68. Schultz, *op. cit.,* p. 111.

69. Quoted in Williams, *West Tennessee,* p. 78.

70. Lorenzo Dow, *History of Cosmopolite; or the four volumes of Lorenzo Dow's Journal Concentrated in One* (Washington, Ohio, 1848), pp. 346-47. The rise of Randolph in the 1820's on the second bluff, to which Dow was probably referring, supports his contention.

Chapter II

1. T. P. Abernethy, *From Frontier to Plantation in Tennessee,* p. 276. Hereafter cited as *Frontier to Plantation.*

2. J. S. Bassett, ed., *Correspondence of Andrew Jackson* (2 vols. Washington, 1926), II, 3; Overton to J. Winchester, Oct. 21, 1830, quoted in J. M. Keating, *History of Memphis,* I, 173.

3. Register's Office of Shelby County, Book A, p. 133.

4. Williams, *West Tennessee,* pp. 12-17.

5. Thomas Pownall, *Administration of the Colonies* (3rd ed., 1776), Appendix, pp. 45-49; Adair, *American Indians,* pp. 483 ff.

6. *Gentleman's Magazine,* XXXIII, 284.

7. Abernethy, *Frontier to Plantation,* pp. 22-23.

8. *Ibid.*, p. 348. Here I am merely dotting the i's and crossing the t's of Abernethy's excellent account, which cannot be touched by anything written so far on Tennessee history. Other works on its early history, and they are legion, are so warped by a filiopietistic attitude that they are almost worthless.

9. Specie certificates could be bought for 2 or 3 shillings a pound.—*State Records of North Carolina,* XVII, 139-40. Since 8 shillings were then equivalent to one Spanish milled dollar (*ibid.*, XXIV, 475-78), 10 pounds of certificates cost only 3 or 4 dollars.

10. *American State Papers, Public Lands,* I, 23-24, Jefferson's Report.

11. Abernethy, *Frontier to Plantation,* pp. 186-89.

12. *Dictionary of American Biography,* XIV, 115.

13. W. W. Clayton, *History of Davidson County, Tennessee* (Philadelphia, 1880), p. 99.

14. There were minor grants south and west of these tracts: see map on p. 28.

15. Davis, *Memphis,* p. 10; Register's Office of North Carolina, Book A, p. 149.

16. Treaty of 1783 with Virginia, *American State Papers, Indian Affairs,* I, 326-432; Treaty of Hopewell, 1786, Malone, *op. cit.*, p. 307.

17. J. H. DeWitt, "General James Winchester," *Tennessee Historical Magazine,* I, 193.

18. The various transactions are as follows: (1) Overton sold half of the Rice tract to Jackson for $100 in 1796; (2) July 3, 1797, Jackson conveyed by deed to Stephen and Richard Winchester an undivided one-eighth each for $312.50 a piece; (3) July 3, 1809, Stephen sold his eighth to his brother William of Baltimore for $500; (4) Feb. 15, 1810, Richard sold his eighth to his brother James for $500; (5) Dec. 12, 1818, Jackson sold another eighth to James Winchester for $5,000.—Register's Office of Davidson County, Book D, pp. 48, 202, 207; Book G, pp. 530, 630; Register's Office of Shelby County, Book 13, p. 218.

19. Overton to J. Winchester, Oct. 25, 1818, *Tenn. Hist. Mag.*, I, 196-97. Hereafter James Winchester will be referred to as General Winchester to distinguish him from his son Marcus.

20. J. Shelby, *The Chickasaw Treaty* (Lexington, Ky., 1828), pp. 3-4.

21. Abernethy, *Frontier to Plantation,* pp. 273-75.

22. *Ibid.*, pp. 172-76.

23. Raleigh, *Register,* Nov. 14, 1818; Williams, *West Tennessee,* p. 102.

24. Quoted, *ibid.*, p. 118.

25. Overton to J. Winchester, Oct. 25, 1818, *Tenn. Hist. Mag.*, I, 197.

26. Memphis Abstract Company, *Records,* Book 340, p. 12.

27. *Old Folks Record,* p. 404; Williams, *West Tennessee,* p. 126. It is erroneously stated by most Tennessee historians that Jackson named the town. Judge J. M. Lea, a contemporary of Jackson's, stated definitely that Winchester chose the name: *Tenn. Bar Assoc. Report, 1891,* pp. 170-77.

28. Davis, *Memphis,* pp. 16-18, 194-96. According to Judge Foy, in 1794 the Wolf entered the Mississippi at the present Jefferson Street, and the Mississippi struck the bluff at the present Union Street. In 1819 the Mississippi struck the bluff at the present Jackson Street, and the mouth of the Wolf was to the north at Cochran's Sawmill.

29. *Old Folks Record,* p. 405.
30. Nashville *Whig,* July 12, 1820.
31. Williams, *West Tennessee,* p. 114.
32. Nashville *Whig,* July 12, 1820.
33. James Brown, in the *Old Folks Record,* p. 407.
34. Davis, *Memphis,* p. 59; J. P. Young, *Standard History of Memphis,* p. 68.
35. Davis, *Memphis,* p. 19; *Old Folks Record,* p. 407.
36. Memphis Abstract Company, *Records,* Book 340, p. 15, deed, Oct. 18, 1823.
37. Davis, *Memphis,* p. 59.
38. J. J. Rawlings, *Reminiscences,* p. 9.
39. Overton to J. Winchester, July 12, 1822, Nov. 1, 1823, *Tenn. Hist. Mag.,* I, 198, 201.
40. Overton to J. Winchester, April 4, 1823, *Tenn. Hist. Mag.,* I, 200.
41. Overton to J. Winchester, Nov. 23, 1823, *Tenn. Hist. Mag.,* I, 200-1.
42. DeWitt, "General James Winchester," *Tenn. Hist. Mag.,* I, 196-97.
43. Overton to J. Winchester, Nov. 1, Nov. 23, 1823, *Tenn. Hist. Mag.,* I, 201-2.
44. Overton to J. Winchester, June 12, 1822, Nov. 23, 1823, *Tenn. Hist. Mag.,* I, 198, 202.
45. Davis, *Memphis,* pp. 59-60. Davis's estimate of 600 in 1824 may have been too high, for the state census of 1825 placed it at only 308.
46. DeWitt, "General James Winchester," *Tenn. Hist. Mag.,* I, 198-99.
47. *Ibid.,* pp. 199-200.
48. Young, *Standard History of Memphis,* p. 78.
49. *Memphis Digest of Ordinances and Charters, 1826-1856,* pp. 5-6.
50. Davis, *Memphis,* pp. 62-63.
51. *Ibid.,* p. 64.
52. *Ibid.,* p. 65.
53. Keating, *Memphis,* I, 142, map.
54. *Ibid.,* pp. 225-27. See map of the Western District about 1830 on page 55.
55. Keating, *Memphis,* I, 222, has a map showing the final division of the Ramsay tract by the county court in 1837.
56. *Rainey's City Directory, 1855,* p. 38; James Phelan, *History of Tennessee,* 339-40; Keating, *Memphis,* I, 185.
57. McLemore to M. Winchester, Nov. 24, 1831, Phelan, *op. cit.,* p. 344.
58. Overton to M. Winchester, May 12, Dec. 27, 1832, Keating, *Memphis,* I, 186.
59. See below, Chapter III.
60. See above, note 28.
61. See above, map on Memphis in the late 1820's.
62. James Brown, in the *Old Folks Record,* pp. 404-5; Davis, *Memphis,* pp. 196-97.
63. *Ibid.,* p. 199.
64. *Ibid.,* pp. 200-20.
65. See above, map on Memphis in the late 1820's.

66. Original Agreement, Articles III and IV, quoted in full in the *Old Folks Record*, p. 557.

67. Overton to M. Winchester, Oct. 21, 1830, Keating, *Memphis*, I, 173.

68. Overton to Lawrence and M. Winchester, Jan. 21, 1828, Keating, *Memphis*, I, 170.

69. Davis, *Memphis*, p. 199.

70. Winchester to P. Miller, Aug. 14, 1834, Keating, *Memphis*, I, 197.

71. Davis, *Memphis*, p. 199; Phelan, *op. cit.*, pp. 335-37.

72. Claybrook to M. Winchester, Sept. 8, 1835, Keating, *Memphis*, I, 199.

73. Davis, *Memphis*, p. 201; *Old Folks Record*, p. 454.

74. New Orleans *Price Current*, Mar. 7, 1827. Mississippi cotton of the best grade was quoted at 14c a pound to 9¼c for the Tennessee and north Alabama staple of the same quality. See also Davis, *Memphis*, p. 202.

75. *Ibid.*, pp. 202-3.

76. Huntington *Advertiser*, Oct., 1841, quoted in Williams, *West Tennessee*, p. 253.

77. Winchester to J. S. Claybrook, Jan. 28, 1834, Keating, *Memphis*, I, 197.

78. Overton to J. Winchester, Mar. 13, 1823, *Tenn. Hist. Mag.*, I, 199; Overton to Memphis editors, Feb., 1832, Keating, *Memphis*, I, 188; letter from Washington in 1832, *ibid.*, p. 186.

79. Overton to J. Winchester, Nov. 23, 1823, *Tenn. Hist. Mag.*, I, 202.

Chapter III

1. *Rainey's City Directory, 1855*, p. 28.

2. James Brown, in the *Old Folks Record*, pp. 403-5. Brown as surveyor arrived at the bluff in March, 1819, and resided in the vicinity for several years.

3. "Journal of Thomas Nutthall," R. G. Thwaites, ed., *Early Western Travels* (Cleveland, 1904), XIII, 88; Davis, *Memphis*, p. 57. Lists of early settlers may be found in J. J. Rawlings, *Reminiscences*, pp. 8-9, Keating, *Memphis*, pp. 155-56, and Davis, *Memphis*, pp. 312-13.

4. *Old Folks Record*, p. 581. Brown (*ibid.*, p. 404), states that there were only twenty settlers there in 1820.

5. Rawlings, *Reminiscences*, pp. 8, 13; *Old Folks Record*, p. 179; *Rainey's City Directory, 1855*, p. 28.

6. Jackson *Gazette*, April 26, 1824.

7. Quoted in J. S. Williams, *Old Times in West Tennessee*, p. 196.

8. E. W. Gould, *Fifty Years on the Mississippi*, p. 75.

9. Davis, *Memphis*, p. 96.

10. A. K. Underwood, in the *Old Folks Record*, p. 542; Rawlings, *Reminiscences*, p. 13.

11. Davis, *Memphis*, p. 96.

12. Minutes of the County Court, *Old Folks Record*, p. 372. See also p. 167.

13. Rawlings, *Reminiscences*, p. 9.

14. Davis, *Memphis*, p. 62.

15. *Ibid.*, p. 66.

16. Frances Trollope, *Domestic Manners of the Americans*, I, pp. 34-35.

17. Davis, *Memphis*, pp. 70-71.

18. *Ibid.*, p. 77. I have accepted Davis's account of Winchester's marriage at face value. As an admirer of the Major he surely would not have invented such a lie, in spite of his undeniable penchant for romance, and in publishing the story he would have been held strictly responsible by the Winchester family had he strayed from the truth in the slightest detail. That he was not challenged by the Winchesters at the time of publication, particularly in an age conspicuous for its duels and its sensitivity to insults, is irrefutable evidence that his account is accurate.

19. Quoted in Davis, *Memphis*, p. 79.

20. J. B. Killebrew, *Resources of Tennessee*, pp. 1014 ff.; S. C. Williams, *West Tennessee*, pp. 94 ff.

21. See map of the Western District about 1830 on page 000.

22. S. C. Williams, *West Tennessee*, p. 174.

23. James F. Cooper, *Notions of the Americans* (2 vols. London, 1828), II, 386.

24. *Old Folks Record*, p. 99.

25. S. C. Williams, *West Tennessee*, pp. 111-12; Abernethy, *Frontier to Plantation*, p. 260.

26. S. C. Williams, *West Tennessee*, p. 114.

27. *Ibid.*, p. 207.

28. *The Cultivator*, VIII, 99, quoted in U. B. Phillips, *Life and Labor in the Old South*, p. 103; *Rainey's City Directory, 1855*, p. 67.

29. *Old Folks Record*, p. 451.

30. *Ibid.*; J. S. Williams, *Old Times in West Tennessee*, p. 194.

31. *Old Folks Record*, pp. 8, 451.

32. *Ibid.*, p. 503, M. Winchester to Overton, Jan. 15, 1826; Davis, *Memphis*, pp. 309-10.

33. Keating, *Memphis*, I, 169.

34. J. S. Williams, *Old Times in West Tennessee*, pp. 194-95.

35. *Old Folks Record*, p. 452. Brown, as supervisor of both roads, had an excellent opportunity to observe this development.

36. Keating, *Memphis*, II, 19.

37. J. S. Williams, *Old Times in West Tennessee*, p. 197; *Old Folks Record*, p. 249.

38. See R. W. Johnson, "Geographical Influences in the Location and Growth of Memphis," *Journal of Geography*, XXVII, 85-97.

39. Squire Richards, city register, was the authority for the story that the name was first applied to denizens of Catfish Bay during a game of "shindy" by their southern opponents as "Pinch Gut," because of their short stature and their pot-bellies.—Keating, *Memphis*, I, 184.

40. Davis, *Memphis*, p. 110.

41. Keating, *Memphis*, I, 184.

42. Davis, *Memphis*, pp. 112-13.

43. See above, map on Memphis in the late 1820's.

44. *Old Folks Record*, p. 376.

45. Davis, *Memphis*, pp. 114 ff.

46. *Old Folks Record*, pp. 375-76.

47. Colonel J. T. Trezevant, quoted in Keating, *Memphis*, I, 230 n.

48. *Old Folks Record*, p. 558.

49. Davis, *Memphis*, p. 118.

50. *Ibid.*, p. 114.

51. *Ibid.*, p. 73; J. J. Rawlings, quoted in Keating, *Memphis*, I, 152.

52. Davis, *Memphis*, pp. 132, 254.

53. J. J. Rawlings, quoted in Keating, *Memphis*, I, 152-53.

54. Davis, *Memphis*, pp. 233, 303; Rawlings, *Reminiscences*, pp. 14, 26.

55. Keating, *Memphis*, I, 151; J. P. Young, *Standard History of Memphis*, p. 539.

56. Rawlings, *Reminiscences*, p. 3.

57. *Ibid.*

58. *Old Folks Record*, p. 102.

59. Davis, *Memphis*, p. 287.

60. Keating, *Memphis*, I, 152.

61. J. S. Williams, *Old Times in West Tennessee*, pp. 131-33.

62. Davis, *Memphis*, pp. 171 ff.

63. *Ibid.*, pp. 171 ff.

64. Jackson *Gazette*, Sept. 5, Oct. 17, 1829.

65. Davis, *Memphis*, p. 219.

66. *Old Folks Record*, p. 101.

67. S. C. Williams, *West Tennessee*, p. 185.

68. Davis, *Memphis*, p. 230.

69. *Rainey's City Directory, 1855*, pp. 41-42.

70. Davis, *Memphis*, pp. 230-32.

71. S. C. Williams, *West Tennessee*, p. 187; *Rainey's City Directory*, 1855, p. 42.

72. *Old Folks Record*, p. 101; Davis, *Memphis*, p. 233.

73. *Ibid.*, pp. 240-42.

74. *Ibid.*, p. 242; Keating, *Memphis*, II, 124; S. C. Williams, *West Tennessee*, p. 188.

75. Davis, *Memphis*, pp. 235-40; *Rainey's City Directory, 1855*, p. 42.

76. Keating, *Memphis*, II, 122-23.

77. S. C. Williams, *West Tennessee*, p. 193.

78. Justin McManus, *Memoir of St. Peters Diamond Jubilee* (Memphis, 1921), pp. 8-10.

79. J. H. Noyes, *History of American Socialism* (Philadelphia, 1870), pp. 62-72; W. R. Waterman, *Frances Wright* (Columbia University Studies, Vol. CXV), I, 117.

80. The present Germantown, Tennessee.

81. Waterman, *op. cit.*, p. 130. Waterman's is the only full account of Miss Wright, but Mrs. Trollope in her *Domestic Manners of the Americans*, I, 38-41, describes Nashoba and includes a sketch of the grounds.

82. Davis, *Memphis*, pp. 274-84. Miss Wright frequently visited Memphis in the 1830's with her husband, Count d'Arusmont of Paris, and when she decided to obtain her freedom, she filed suit for divorce in the circuit court at Raleigh, Tennessee, county seat of Shelby.

83. Davis, *Memphis*, p. 73.

84. Philip M. Hamer, *History of Tennessee*, I, 321.

85. S. C. Williams, *West Tennessee*, p. 213.

86. Virgil A. Stewart, *History of the Detection, Conviction, Life, and Designs of John A. Murrell* (Cincinnati, 185-?). See J. S. Williams, *Old Times in West Tennessee,* pp. 201-5, and Keating, *Memphis,* I, 157-68, for the myths about Murrell which these authors accept as authentic. S. C. Williams, *West Tennessee,* pp. 246-49, gives the best estimate of Murrell and an account of his trial in which he was sentenced to a brief term in jail. Robert Coates in *The Outlaw Years* catches the true spirit of the times, but he accepts all these "tall tales" at face value.

87. Davis, *Memphis,* pp. 125-27.

88. *Ibid.,* pp. 128 ff. Davis is wrong when he states that the fight between Jackson and the Bentons occurred in Memphis, for it took place at the more famous Bell Tavern in Nashville.

89. Davis, *Memphis,* pp. 164 ff.

90. Reuben Davis, *Recollections of Mississippi and Mississippians,* p. 24.

91. A. Levasseur, *Lafayette en Amérique* (2 vols. Philadelphia, 1829), II, 262.

92. Bernhard, Duke of Saxe-Weimar-Eisenach, *Travels through North America, 1825-1826* (2 vols. Philadelphia, 1828), II, 90.

93. Alexis de Tocqueville, *Democracy in America* (tr. Henry Reeve. 2 vols. New York, 1904), I, 367.

94. J. E. Alexander, *Transatlantic Sketches* (2 vols. London, 1833), II, 73-87.

95. Frances Trollope, *Domestic Manners of the Americans,* I, 32-43.

96. *Old Folks Record,* p. 558; Keating, *Memphis,* II, 199.

97. *Ibid.,* p. 242.

98. *Rainey's City Directory, 1855,* p. 68; S. C. Williams, *West Tennessee,* p. 204.

99. S. G. L. Sioussat, "Memphis as a Gateway to the West," *Tenn. Hist. Mag.,* III, 6-7; Davis, *Memphis,* pp. 75-76.

100. Keating, *Memphis,* II, 191.

101. *Old Folks Record,* p. 249; Winchester to Overton, Jan. 15, 1826, *ibid.,* pp. 563-64.

102. *Ibid.,* pp. 8, 9, 100; Keating, *Memphis,* II, 209-25.

103. *Ibid.,* II, 142; *Old Folks Record,* pp. 534-35.

104. Keating, *Memphis,* II, 302.

105. *Ibid.,* II, 307. Horse-racing and blooded stock appeared early in Tennessee. In January, 1807, James Winchester offered to sell his "Volunteer" for $1,500.—Keating, *Memphis,* I, 153 n.

106. Davis, *Memphis,* pp. 245-54.

107. Young, *Standard History of Memphis,* p. 75.

108. *United States Census,* 1840, p. 58; see above, Table I, p. 45.

109. Keating, *Memphis,* I, 213; II, 20.

110. Davis, *Memphis,* p. 97. Davis speaks from the heart here, for he was wharfmaster himself for a long time.

111. *Ibid.,* pp. 97-99.

112. *Ibid.,* pp. 96-103. There is no record of such resolutions having been passed by the state of Indiana.

Chapter IV

1. See above, Table I. The seven cities not included for 1860 were Norfolk, Va., 14,620; Wheeling, Va., 14,083; Alexandria, Va., 12,654; Augusta, Ga., 12,493; Donaldsonville, La., 11,484; St. Landry, La., 10,346; Newport, Ky., 10,046.

2. *United States Census,* 1820, 1860.

3. Mayor Baugh in 1858 sent the following message over the newly completed Atlantic cable: "The city of Memphis on the shore of the Mississippi, the largest interior depot of cotton in America, sends her greetings to the city of Manchester, the largest manufacturing city of that staple in Great Britain." —Keating, *Memphis,* I, 422.

4. *Rainey's City Directory, 1855,* p. 67; *Appeal,* Oct. 26, 1858.

5. *City Directory, 1857,* pp. 223-24.

6. Quoted in Keating, *Memphis,* I, 302.

7. Quoted in the *Appeal,* Jan. 17, 1855.

8. Report of the Chamber of Commerce, 1860-61, *Appeal,* Sept. 8, 1861; Keating, *Memphis,* I, 438 (corrected).

9. *Rainey's City Directory, 1855,* p. 43.

10. Keating, *Memphis,* I, 438. Twelve-year-old males sold for $700, and females between the ages of twelve and eighteen brought from $600 to $800. According to U. B. Phillips, *American Negro Slavery,* p. 370, a good field hand in the fifties sold from $750 in Virginia to $1,200 in New Orleans.

11. See below, Chapter VI.

12. S. G. L. Sioussat, "Memphis as a Gateway to the West," *Tenn. Hist. Mag.,* III, 8 ff.

13. *Ibid.,* III, 17; 25 Congress, 2 Session, *Executive Documents,* IX, 311.

14. Quoted in *Tenn. Hist. Mag.,* III, 14.

15. *Southern Literary Messenger,* V, 2-12, 233-306.

16. Davis, *Memphis,* p. 206.

17. Sioussat, "Memphis as a Gateway to the West," *Tenn. Hist. Mag.,* III, 23-24.

18. 5 *U. S. Statutes at Large,* p. 626.

19. 28 Congress, 1 Session, *Reports of Committees,* I, Report 120. Davis (*Memphis,* pp. 207-11), gives an amusing description of this inspection.

20. *Ibid.,* pp. 210-11; Keating, *Memphis,* I, 237.

21. 28 Congress, 1 Session, *Executive Documents,* III, Doc. 33.

22. Goodspeed Publishing Company, *History of Tennessee* (Shelby Co. Edition), p. 870.

23. *Tenn. Hist. Mag.,* III, 25; Davis, *Memphis,* p. 207.

24. Memphis, *Enquirer,* Jan. 20, 27, 1844; 5 *U. S. Statutes at Large,* p. 665.

25. James K. Polk, *Diary* (ed. M. M. Quaife. 4 vols. Chicago, 1910), I, 54.

26. 29 Congress, 1 Session, *Executive Documents,* I, 648.

27. *Tenn. Hist. Mag.,* III, 26 n.

28. Keating, *Memphis,* I, 356.

29. 10 *U. S. Statutes at Large,* pp. 586-87; *Appeal,* Aug. 16, 1854; Davis, *Memphis,* p. 211.

30. Secretary of the Navy Dobbin to President Pierce, Dec. 26, 1854, quoted in Keating, *Memphis,* I, 308-9.

31. *Appeal,* Aug. 16, 1854.

32. Davis, *Memphis,* pp. 212-18.

33. Little Rock *Banner,* April 9, 1845, citing the Memphis *Enquirer.*

34. McLemore to A. J. Donelson, Jan. 8, 1838, *Tenn. Hist. Mag.,* III, 7-8 n.

35. Little Rock *Banner,* Feb. 5, 1845.

36. *Appeal,* April 26, 1845; *Enquirer,* March 29, 1845.

37. S. G. L. Sioussat has written an excellent short summary of the convention, "Memphis as a Gateway to the West," *Tenn. Hist. Mag.,* III, 77-114. A full bibliography would include the *Journal of the Proceedings of the Western and Southwestern Convention of 1845* (127 pages); *DeBow's Review,* Vol. I; *Niles' Register;* and the files of Memphis newspapers.

38. *Appeal,* July 11, 18, 1845; *Niles' Register,* LXVIII, 312.

39. *Appeal,* July 4, 1845; *Tenn. Hist. Mag.,* III, 82. Douglas and Lincoln were both selected as delegates from Illinois to the November session, but neither came.

40. Nashville *Union,* Nov. 25, 1845; *DeBow's Review,* I, 10-14.

41. Sioussat, "Memphis as a Gateway to the West," *Tenn. Hist. Mag.,* III, 85-89, 103-6.

42. *Ibid.,* p. 87.

43. Sioussat suggests that the absence of Clay, Cass, and Benton can be accounted for by the fact that the 29th Congress was to convene in a few weeks.

44. *DeBow's Review,* I, 15. The Mobile *Advertiser,* speaking for the extreme states' rights school, made this drastic comment on Calhoun's inconsistency: "It is certainly a little singular that the ultra strict constructionist of the State's Rights party par excllence should be the most enthusiastic advocate of a convention, the avowed object of which is to induce the General Government to engage in the most vast and stupendous scheme of internal improvements that has ever originated in this country." Quoted in the *True American,* Lexington, Nov. 11, 1845.

45. *DeBow's Review,* I, 18-19.

46. *Journal of the Proceedings of the Southern Convention Assembled Oct. 23, 1845,* pp. 25-27.

47. *Ibid.,* pp. 25-28.

48. *Tenn. Hist. Mag.,* III, 108-11.

49. *Ibid.,* 112.

50. R. S. Cotterill, "Southern Railroads and Western Trade, 1840-50," *Mississippi Valley Historical Review,* III, 431-33.

51. R. S. Cotterill, "Memphis Railroad Convention, 1849," *Tenn. Hist. Mag.,* IV, 83.

52. *Ibid.,* IV, 83.

53. *Ibid.,* IV, 93.

54. *Appeal,* Oct. 27, 1849.

55. *Ibid.,* June 10, 1853.

56. *Ibid.,* Feb. 9, 1859.

57. R. S. Cotterill, "Southern Railroads and Western Trade," *Miss. Val. Hist. Rev.,* III, 427.

58. R. B. Way, "Commerce of the Lower Mississippi in the Period 1830-1860," *Proceedings of the Mississippi Valley Historical Association,* X, 59.

59. *Ibid.*

60. A. Hulburt, *Paths of Inland Commerce* (Vol. XXI of "The Chronicles of America" Series, New Haven, 1920), pp. 480-81.

61. *DeBow's Review,* I, 160; *Cist's Weekly Advertiser,* Jan. 4, 1848.

62. U. B. Phillips, *Transportation in the Eastern Cotton Belt to 1860* (New York, 1908), covers this subject thoroughly.

63. Charleston *Courier,* Sept. 30, 1845.

64. Cotterill, "Southern Railroads and Western Trade," *Miss. Val. Hist. Rev.,* III, 471-73.

65. Way, "Commerce on the Lower Mississippi," *Proceedings of the Mississippi Valley Historical Association,* X, 67; Memphis *Bulletin,* Oct. 31, 1857.

66. R. S. Cotterill, "Beginnings of Railroads in the Southwest," *Miss. Val. Hist. Rev.,* VIII, 318-26. The only road of any importance constructed in the Southwest before 1840 was the Tuscumbia and Decatur in Alabama, 46 miles in length, around the great shoals (Muscle Shoals) of the Tennessee.

67. U. B. Phillips, "Transportation and Commerce," *The South in the Building of the Nation,* V, 362.

68. *American Railroad Journal,* XXXIV, 393.

69. R. S. Cotterill, "Southern Railroads, 1850-60," *Miss. Val. Hist. Rev.,* X, 401.

70. Way, "Commerce on the Lower Mississippi," *Proceedings of the Mississippi Valley Historical Association,* X, 62-68.

71. A. L. Brooks, "Early Plans for Railroads in West Tennessee," *Tenn. Hist. Mag.,* Oct., 1932, pp. 37-38.

72. Sioussat, "Memphis as a Gateway to the West," *Tenn. Hist. Mag.,* III, 10.

73. S. C. Williams, *West Tennessee,* p. 171.

74. Fort Pickering *Eagle,* May 6, 1842; Brooks, "Early Plans for Railroads in West Tennessee," *Tenn. Hist. Mag.,* Oct., 1932, pp. 36-37.

75. *American Railroad Journal,* XXXIII, 626.

76. Keating, *Memphis,* II, 204.

77. Report of the Chamber of Commerce, 1860-61, *Appeal,* Sept. 8, 1861.

78. *Ibid.*

79. *Ibid.* In 1861 fifteen miles had been laid on the western end out of Little Rock.—Arkansas Historical Society, *Publications,* I, 207. This support of an Arkansas road was due to the desire of Memphis to become the eastern terminal of the transcontinental road.

80. 27 Congress, 3 Session, *Executive Documents of the House,* p. 126; F. H. Dixon, *Traffic History of the Mississippi River System,* p. 14; Davis, *Memphis,* p. 117. E. W. Gould, *Fifty Years on the Mississippi,* pp. 393-94, gives an excellent description of the Memphis flatboat market.

81. *Ibid.,* pp. 390-404; Keating, *Memphis,* II, 193. Keating lists the names of more than one hundred of the earlier independent steamboats with accounts of several terrible accidents which occurred near by.

82. *Ibid.,* II, 177.

83. Brooks, "Early Plans for Railroads in West Tennessee," *Tenn. Hist. Mag.,* Oct., 1932, p. 23.

84. John Hallum, *Diary of an Old Lawyer,* p. 18; *Old Folks Record,* p. 116.

85. *The South in the Building of the Nation,* V, 349.

86. Keating, *Memphis,* II, 200; *Rainey's City Directory, 1855,* p. 85; *Twyman's Directory, 1849,* p. 111; Hallum, *op. cit.,* 19.

87. Way, "Commerce on the Lower Mississippi," *Proceedings of the Mississippi Valley Historical Association,* X, 68.

88. *Appeal,* Oct. 28, 1858.

89. *Ibid.,* Oct. 26, 1858, quoting a letter to the St. Louis *Republican* from a resident of that city who had visited Memphis.

90. *Ibid.,* Oct. 28, 1858.

91. *Ibid.,* Aug. 19, 1860.

92. Petersburg *Express,* quoted in the *Appeal,* Mar. 1, 1861.

93. According to the Buffalo *Republican* of April 6, 1861, quoted in the *Appeal,* April 10, 1861, 18,000 bales of Memphis cotton had recently been shipped from Buffalo to Boston in three days. It had come to Buffalo via Cincinnati.

94. The exhaustive report of the Memphis Chamber of Commerce, compiled by John S. Toof, its secretary in 1860. It is to be found only in the *Appeal* of Sept. 8, 1861, where it occupies two full pages.

95. See Table VI.

96. *Appeal,* Feb. 21, 28, April 17, 1845.

97. *Ibid.,* Aug. 20, 1846; see map, Keating, *Memphis,* I, 236. The plan was to dig a canal from Raleigh to the Mississippi, a distance of eleven miles instead of the forty-odd taken by Wolf River, and to erect a dam which would produce 400 horsepower for the navy yard, eight pair of six-foot millstones, 500,000 spindles for spinning cotton, and 100 power looms.

98. *Appeal,* Jan. 26, Feb. 2, 1847.

99. *The South in the Building of the Nation,* V, 317.

100. *DeBow's Review,* X, 525-29.

101. See above, note 7.

102. *DeBow's Review,* X, 527; *Twyman's Directory, 1849,* p. 112.

103. *Ibid.,* p. 112. This cotton mill was described at length in 1846 in *DeBow's Review,* X, 527, but in 1849 it was still uncompleted.—*Twyman's Directory, 1849,* p. 112. In the early fifties, however, it began operation.—*Appeal,* July 12, 1854.

104. Keating, *Memphis,* II, 233.

105. *Ibid.,* II, 239.

106. *Rainey's City Directory, 1855,* p. 210; *City Directory, 1859,* p. 20; *American Railroad Journal,* XXIV, 712.

107. *City Directory, 1855,* pp. 5, 214; *ibid., 1857,* pp. 58, 86; *ibid., 1859,* pp. 109, 133, 137, 221.

108. *Appeal,* Sept. 8, 1861.

109. *Rainey's City Directory, 1855,* p. 84; Keating, *Memphis,* I, 236, 422; Young, *Standard History of Memphis,* p. 95.

110. Keating, *Memphis,* II, 19; Memphis *Evening Ledger,* Oct. 22, 1857.

111. Keating, *Memphis,* II, 244-45. The Union bank and the Planters bank, which formed a merger after the war, still exist.

112. S. C. Williams, *West Tennessee,* p. 216; *City Directory, 1859,* p. 23.

113. *Rainey's City Directory, 1855,* p. 61; Keating, *Memphis,* II, 244-48; Phelan, *History of Tennessee,* p. 272.

114. *City Directory, 1859,* index; Keating, *Memphis,* II, 181 ff.

115. These figures are taken from the Report of the Chamber of Commerce, 1860-1861, in the *Appeal,* September 8, 1861, compiled by John S. Toof, who seems to have been a fairly careful statistician for his day.

116. F. Bancroft, *Slave-Trading in the Old South,* pp. 250-51. Chapter XII is devoted to the Memphis market.

117. *Ibid.,* pp. 250-51.

118. *Ibid.,* pp. 253-56; Hallum, *op. cit.,* pp. 77 ff.; Goodspeed Publishing Company, *History of Tennessee* (Shelby Co. Edition), pp. 822-24.

119. Bancroft, *op. cit.,* pp. 262-64; J. A. Wyeth, *Life of Forrest* (New York, 1899), p. 22.

120. L. Lewis and H. J. Smith, *Chicago, a History of its Reputation,* pp. 1-85.

121. *Rainey's City Directory, 1855,* p. 43.

Chapter V

1. See notes 5 and 6, below.

2. *Old Folks Record,* p. 47. This perennial interest in music and drama can be appreciated only by reading the Memphis newspapers over a period of years. For a catalogue of the plays see *Memphis Theater Programs, 1859-60.*

3. Davis, *Memphis,* pp. 178-82; *Appeal,* Dec. 10, 1859.

4. *Rainey's City Directory, 1855,* p. 194; Keating, *Memphis,* II, 307.

5. *United States Census,* 1860, Introduction, p. xxxii.

6. *Ibid.,* pp. xxxi-xxxii. In 1860 St. Louis led the nation with 60 per cent foreign-born; San Francisco had 50 per cent, and of the older Tidewater cities, New York had 47 per cent, Boston 36 per cent, Philadelphia 29 per cent, Baltimore 25 per cent, Charleston 15 per cent, and Richmond 13 per cent. In this respect Memphis was definitely a western and not a southern town.

7. *Ibid.,* pp. xxxii, 467.

8. Keating, *Memphis,* I, 246.

9. *Appeal,* Aug. 17, 1854.

10. Keating (*Memphis,* II, 139) states that there were not many Germans in Memphis before 1855.

11. *City Directory, 1860,* pp. 25, 39.

12. Memphis *Press Scimitar,* March 19, May 7, 1927.

13. Keating, *Memphis,* II, 249. The Lowenstein concern is still in operation.

14. *Ibid.,* II, 293.

15. *Ibid.,* II, 227-28.

16. *Ibid.,* II, 284-85.

17. For a general discussion of town slaves see U. B. Phillips, *American Negro Slavery,* pp. 402-24.

18. *United States Census,* 1850, p. 575; *ibid.,* 1860, I, 467. The municipal tax report for 1856 placed the number of slaves at 1,459 (*City Directory, 1856,* p. 8) and that for 1860 at 1,875.

19. In Shelby County outside of Memphis there were 12,120 whites to 13,347 Negroes, making a total of 25,467 persons.

20. *United States Census,* 1850, p. 575; *ibid.,* 1860, I, 467. It is odd that Nashville, which had fewer Negroes in 1860 than Memphis, should have had

719 free Negroes to the latter's 198. Since Memphis was such a large slave market, there may have been considerable kidnapping of free Negroes.

21. Keating, *Memphis*, I, 381.

22. S. C. Williams, *West Tennessee*, p. 209.

23. T. P. Abernethy, "Origin of the Whig Party in Tennessee," *Miss. Val. Hist. Rev.*, XII, 504-22.

24. S. G. L. Sioussat, "Tennessee and National Political Parties," *American Historical Association, Report, 1914*, I, 252. Tennessee gave its electoral vote to every Whig presidential candidate from 1836 through 1860 with the exception of the year 1856. In state elections, however, the Democrats were more successful.

25. Abernethy, *Frontier to Plantation*, pp. 303-7.

26. See also maps in A. C. Cole, *The Whig Party in the South*, Appendix.

27. Davis, *Memphis*, p. 203.

28. A. C. Cole, *op. cit.*, Appendix.

29. This table has been compiled from the statistics in the local Memphis papers. It is evident that Memphis and Shelby County may be considered as practically a single political entity.

30. A. C. Cole, "Nativism in the Lower Mississippi Valley," *Proceedings of the Mississippi Valley Historical Association*, VI, 259-60.

31. Keating, *Memphis*, I, 349.

32. *Appeal*, July 6, 1854. The Louisville *Times* put the majority at 774, but the *Appeal* stated that it was only 73.

33. Keating, *Memphis*, I, 363 ff.

34. *Appeal*, June 25, 29, 1856.

35. Cole, "Nativism in the Lower Mississippi Valley," *Proceedings of the Mississippi Valley Historical Association*, VI, 272.

36. Keating, *Memphis*, I, 370; *Appeal*, April 25, 1855.

37. *Ibid.*, August 27, 1856.

38. Keating, *Memphis*, I, 379.

39. See Table VIII.

40. Keating, *Memphis*, II, 209-25; *Old Folks Record*, pp. 8, 9, 100. There were other spasmodic attempts to establish newspapers, and many journals of a religious or technical nature were also published locally.

41. The Christians formed a congregation in 1843 and acquired a resident pastor five years later.—Memphis *Press Scimitar*, Jan. 8, 1927. The Jews erected a synagogue in the fifties.

42. *City Directory, 1860*, pp. 26-28.

43. Davis, *Memphis*, p. 240.

44. Abernethy, *Frontier to Plantation*, pp. 219-20.

45. *Rainey's City Directory, 1855*, p. 53.

46. M. Hamilton, *History of St. Agnes Academy*, p. 29.

47. *Rainey's City Directory, 1855*, p. 54.

48. *Ibid.*, p. 50.

49. *Ibid.*, pp. 57-59; Keating, *Memphis*, I, 260-61, II, 152.

50. Memphis *Bulletin*, Nov. 10, 1856; *City Directory, 1856*, p. 9.

51. *City Directory, 1860*, p. 37.

52. Keating, *Memphis*, I, 299.

53. This information on the public school system has been taken from an article in the *City Directory, 1856*, pp. 11-17. See also the table in Keating, *Memphis*, II, 151.

54. *City Directory, 1860*, pp. 24-25.

55. Keating, *Memphis*, I, 419.

56. *Ibid.*, 300-1; *City Directory, 1856*, pp. 21-22. There is copious evidence in numerous sources of increasing temperance agitation in the two decades before 1860.

57. *Appeal*, April 11, 1857.

58. *Ibid.*, May 19, 1846.

59. Keating, *Memphis*, II, 292-95.

60. See above, Chapter IV.

61. Keating, *Memphis*, I, 260; *Eagle*, Feb., 1842.

62. *Ibid.*, April 14, 1852.

63. *Memphis Digest, 1867*, pp. 80-85.

64. *Old Folks Record*, p. 558; see above, map on the early land grants in the Memphis area.

65. Keating, *Memphis*, I, 277.

66. *Memphis Digest, 1867*, p. 92.

67. Keating, *Memphis*, I, 279-81.

68. *Old Folks Record*, p. 160.

69. Davis, *Memphis*, p. 98.

70. *Twyman's Directory, 1849*, p. 108.

71. Keating, *Memphis*, I, 294, 350.

72. *Appeal*, Feb. 23, 1858. See also editorials of March 7 and 9.

73. *Ibid.*, quoted in Keating, *Memphis*, I, 412.

74. *Memphis Digest, 1867*, p. 132.

75. See Table XI, p. 182.

76. Keating, *Memphis*, I, 269; Young, *Standard History of Memphis*, p. 110.

77. *Appeal*, April 14, 1860, April 2, 1861; Keating, *Memphis*, I, 413-15. These charges were not mere propaganda of enemies of the administration, but facts generally known at the time. Neither the *Appeal* nor Keating, who came to Memphis later, had any ax to grind.

78. Keating, *Memphis*, II, 20.

79. *Ibid.*, I, 274.

80. Goodspeed Publishing Company, *History of Tennessee* (Shelby Co. Edition), p. 875.

81. See Table XIII, p. 189.

82. Keating, *Memphis*, I, 441.

83. *Twyman's Directory*. This amusing notice appears on page 43: "Addenda —The following were omitted by the young man who took the names in the 2nd district. There are a few new citizens and some old ones who were not here when the names were taken, and if we were to attempt to give every name we would never get through the work."

84. *City Directory, 1860*, p. 69.

85. Descriptions of Memphis in 1848 and 1852 by contemporaries appear ir the *Old Folks Record*, pp. 57, 115.

86. See above, note 2.

87. *Appeal*, Aug., 1847, Sept., 1856, Oct. 6, 1858.

88. The war prevented construction and the city had to wait until the eighties for good water.

89. *Old Folks Record*, p. 116; *Appeal*, Mar. 27, 1860.

90. *Rainey's City Directory, 1855*, p. 43.

91. See the description of the Topp mansion in an article by William McCaskill in the Memphis *Commercial Appeal*, Jan. 17, 1934.

92. F. L. Olmsted, *Journey in the Back Country*, I, 137-40.

93. Some instances of this antipathy have been mentioned above; e.g., the discrimination against Memphis in the matter of the location of state banks. This paragraph, however, is based upon the testimony of several octogenarians of the interior counties with whom I have conversed, who recall vividly the contempt of their parents for Memphis.

Chapter VI

1. *Appeal*, Oct. 24, 1860.
2. *Ibid.*, Oct. 25, 1860.
3. *Ibid.*, July 3, 1860.
4. *Ibid.*, Nov. 13, 1860.
5. Presidential vote in 1860 of Memphis, West Tennessee, and Tennessee:

	Bell	Douglas	Breckenridge
Memphis	2,250	2,319	572
West Tennessee	15,000	7,000	10,000
Tennessee	69,176	11,330	64,809

6. S. G. L. Sioussat, "Tennessee and National Political Parties, 1850-60," *Report of the American Historical Association, 1914*, p. 230; *Eagle*, June 7, 1849.
7. *Appeal*, Nov. 17, 1850.
8. Abernethy dismisses this increased Democratic strength in Memphis as natural in view of the fact that Harris was its own citizen; yet it must be remembered that the state voted against Polk, its native son, in 1844.
9. See above, Chapter IV.
10. *Appeal*, Dec. 28, 29, 1860.
11. *Ibid.*, Jan. 9, 1861; J. W. Patton, *Unionism and Reconstruction in Tennessee*, p. 10.
12. *Enquirer*, Nov. 13, 1860.
13. *Appeal*, Dec. 1, 1860.
14. *Ibid.*, Dec. 23, 1860.
15. *Ibid.*, Jan. 9, 1861.
16. Patton, *Unionism and Reconstruction*, p. 12.
17. *Appeal*, Feb. 10, 12, 1861.
18. *Ibid.*, Jan. 30, Feb. 10, 13, 1861.
19. Keating, *Memphis*, I, 481.
20. *Appeal*, April 3, 1861.
21. *Ibid.*, April 16, 17, 18, 1861; J. A. Minnis of Memphis to A. R. Nelson, April, 1861, Nelson Papers.
22. *Appeal*, June 12, 1861.
23. John G. Nicolay and John Hay, *Abraham Lincoln: A History* (10 vols. New York, 1890), IX, 250.

24. See maps in Abernethy, *Frontier to Plantation,* p. 343, showing the shift in the vote by county from February to June. Middle Tennessee, which defeated the convention by a majority of 1,382 in February—and secession by a much larger majority—voted 58,265 to 8,198 for secession in June.—J. W. Fertig, *The Secession and Reconstruction of Tennessee* (Chicago, 1898), pp. 20, 27. In June the relative Union strength in West Tennessee was greater than that in the middle section of the state, as the following figures show:

JUNE VOTE

West Tennessee		Middle Tennessee		East Tennessee	
For	Against	For	Against	For	Against
29,167	6,117	58,265	8,198	14,780	32,923

25. See below, Chapter VII.

26. Frank Moore, comp., *The Rebellion Record: A Diary of American Events . . .,* II, D. 42. The greater part of this description of Memphis prior to June, 1862, is taken from the *Appeal,* but only upon special points will the exact reference be given.

27. T. W. Knox, *Campfire and Cottonfield,* p. 145.

28. *Appeal,* May 5, 1861; *Rebellion Record,* II, P. 58.

29. *Appeal,* May 24, 1861; Cincinnati *Daily Gazette,* June 10, 24, 1861.

30. *War of the Rebellion,* Series I, Vol. IV, p. 362. Hereafter cited as *W. R.*

31. *Appeal,* Aug. 15, 1861.

32. Knox, *Campfire and Cottonfield,* pp. 187-88; *Rebellion Record,* II, P, 31; *Appeal,* July 18, 1861. Ardent supporters of the Confederacy took blankets off their own beds to send them to the soldiers.

33. *Rebellion Record,* III, P. 23; IV, D. 3-4; *Appeal,* Sept. 5, 1861.

34. *Appeal,* April 18, 1862.

35. Young, *Standard History of Memphis,* p. 327; *Argus,* June 2, 1862. Judging by the election returns of 4,929 in February, 1861, and 3,386 in August of the same year, only 1,600 men left the city in the first five months of war. The final total of volunteers cannot be determined on this basis, however, for many of the voters in August were recent arrivals who came to work in the factories. Keating (*Memphis,* I, 504) carelessly mistook the August vote of 731 in the county outside of Memphis for the 3,386 vote in the city, and upon this error he bases his statement that Memphis had as many soldiers as it had voters. Young (*Standard History of Memphis,* p. 125) follows him in this error, though Young's estimate of the number of soldiers was not based upon the election returns.

36. *Appeal,* April 18, 1862.

37. *Ibid.,* April 18, 1862.

38. Report of the Chamber of Commerce, 1860-61, *Appeal,* Sept. 8, 1861.

39. *Ibid.,* Sept. 8, 1861.

40. *Ibid.,* May 3, Oct. 6, 1861; Keating, *Memphis,* I, 504-5.

41. *Rebellion Record,* II, D. 42; *Appeal,* Sept. 28, Oct. 2, 1861.

42. Knox, *Campfire and Cottonfield,* p. 173; *W. R.,* Series I, Vol. X, Pt. II, p. 591. Ed Porter, captain of a company of irregulars, reported that he had burned 40,000 bales in this vicinity early in June.

43. "The Peculiarities of the Day," *Appeal,* April 11, 1862.

44. *Rebellion Record,* II, D. 52; IV, D. 37, 53; *Argus,* March 8, 1862; *W. R.,* Series I, Vol. X, Pt. II, p. 298.

45. Correspondent of the Charleston *Courier, Appeal,* May 22, 1862; for the story of the *Appeal's* odyssey, see R. A. Halley, "A Rebel Newspaper's War Story." *Tenn. Hist. Mag.,* VIII, 124-53.

46. *W. R.,* Series I, Vol. X, Pt. II, p. 57; *Rebellion Record,* V, D. 22.

47. Good accounts of the battle by participants and spectators may be found in Knox, *Campfire and Cottonfield,* pp. 174-80; *Battles and Leaders of the Civil War,* I, 449-60; *Appeal,* June 9, 1862; and *W. R.,* Series I, Vol. X, Pt. I, pp. 906-11.

48. Knox, *Campfire and Cottonfield,* p. 182.

49. *W. R.,* Series I, Vol. X, Pt. I, p. 910.

50. *Ibid.,* pp. 912-13; Knox, *Campfire and Cottonfield,* p. 179.

51. *Ibid.,* p. 181.

52. London *Times,* Oct. 9, 1861; Oct. 8, 9, 1862.

53. On this point see J. F. C. Fuller, *Grant and Lee* (London, 1933), pp. 38-42.

54. B. H. Liddell Hart, *Sherman: Soldier, Realist, American* (New York, 1929), p. 144.

55. *W. R.,* Series I, Vol. XXXIX, Pt. I, pp. 469-84. Forrest had no intention of capturing the city but merely of forcing the retreat of the cavalry detachment under A. J. Smith near Grenada, and his ruse succeeded perfectly. For a vivid description of the panic he caused in Memphis see the letter of A. W. Pearson, a Federal officer, in Keating, *Memphis,* I, 541-44.

56. There was skirmishing near Memphis as late as February, 1865: *W. R.,* Series I, Vol. XLIX, Pt. I, p. 37.

57. *Congressional Globe,* 38 Cong., 1 Sess., IV, 3324.

58. E. M. Coulter, "Commerce with the Confederacy," *Miss. Val. Hist. Rev.,* V, 378-83.

59. *W. R.,* Series I, Vol. XVII, Pt. II, p. 424; J. W. Garner, *Reconstruction in Mississippi* (New York, 1901), p. 31. Grant's order concerning the Jews was immediately rescinded by Lincoln.

60. *W. R.,* Series III, Vol. II, p. 349.

61. *Ibid.,* Series I, Vol. XVII, Pt. II, p. 158; Knox, *Campfire and Cottonfield,* p. 184; Keating, *Memphis,* I, 517. John Hallum, author of *Diary of an Old Lawyer,* was the middleman in many of these illegal transactions, and his diary gives an intimate picture of Memphis during the war. See particularly pp. 284-336.

62. Knox, *Campfire and Cottonfield,* p. 193; *Bulletin,* August 28, 1862; *W. R.,* Series I, Vol. XVII, Pt. II, p. 187.

63. *Ibid.,* p. 141.

64. General Order No. 4, Keating, *Memphis,* I, 514, 518; General Order No. 64. *W. R.,* Series I, Vol. XVII, Pt. II, p. 123.

65. *Ibid.,* 171, 186.

66. *Bulletin,* July 19, 1864.

67. *W. R.,* Series I, Vol. XVII, Pt. II, p. 140.

68. Knox, *Campfire and Cottonfield,* pp. 217-18.

69. C. A. Dana to Secretary of War Stanton, Jan. 21, 1863, quoted in J. S. McNeily, "War and Reconstruction in Mississippi," *Miss. Hist. Pub.,* Centenary Series, II, 178.

70. Testimony of General Canby before the House Committee, *Miss. Val. Hist. Rev.,* V, 390.

71. *Congressional Globe*, 38 Cong., 2 Sess., II, 1354.

72. Coulter, "Commerce with the Confederacy," *Miss. Val. Hist. Rev.*, V, 390.

73. W. T. Sherman, *Memoirs*, I, 313.

74. Hallum, *Diary*, p. 307.

75. *W. R.*, Series I, Vol. XXXIX, Pt. II, 22.

76. Keating, *Memphis*, I, 517; Knox, *Campfire and Cottonfield*, p. 193; Sherman, *Memoirs*, I, 293.

77. *Rebellion Record*, V, D. 28; Keating, *Memphis*, I, 517.

78. The correspondent of the Cairo *Gazette*, writing in the *Appeal*, June 16, 1862; Knox, *Campfire and Cottonfield*, p. 184; *W. R.*, Series I, Vol. XVII, Pt. II, pp. 41, 122, 910.

79. *Ibid.*, p. 29.

80. Keating, *Memphis*, I, 517.

81. *Rebellion Record*, V, D. 38; *Bulletin*, July 18, 1862.

82. Keating, *Memphis*, I, 517, estimates their number at 1300, but the *Bulletin*, July 25, states that only 250 left. The *Avalanche* and the *Argus* had been suppressed.—Knox, *Campfire and Cottonfield*, pp. 189-93. They were succeeded by the *Bulletin*, which in spite of its sincere Union sentiment aroused the ire of the military authorities on more than one occasion. The *Appeal* is of little value for this period, since it was hopelessly biased and published away from Memphis.

83. Knox, *Campfire and Cottonfield*, p. 184.

84. Sherman, *Memoirs*, I, 288.

85. *W. R.*, Series I, Vol. XVII, Pt. II, p. 82.

86. *Ibid.*, Vol. XLIX, Pt. II, pp. 889-901. These works were located in Fort Pickering.

87. *W. R.*, Vol. XLVII, Pt. II, pp. 470, 471.

88. Sherman, *Memoirs*, I, 293.

89. *Bulletin*, July 3, 1862.

90. General Order No. 61, *W. R.*, Series I, Vol. XVII, Pt. II, p. 117.

91. A dog with a bad name rarely receives justice. Both Young and Keating indulge in a silly and childish tirade on Sherman which is unjust and untrue so far as his treatment of Memphis is concerned.

92. Sherman, *Memoirs*, I, 304-6; *W. R.*, Series I, Vol. XVII, Pt. II, p. 113.

93. *Ibid.*, p. 127.

94. *Ibid.*, p. 122.

95. *Ibid.*, pp. 122, 156.

96. *Ibid.*, pp. 201-2. The following spring 63 persons were sent south by his successor.—*Bulletin*, April 2, 1863.

97. *Ibid.*, Oct. 18, 1862.

98. *Ibid.*, Oct. 26, 1862; *W. R.*, Series I, Vol. XVII, Pt. II, pp. 856-57, 861-69, 875.

99. *Ibid.*, pp. 15, 16, 60, 179, 856.

100. *Ibid.*, pp. 158-59.

101. Lloyd Lewis, *Sherman, Fighting Prophet* (New York, 1932), p. 244.

102. *Ibid.*, p. 332; *Bulletin*, Oct. 8, 1862; Feb. 21, 1863.

103. *W. R.*, Series I, Vol. XVII, Pt. II, p. 188.

104. *Ibid.*, p. 261.

105. Memphis had ten different commanders during the war.—*Argus*, May 30, 1865.

106. Keating, *Memphis*, I, 534; Sherman (*Memoirs*, I, 312) admitted that Van Dorn's spies entered the town without difficulty.

107. Special Order No. 13, *Bulletin*, May 1, 1863.

108. *Ibid.*, July 7, 1862. The editor of the 1865 city directory, himself a Union man, inadvertently reveals the true character of those who remained. In an article describing conditions in June, 1862, he enumerates the various classes of citizens who had fled, and concludes in this vein: "Who lives in Memphis? Its civilians . . . the men with whom the duties and inclination of domesticity have rendered business, home, and pursuits of literature and art paramount to the most boisterous attraction of military distinction. Civilians in taste as in occupation form now the population of Memphis."—*City Directory, 1865*, pp. 104-5.

109. *Bulletin*, Jan. 2, 1863.

110. *Ibid.*, July 11, 1864; *Rebellion Record*, Vol. XI, Doc. 591.

111. *Ibid.*, V, D. 43; VIII, D. 8; Hallum, *Diary*, 312, 318; *W. R.*, Series I, Vol. X, Pt. II, p. 507.

112. Letter of Emerson Etheridge, quoted in Keating, *Memphis*, I, 527.

Chapter VII

1. Taxable property had been assessed at $18,297,545 in 1860, including $1,320,625 in slaves; in 1865 it was assessed at $17,814,930: *Commercial*, Jan. 27, 1866.

2. *Ibid.*, Jan. 27, 1866; Keating, *Memphis*, I, 544.

3. See above, Table I.

4. United States Census Reports.

5. *American Historical Magazine*, VIII, 151-52.

6. Hamer, *History of Tennessee*, II, 631. The legislature of 1865 contained 78 members; 55 of these were born in Tennessee, 11 in other southern states, 9 in the North, and 3 abroad. Forty-three had served in the Union army.

7. J. W. Patton, *Unionism and Reconstruction in Tennessee*, p. 24.

8. *Ibid.*, pp. 58-74.

9. T. W. Humes, *The Loyal Mountaineers of Tennessee* (Knoxville, 1888), p. 78.

10. Hamer, *History of Tennessee*, II, 584.

11. A. A. Miller, *Official and Political Manual of Tennessee* (Nashville, 1890), p. 48.

12. Patton, *Unionism and Reconstruction*, p. 212.

13. *Ibid.*, p. 104, quoting from *Proclamation Book*, p. 10.

14. Quoted in Patton, *Unionism and Reconstruction*, p. 87.

15. In parts of East Tennessee, even today, a Negro is not allowed to stay overnight.

16. 34th Tennessee General Assembly, *Acts*, 2 Session, 1865-66, pp. 52-62; Extra Session, 1866, pp. 17-19.

17. *American Annual Cyclopaedia, 1867* (New York, 1869-76), p. 709.

18. Hamer, *History of Tennessee*, II, 611.

19. *Ibid.*, II, 619.

20. Patton, *Unionism and Reconstruction*, pp. 142-43.

21. Quoted in Knoxville *Daily Free Press and Herald*, Sept. 25, 1868.

22. Hamer, *History of Tennessee,* II, 645 ff.
23. See below, Table X, p. 174.
24. Letter of P. T. Scruggs, *Avalanche,* April 20, 1868.
25. Keating, *Memphis,* I, 562.
26. *Memphis Digest, 1867,* pp. 149-63.
27. *Argus,* May 22, 1866; *Post,* Nov. 7, 1866; *Appeal,* Feb. 8, 1867.
28. See the Nashville *Banner* on "Unhappy Memphis," quoted in the *Public Ledger,* Oct. 23, 1868; *ibid.,* Feb. 24, March 12, 13, 1867.
29. *Ibid.,* May 15, 1866; Oct. 10, 1868.
30. *Ibid.,* Dec. 5, 1867; *Memphis Digest, 1867,* 140 ff.
31. *Appeal,* Feb. 26, 1867.
32. See below, note 35, for sources of these figures.
33. *Public Ledger,* Jan. 3, 1868.
34. *Ibid.,* Nov. 4, 1868.
35. Hamer, *History of Tennessee,* II, 597, 645, 628; *Argus,* Aug. 3, Dec. 29, 1865; Mar. 29, April 3, Oct. 14, 1866; *Public Ledger,* Aug. 2, 1867; Nov. 4, 1868; Nov. 4, 1870; *Appeal,* Aug. 6, 1869; *Commercial,* Dec. 29, 1865.
36. *Report of the Secretary of War, 1868,* p. 1057; J. H. Robinson, "A Social History of the Negro in Memphis and Shelby County" (unpublished Yale doctoral dissertation in Sociology, 1934), p. 88.
37. Patton, *Unionism and Reconstruction,* p. 166.
38. *Public Ledger,* March 7, 1867. A Mississippi planter who had been in the city three weeks trying to obtain hands complained in a letter to the *Ledger* that "the cities are ruining the farmers by hiring the laborers and giving them small jobs about town. Some are kept by steamboatmen on the levee to unload boats; the merchants have them for porters and clerks in every house in town."
39. "Africa in Memphis," *Public Ledger,* March 7, 1867.
40. Patton, *Unionism and Reconstruction,* p. 160.
41. *Public Ledger,* Sept. 6, 1867; Robinson, *op. cit.,* pp. 96-97.
42. Keating, *Memphis,* II, 148.
43. Robinson, *op. cit.,* p. 97.
44. General Stoneman, commanding the District of Tennessee, to General Grant, May 12, 1866, published in the *Argus* of that date.
45. *Argus,* Sept. 20, 1865; Keating, *Memphis,* I, 568.
46. Stoneman to Grant, *Public Ledger,* May 12, 1866. The *Ledger* and the *Argus* give different accounts of the origin of the riot, as do all other sources. General Runkle of the Freedmen's Bureau admitted that the Negro troops started it.—Letter to Gen. C. B. Fisk, *Argus,* May 2, 1866.
47. Hamer, *History of Tennessee,* II, 613.
48. *Argus,* May 2, 3, 12, 1866; Stoneman to Grant, *Argus,* May 12, 1866; Report of Major H. W. Hildreth, aide to Gen. Howard, *Argus,* July 3, 1866. See also the excerpts from northern papers quoted in the *Argus,* May 12, 1866.
49. A Report of the "Memphis Riots and Massacres" was prepared under congressional guidance but, as its name suggests, it was prejudiced and inaccurate.
50. The vote in the municipal election of January, 1868, was 4,301, while that of the previous August was 6,495 and that of the following November was 7,340.
51. *Bulletin,* April 7, 1867; *Avalanche,* April 14, 1867.
52. Knoxville *Whig,* Sept. 18, 1867.

53. *Public Ledger,* March 18, 1867; Keating, *Memphis,* I, 585.

54. The late Judge J. P. Young, the late Captain Walter L. Vesey, and the late General A. R. Taylor, with whom I have discussed the matter, all agree that every ex-Rebel joined the order, and as members themselves they should know whereof they speak.

55. Robinson, *op. cit.,* p. 171.

56. Keating, *Memphis,* II, 154.

57. *Post,* Aug. 6, 1869.

58. Keating, *Memphis,* I, 622-24.

59. *Ibid.,* I, 626.

60. Quoted in Young, *Standard History of Memphis,* p. 131.

61. *Public Ledger,* July 15, 1867.

62. *Argus,* May 16, 1866.

63. Hildreth's Report, *Argus,* July 3, 1866; *ibid.,* Aug. 12, 1866.

64. Stoneman's Report, *Argus,* June 3, 1866.

65. *Argus,* May 16, July 6, 1866; *Public Ledger,* July 2, 9, 1867.

66. *Argus,* May 20, 1866.

67. Keating, *Memphis,* I, 595.

68. E. B. Pickett to Jerry Frazer in the State Archives, quoted in Patton, *Unionism and Reconstruction,* p. 239.

69. *Municipal Report for 1872,* p. 56.

70. See Johnson's statement, *ibid.,* p. 56.

71. Keating, *Memphis,* I, 581.

72. *Public Ledger,* Aug. 3, 1867.

73. *Ibid.,* March 20, 1867.

74. *Ibid.,* March 14, 1868.

75. *Ibid.,* Aug. 29, 1867; Report of the Grand Jury, *ibid.,* March 25, 1868; *Argus,* Nov. 9, 1865.

76. Report of the Chief of Police, *Municipal Report for 1872,* p. 40.

77. *Argus,* June 27, 1865; Extract 3, General Order No. 170, Keating, *Memphis,* I, 559.

78. *Argus,* Nov. 4, 1865. The Nashville *Banner* also commented on this remarkable recovery.—*Ibid.,* Nov. 7, 1865.

79. History of Memphis Cotton Mills, *Argus,* May 13, 1866.

80. *Ibid.,* June 19, 1866.

81. Keating, *Memphis,* I, 576; *Commercial,* March 13, 1866.

82. *Bulletin,* May 7, 1863; *Argus,* April 17, 1866; *Public Ledger,* Oct. 5. 1867.

83. *Public Ledger,* June 5, 1869; Report of the Chamber of Commerce, 1866-67, Keating, *Memphis,* II 167.

84. *Public Ledger,* Feb. 6, 12, June 28, 1868; Nashville *Daily Free Press and Times,* May 6, 1868.

85. Pickett to Frazer, Patton, *Unionism and Reconstruction,* p. 239.

86. *Public Ledger,* Mar. 8, 1870; Keating, *Memphis,* II, 166-67. Memphis merchants constantly made formal protests against the cotton tax *(Argus,* May 31, 1866; *Public Ledger,* Oct. 24, 1867), and it was finally repealed in 1868.

87. *Public Ledger,* June 7, 1867.

88. Reports of the Chamber of Commerce for the years designated, Keating, *Memphis,* II, 162-68.

89. Half of the 1870 crop came from Arkansas.—*Avalanche,* Sept. 6, 1870. During this year the price at Memphis, prophetic of what the American farmer was to experience for the rest of the century, dropped from 33 cents to 18 cents a pound.

90. Keating, *Memphis,* I, 611.

91. *Ibid.,* I, 611.

92. See the extracts from Mississippi papers quoted in the *Public Ledger,* Sept. 15, Oct. 11, 1870.

Chapter VIII

1. Denis A. Quinn, *Heroes and Heroines of Memphis,* p. 18. Hereafter cited as *Heroes.* The best treatment of the subject in the nineteenth century was Daniel Drake, *A Systematic Treatise . . . on the Principal Diseases of the Interior Valley of North America* (Cincinnati, 1850).

2. *Report of the Board of Health, 1879,* pp. 19-20; Keating, *Memphis,* II, 300.

3. *Public Ledger,* Sept. 18, 1867.

4. "Memphis Mud and Filth," *Public Ledger,* Aug. 10, 20, 1867.

5. These figures, taken from Keating, *Memphis,* I, 677, are only approximate, and they have been corrected wherever possible.

6. Davis, *Memphis,* p. 310.

7. *Encyclopaedia Britannica* (14th edition), XXIII, 883.

8. On Reed's work see 61 Congress, 3 Session, *Senate Documents,* Vol. LXI.

9. When the sanitary measures of the eighties and nineties destroyed (accidentally) the breeding places of the mosquitoes in Memphis, yellow fever ceased to be a menace. *Aëdes aegypti,* however, may still be found in the Mississippi bottoms.

10. J. P. Dromgoole, *Yellow Fever Heroes, Heroines, and Horrors of 1873,* pp. 16 ff. Hereafter cited as *Yellow Fever.* Quinn, *Heroes,* pp. 231-34.

11. See the testimony of various doctors, nurses, and other individuals who had observed the fever at work, Dromgoole, *Yellow Fever,* pp. 19-60.

12. 61 Congress, 3 Session, *Senate Documents,* LXI, 207; Dromgoole, *Yellow Fever,* p. 10. Disinfectants were useless, and a single person with the germ in his blood could infect an entire community.

13. Dromgoole, *Yellow Fever,* p. 47.

14. J. M. Keating, *History of the Yellow Fever,* p. 103; Quinn, *Heroes,* p. 126; *Public Ledger,* March 1, 1878.

15. Quinn, *Heroes,* pp. 14-16.

16. Dromgoole, *Yellow Fever,* p. 17.

17. Richard Edwards, *In Memoriam of the Lamented Dead Who Fell in the Epidemic of 1873,* p. 25 (hereafter cited as *Epidemic of 1873*); *Report of the Yellow Fever among the Odd Fellows of Memphis in 1873,* p. 3. Hereafter cited as *Odd Fellows Report.*

18. *Louisville Medical Journal,* May, 1874, quoted in the *Odd Fellows Report,* pp. 3-5. Happy Hollow lay west of Front Street between Poplar and Market.

19. Edwards, *Epidemic of 1873,* p. 27.

20. *Odd Fellows Report,* p. 5.

21. *Ibid.,* p. 23; Edwards, *Epidemic of 1873,* p. 26.

22. Quinn, *Heroes,* p. 47; *Appeal,* Sept. 1, 1878.

23. Edwards, *Epidemic of 1873*, p. 59.

24. *Ibid.*, p. 60; *Odd Fellows Report*, p. 22. These two sources give detailed accounts of the work of all relief organizations.

25. Edwards, *Epidemic of 1873*, pp. 28-29. Quinn's memoir, definitely prejudiced since its author was a priest, is nevertheless the most valuable source for the real story of these epidemics of the seventies. Better still, it gives a graphic picture of the Irish Catholics in Memphis and of their relations with the Protestants.

26. *Odd Fellows Report*, p. 22; Edwards (*Epidemic of 1873*, p. 59) admits that his estimate of 1,664 deaths in 57 days is too conservative. The board of health reported a lower mortality (Young, *Standard History of Memphis*, p. 157), but its figures were always too low.—Quinn, *Heroes*, p. 216.

27. *Ibid.*, p. 43; Edwards, *Epidemic of 1873*, p. 59.

28. Reports of the Chamber of Commerce, Keating, *Memphis*, I, 645; II, 168. The assessment and tax rate varied from $24,542,315 at $2.00 per $100 in 1871 to $29,971,045 at $2.64 in 1875 to $19,998,166 at $3.00 in 1878.

29. Keating, *History of the Yellow Fever*, pp. 103-5.

30. *Report of the Central Relief Committee, 1878*, p. 6.

31. *Ibid.*, p. 7; Keating, *History of the Yellow Fever*, p. 107 n. By Aug. 13 there were already a dozen cases in the city.

32. *Report of the Central Relief Committee, 1878*, pp. 7-8; Keating, *History of the Yellow Fever*, p. 149; Quinn, *Heroes*, p. 130.

33. *Ibid.*, pp. 155-56; Keating, *History of the Yellow Fever*, pp. 107-8.

34. Quinn, *Heroes*, pp. 131-33.

35. *Ibid.*, p. 226. Jackson had only 8 cases of fever during the epidemic.

36. *Ibid.*, p. 27.

37. *Report of the Central Relief Committee, 1878*, pp. 9, 45.

38. Quinn, *Heroes*, p. 139. The *Avalanche* of Sept. 1 stated that there were 5,000 left. Quinn's figure represents the maximum population, and at times less than half that number were in the city.

39. *Report of the Central Relief Committee, 1878*, pp. 9, 18; *Avalanche*, Sept. 3, Oct. 2, 1878.

40. *Appeal*, Sept. 20, 1878.

41. *Public Ledger*, Sept. 20, 1878.

42. Keating, *History of the Yellow Fever*, p. 668; Dromgoole, *Yellow Fever*, p. 77.

43. *Ibid.*, p. 64.

44. Keating, *History of the Yellow Fever*, p. 113.

45. *Ibid.*, p. 130.

46. *Ibid.*, p. 130.

47. Dromgoole and Keating both recount vivid anecdotes of the plague which would fill a book by themselves.

48. Quinn, *Heroes*, p. 191.

49. Dromgoole, *Yellow Fever*, p. 63.

50. Keating, *History of the Yellow Fever*, p. 109.

51. *Avalanche*, Sept. 21, 1878; Dromgoole, *Yellow Fever*, pp. 107-25. In these pages appear reports from all tri-state towns.

52. *Avalanche*, Oct. 5, 10, 1878; Dromgoole, *Yellow Fever*, pp. 110-16; Keating, *History of the Yellow Fever*, pp. 142-43.

53. *Ibid.*, p. 116 n.; Quinn, *Heroes*, p. 216. One undertaker stated that he would testify under oath that more than 200 were buried in a single day, though the highest estimate of the board of health was little more than 100. On Sept. 17 the *Avalanche* listed the names of 208 persons alleged to have died on the previous day, but the estimate of the Associated Press for the same date was 127.—*Public Ledger*, Nov. 26, 1878.

54. Whites, 4,204 out of 5,600; blacks, 946 out of 12,000.

55. Quinn, *Heroes*, p. 214.

56. *Report of the Board of Health, 1879*, p. 5; Keating, *Memphis*, I, 676.

57. *Public Ledger*, Sept. 3, Oct. 18, 1879.

58. The secretary of the state board of health, ex-Mayor Johnson, estimated the mortality at 587 out of 2,010 (whites, 470 out of 1,298; blacks, 117 out of 702). Quinn (*Heroes*, p. 214) estimated the dead at 800.

59. See particularly T. J. Wertenbaker, *Norfolk, Historic Southern Port* (Durham, N. C., 1931), pp. 206-16.

60. H. E. Sigerist, *History of American Medicine*, pp. 234, 239.

61. C. E. A. Winslow, *Hermann Biggs* (Philadelphia, 1929) is an exhaustive study of Biggs' work in public health.

62. Sigerist, *op. cit.*, pp. 235-36.

63. Winslow, *op. cit.*, p. 41.

64. At once Norfolk and Nashville installed sewerage systems, and within a few years numerous cities followed their example.—Wertenbaker, *op. cit.*, p. 273. G. E. Waring, *Sewerage and Land Drainage* (New York, 1889) gives a general history of this movement.

65. Keating, *Memphis*, I, 624. Two thirds of this amount consisted of taxes due since 1870.

66. Report of the President of the Taxing-District, Dec. 31, 1885, *Memphis Merchants' Exchange Directory, 1885*, p. 40.

67. This report is printed in full in the *Appeal*, Jan. 12, 1875, under the caption "A Bad Movement—The Liberties of the People Endangered."

68. Keating, *Memphis*, I, 623-43. Though a prominent local journalist, Keating sided with the conservatives and took an active part in the fight to repeal the charter. He therefore is an excellent authority for the intimate details of the movement.

69. *Memphis Digest, 1876*, pp. 9-35.

70. *Acts of the State of Tennessee*, 41 General Assembly, Chap. X.

71. A taxing-district bill was drawn up by City Attorney S. P. Walker in the middle seventies, but the final bill was the work of George Gantt, who was assisted by other local lawyers, Judge C. W. Heiskell in particular.

72. *Digest of the Taxing-District, 1879*, pp. 1-43.

73. The State Supreme Court rendered its decision in 1879.—*Luehrmann* vs. *the City of Memphis*, 2 Lea 425. The decision of the Federal Supreme Court came in 1880.—102 U. S. 472. Since 1879 there have been three major modifications of this act. In 1893 the state surrendered direct control over the local government and the name "City of Memphis" was restored. In 1905 both boards were enlarged and a bicameral council established. In 1909 the commission form of government was adopted.—*Memphis Digest, 1931*, Preface, p. ix.

74. C. F. Vance, *Past and Future of Memphis*, p. 7.

75. Department of the Interior, *Bulletin of the Bureau of Education*, L, 13.

76. Quinn, *Heroes*, pp. vii, 214.

77. Keating, *Memphis*, II, 288. Its membership was formerly 350.

78. See above, Table IX, p. 164.

79. See above, Table I, p. 45.

80. In the seventies the *Iron Age*, a New York industrial sheet, made this comment: "At Memphis coal from Kentucky, used with iron ores of like cast, should make it one of our greatest manufacturing centers—coal and iron being obtainable from the Alabama fields cheaper than they can be delivered at St. Louis."—*Memphis: Past, Present, and Future*, p. 82.

81. Rice-Stix & Co. (wholesale dry goods) was the largest concern to move to St. Louis, but Hill-Fontaine & Co. (cotton), Hill, Ferry, & Mitchell (wholesale shoes), Thomas Hallen & Co. (cotton), and several other firms joined the exodus.

Chapter IX

1. Keating, *Memphis*, I, 678.

2. *Report of the Board of Health, 1879*, pp. 8-12; *Commercial Appeal*, Oct. 31, 1900. Colonel George A. Waring of Newport, R. I., presented his plan in 1879 to a meeting of the American Public Health Association in Nashville, at which representatives from Memphis were present. The bluff city was the first to install it, but within a decade 37 other towns had followed its example and Europe watched the experiment with interest.

3. *Report of the Taxing-District, 1880-82*, map; *Memphis Digest, 1892*, p. 7.

4. *Art Supplement to the Evening Scimitar*, Oct., 1891, pp. 50-52; John Lundie, *Report on the Waterworks System of Memphis*, 1898. The water company was privately owned until 1903, when it was purchased by the city.

5. Nineteen for whites, 25 for Negroes. There are complete board of health reports for the years 1879-1900. See in particular the reports for 1879 (p. 12), and 1898 (pp. 7-9). See also *Survey of Health Problems and Facilities in Memphis and Shelby Co., 1929*, pp. 11-13.

6. Fever threatened in 1888, 1897, 1898, and 1905.

7. *Taxing-District Report, 1880-82*, p. 8.

8. *Meriwether* vs. *Garrett*, 102 U. S. 472 (Oct., 1880); *Amy* vs. *Shelby Co.*, 114 U. S. 387 (1884).

9. *O'Connor* vs. *the City of Memphis*, 6 Lea 730. The debt of the old city was in the hands of two receivers, one appointed by federal and the other by state courts.

10. *Acts of the General Assembly of Tennessee, 1883*, Chap. 170; *1885*, Chap. 14; *Extra Sess., 1885*, Chap. 2; *1887*, Chap. 41; *1895*, Chap. 56.

11. Report of the President of the Taxing-District, *Memphis Merchants' Exchange Report, 1885*, pp. 40-45.

12. *Art Supplement*, 1891, pp. 49, 54.

13. *Art Supplement of the Evening Scimitar*, 1899, p. 55.

14. *City Directory, 1893*, pp. 33-34.

15. This library, endowed by F. H. Cossitt, a native son who had prospered in New York, was the first institution of its kind large enough to serve the needs of the city. The endowment was later supplemented by annual appropriations from municipal taxes. Prior to the founding of the Cossitt Library, the Bar Association and the Odd Fellows each operated a small library.

16. Andrew Morrison in his *Memphis, the Bluff City,* gives a vivid description of the physical appearance of Memphis in 1891. His work contains many illustrations, as do also the art supplements of the *Scimitar* for 1891 and 1899. Volume I of *Art Work in Memphis* includes hundreds of etchings of public buildings and private homes.

17. *Appeal-Avalanche,* July 3, 1891, p. 4.

18. C. D. Warner, "Studies in the South and West," *Harper's Magazine,* LXXVII, 351-57; Young, *Standard History of Memphis,* p. 230.

19. *Memphis Digest, 1898,* pp. 79-85. There were further amendments in 1895 and 1899.

20. Letter of L. B. McFarland in the *Commercial Appeal,* Dec. 29, 1899.

21. L. B. McFarland, *Memoirs and Addresses,* pp. 117-43. Later an eleven-mile strip between these parks was bought and converted into a driveway.

22. *Art Supplement, 1899,* pp. 6-7. The actual gain in population within the old corporation limits between 1890 and 1900 was therefore nearer twenty than forty thousand, and part of the increase in the percentage of Negroes was due to the annexation of the formerly untaxed districts outside the city where they had congregated: see above, map on the territorial growth of Memphis. The National Bureau of Education rejected the federal census returns of 1900 for Memphis as unreliable.

23. *Twelfth Census of the United States,* Vol. VI, plate 18.

24. *Prosperity Edition of the Commercial Appeal,* Dec. 30, 1913, p. 8; *Call of the Alluvial Empire* (Pamphlets published by the Southern Alluvial Land Assoc. in 1917 and 1919); see also accompanying map on the Memphis hinterland.

25. Nashville and Atlanta, several hundred miles to the east, were unfavorably located for this trade and the Texas towns were as yet too small.

26. Reports of the Memphis Merchants' Exchange, 1883-88. Those for 1889-1900 have been lost.

26a. Increase in Population in Memphis Hinterland with Density Per Square Mile

Section	Area in square miles	1840 Total population	1840 Population per square mile	1860 Total population	1860 Population per square mile
Shelby County	801	14,721	18.4	48,092	60.0
Tennessee Hinterland	2,721	60,169	22.1	79,592	29.3
West Tennessee	6,632	102,687	15.5	165,505	24.9
Yazoo Delta	5,516	18,396	3.3	63,825	11.6
North Mississippi	12,192	116,783	9.6	293,329	24.1
St. Francis Basin	2,360	2,971	1.3	18,803	7.1
East Arkansas	9,193	18,153	2.0	73,007	7.9
Total	39,415	333,880	8.4	742,052	18.8

Section	1880 Total population	1880 Population per square mile	1900 Total population	1900 Population per square mile	1930 Total population	1930 Population per square mile
Shelby County	78,430	97.9	153,557	191.7	306,482	382.6
Tennessee Hinterland	116,796	42.9	129,110	47.7	128,051	47.1
West Tennessee	237,460	35.8	300,140	45.3	337,251	50.9
Yazoo Delta	121,580	22.0	231,388	41.9	402,311	72.9
North Mississippi	408,553	33.5	465,463	38.2	507,442	41.6
St. Francis Basin	30,650	13.0	64,734	27.4	182,089	77.2
East Arkansas	130,788	14.2	230,906	25.1	393,101	42.8
Total	1,124,257	28.7	1,575,298	39.9	2,256,727	57.2

27. *Memphis: Past, Present, and Future* (1883), p. 76; Morrison, *Memphis, the Bluff City,* p. 101. For the period between 1878 and 1883 there are no local statistics except on cotton. The Chamber of Commerce dissolved in 1878 and the Merchants' Exchange was not formed until 1883. Until the organization of the Business Men's Club in 1900, half a dozen trade associations carried on the work of the old Chamber of Commerce.

28. *City Directory, 1891,* p. 25; *Cotton Exchange Directory, 1897,* p. 78.

29. *Art Supplement, 1899,* p. 16.

30. *Ibid.,* p. 65; *Cotton Exchange Directory, 1897,* p. 43; *Appeal-Avalanche,* Oct. 31, 1900.

31. U. B. Phillips, "Railway Transportation in the South," *The South in the Building of the Nation,* VI, 315.

32. See above, Chapter VII.

33. *Merchants' Exchange Report, 1883,* pp. 10-11; *Memphis: Past, Present, and Future,* pp. 21, 42.

34. This Birmingham road, started soon after the war by General Forrest as the Memphis and Holly Springs, became successively the Memphis, Selma, and Brunswick, the Memphis and Atlantic, and finally the Kansas City, Memphis, and Birmingham.

35. *Art Supplement, 1899,* p. 24. Jay Gould was particularly interested in Memphis.

36. *Merchants' Exchange Report, 1883,* p. 48; *1887,* p. 29.

37. *Ibid., 1884,* p. 49; *Art Supplement, 1899,* p. 73.

38. *Art Supplement, 1891,* p. 47; *Merchants' Exchange Report, 1886,* pp. 332-34; Morrison, *Memphis, the Bluff City,* p. 16.

39. See the proceedings of the conventions at Memphis in 1887, 1899, and 1907.

40. *The South in the Building of the Nation,* VI, 347.

41. Morrison, *Memphis, the Bluff City,* pp. 90-98.

42. *Ibid.,* p. 101. The various sources referred to above contain much information on the character and history of individual firms. Some of the more famous were: J. T. Fargason & Co.; Oliver-Finnie; Fly, Hern, & Hobson; Hill-Fontaine & Co.; Brooks-Neely & Co.; Geo. Arnold & Co.; M. Gavin & Co.; J. R. Godwin & Co.; Schoolfield-Hanauer & Co.; Porter & McRae; E. M. Apperson & Co.; P. McCadden & Co.; Fulmer-Thornton & Co.; Taylor & Duffin; J. G. Frank & Co.; Mallory-Crawford & Co.; Toof, McGowan & Co.

43. Morrison, *Memphis, the Bluff City,* pp. 85-89; *Art Supplement, 1899,* p. 9.

44. *Ibid.,* p. 10.

45. *Merchants' Exchange Report, 1888,* p. 25; Morrison, *Memphis, the Bluff City,* p. 101.

46. *Ibid.,* pp. 101-2.

47. *Ibid.,* pp. 105-8; *Merchants' Exchange Report, 1885,* pp. 103-6; *1888,* p. 23.

48. *The South in the Building of the Nation,* VI, 152-53.

49. *Art Supplement, 1899,* p. 63; J. T. Grady, *City of Memphis, Tennessee, and Vicinity, and their Resources,* section on lumber. Hereafter cited as *City of Memphis.*

50. *Art Supplement, 1899,* p. 63; *Merchants' Exchange Report, 1883,* p. 24; *1887,* p. 65.

51. *Ibid.,* p. 65.

52. Grady, *City of Memphis,* section on lumber.

53. *Art Supplement, 1899,* p. 65.

54. *Southern Lumberman's* estimate of lumber handled in Memphis during the year 1906:

	Feet	*Value*
Sawed in Memphis	445,875,000	$11,440,200
Logs to cooperage plants by water	46,920,000	434,700
Logs to cooperage plants by rail	42,400,000	625,950
Sawed by Memphis firms outside city	200,675,000	4,281,200
Direct shipments from mills and yards outside city	116,900,000	2,925,500
Handled through Memphis firms	41,400,000	1,875,000
Total	894,210,000	$21,582,550

55. *Merchants' Exchange Report, 1886,* p. 37. These reports describe the manufacturing interests fully. See particularly C. O. Shepherd, "Our Lumber Interests," and R. Gates, "Needs of Memphis"; *Art Supplement, 1899,* pp. 42-43, 52. These articles were written by northerners who settled in Memphis.

56. *Tenth Census of the United States, Manufactures,* p. 411; *Eleventh Census,* II, 330-33; *Twelfth Census,* II, 858-59.

57. Morrison, *Memphis, the Bluff City,* p. 132; *Memphis: Past, Present, and Future,* pp. 20-22.

58. *The South in the Building of the Nation,* VI, 282.

59. *Merchants' Exchange Report, 1883,* p. 30; *1885,* p. 64.

60. See note 56, above.

61. National Board of Education, *Bulletin,* 1919, L. Between 1880 and 1900 neither the migration from the North nor that from abroad was considerable. Of the Negro parents in 1918, 4 per cent were born in Memphis and 80 per cent in the tri-states outside.

62. *Art Supplement, 1899,* p. 22.

63. A memorandum might be scrawled in longhand for purposes of record, however. This statement is based on the unanimous testimony of all the survivors of the nineties whom I have interviewed, and it is certainly no old wives' tale.

64. Morrison, *Memphis, the Bluff City,* p. 9.

65. *Art Supplement, 1899,* pp. 61-64.

66. *Ibid.*

67. Morrison, *Memphis, the Bluff City,* pp. 24 ff.; *Harper's Magazine,* LXXVII, 55 ff.

68. *Art Supplement, 1899,* p. 57. The Nineteenth Century Club was organized in 1890, three years after the formation of the Beethoven Club, a musical society for women only.

69. *Prosperity Edition of the Commercial Appeal,* Dec. 30, 1913, p. 16.

70. *Art Supplement, 1891,* p. 41.

71. In 1899 there were only three public school buildings, two white and one colored, the first of which was erected in 1869. During the nineties appropriations were increased and several new schools were constructed, but the

system remained in dire need of reform.—*Art Supplement, 1891*, pp. 33 ff.; *1899*, p. 58. The following figures are from the *Report of the Tennessee Department of Public Instruction, 1895-96*, pp. 245-46.

Statistics for 1895		
Scholastic population		17,000
	White	*Negro*
Enrollment	4,200	2,677
Average attendance	2,908	1,386
Teachers	91	33

72. The Memphis Typographical Union No. 11, formed in the fifties, was apparently the only local trade union until the Marine Engineers organized a chapter in 1880. In 1883 for the first time, the city directory lists 35 local unions, unconnected with the Knights of Labor or any other national body. Trade unions affiliated with a national organization increased slowly in the eighties.—*City Directories* for 1880-1900.

73. G. W. Lee, *Beale Street, Where the Blues Began*, p. 287.

74. *Ibid.*, p. 240. Since 1905 there have been no black policemen.

75. Quinn, *Heroes*, p. 186. In 1891 the Negroes had 23 Baptist and 10 Methodist churches. Their 37 churches, all Protestant, equalled the total number of white churches, both Protestant and Catholic.—*Art Supplement, 1891*, pp. 33 ff.

76. *City Directory, 1893*.

77. Lee, *Beale Street*, p. 1.

78. *Art Supplement, 1891*, p. 49; *1899*, p. 70.

79. Lee's book is valuable as a subjective work that reveals what the Negro thinks about himself, but not as an objective study of Beale Street. The author is an intelligent man, but obviously one without the training necessary for the task to which he set himself. In spots his treatment lacks realism and there is no reference whatever to sources. His book suffers from his own prejudice and vanity, and it pictures Beale Street as Broadway likes to think it is. In spite of its faults, however, it is a better piece of work than many white men could have done.

80. *City Directory, 1892*, p. 59. The Chickasaw Guards won first honors in several nation-wide meets.

81. Hamer, *History of Tennessee*, II, 705.

82. See election returns in the *Appeal-Avalanche*, 1880, 1884, 1888.

83. Hamer, *History of Tennessee*, II, 694.

84. *Appeal-Avalanche*, Oct. 26, 1892; *Art Supplement, 1899*, p. 14.

85. *Appeal-Avalanche*, Oct. 26, 1892.

86. *Ibid.*, Nov. 5, 1896; the vote was 2,805 to 2,653. The county as a whole gave Bryan a 600 majority.

87. In 1900, Memphis voted two-to-one for Bryan.—*Commercial Appeal*, Nov. 7, 1900. In 1904 it voted four-to-one for Parker.—*Morning News*, Nov. 10, 1904.

88. *Appeal-Avalanche*, July 6, 1891.

BIBLIOGRAPHICAL STATEMENT

The sources used in this study are located in the Cossitt Library in Memphis, the Tennessee State Library in Nashville, and the Library of Congress. The last has only a few items which cannot be duplicated in Memphis, and what little material exists in the state archives in Nashville is in such a poor state of organization that it was not feasible to attempt to use it. When the archives are properly catalogued, some new material may come to light, but at present practically all the sources for the history of Memphis are to be found in the Cossitt Library.

A. Primary Sources

I. GENERAL

Local newspapers, including quotations from papers in other cities, are the chief primary source used in this study. Those cited are to be found in the stacks of the Cossitt Library, where there are files covering almost completely the period from 1836 to 1900. Omissions can often be supplied from the Collier file in the basement or from the files of the state library. The *Appeal* is used consistently for the ante-bellum period, but such numbers of the *Enquirer* as still exist are valuable for the Whig viewpoint. The *Bulletin,* the *Eagle,* and the *Avalanche* are also cited for this period.

Since the *Appeal* was published outside of Memphis after May, 1862, its value ceases during the war period, and the *Argus,* the *Public Ledger,* the *Bulletin,* the *Avalanche,* the *Commercial,* and the *Post* have been substituted. For the years after 1870 the *Appeal-Avalanche* is most reliable, and the *Evening Scimitar* and the *Commercial Appeal* are full of information.

Belonging with the newspapers, also, is J. D. Davis's *History of Memphis and the Old Times Papers,* Memphis, 1873. It is by far the most valuable source for the period prior to 1850. This work is not an actual history but a memoir, consisting of scores of articles written for the newspapers over a thirty-year period, by a man who took an active part in municipal affairs from 1824 until the late seventies. Though often inaccurate as to dates, this memoir is unerring as to the sentiments of the inhabitants on various questions. It catches the flavor of the times, and it is written with such catholicity of taste and ease of style that it reads like a novel.

The Old Folks Record, published monthly from October, 1874, to September, 1875, by the Old Folks of Shelby County, contains hundreds of articles on early history written by contemporaries. In it may be found also a few official records.

J. M. Keating's *History of Memphis* (2 vols. Syracuse, 1886. Vol. II ed. by O. F. Vedder) is included among the primary sources because it contains quotations from numerous sources no longer in existence, and because it is a memoir for the post-bellum period. Keating is highly unreadable—his work is really a fourth-rate history of Tennessee and the United States, with Memphis coming in for mention on every third page. Its paragraphs run on for pages; it is often inaccurate and lacks any semblance of organization other than a rough chronological one. Nevertheless, it is an encyclopedia of Memphis history if used with discrimination.

Numerous letters have been used, particularly for the proprietary era; their location is indicated in the footnotes.

DeBow's Review (46 vols., 1846-1880) and the *American Railroad Journal* (1832-1911) have been cited frequently for the economic history of the ante-bellum period.

The following works deal with the yellow fever epidemics:

Dromgoole, J. P. *Yellow Fever Heroes, Heroines, and Horrors of 1878.* Louisville, 1879.

Edwards, Richard. *In Memoriam of the Lamented Dead Who Fell in the Epidemic of 1873.* Memphis, 1873.

Keating, J. M. *History of the Yellow Fever.* Memphis, 1879.

Quinn, Denis A. *Heroes and Heroines of Memphis.* Providence, 1887. (This deserves special mention. Quinn as a Catholic priest who labored in Memphis for many years gives an intimate picture of its several thousand Irish inhabitants, and his memoir, therefore, is valuable entirely apart from the story it tells of the yellowjack.)

Report of the Central Relief Committee. Memphis, 1878.

Report of the Yellow Fever among the Odd Fellows of Memphis in 1873. Memphis, 1874.

For the study of the new city, 1880-1900, the sources increase. The *Art Supplement* of the *Evening Scimitar* for 1891, 1899, and 1903, as well as the "Prosperity Edition" of the *Commercial Appeal,* December 30, 1913, are mines of information, containing authentic articles on many phases of contemporary economic and social life. The Reports of the Memphis Merchants' Exchange, of which only those for the years 1883-1888 remain, and the *Memphis Cotton Exchange Directory,* 1897, are even fuller of economic history.

After 1880 several surveys of Memphis were made by contemporaries, both natives and outsiders. These works are as objective as their authors were capable of making them, and if the proper discount is subtracted for enthusiasm, they may be considered legitimate source material. Included in these surveys are the following:

Grady, J. T. *City of Memphis, Tennessee, and Vicinity, and Their Resources.* Memphis, 1907.

Memphis, Past, Present, and Future. Memphis, 1883.

Morrison, Andrew. *Memphis, the Bluff City* ("Englehart Series of American Cities"). St. Louis, 1892.

Rippy, J. *Index, Map, and Business Guide of Memphis.* Memphis, 1888.

Warner, C. D. "Studies in the South and West," *Harper's Magazine,* Vol. LXXVII (1889).

Other general primary sources consist of several volumes of *Memphis Theater Programs* for the years, 1859-60, 1871-78, and of *Art Works of Memphis,* Vol. I (Chicago, 1895), which contains hundreds of etchings of private homes and public buildings.

II. OFFICIAL AND SEMI-OFFICIAL RECORDS OF MEMPHIS

Official municipal documents of Memphis are scarce, and there has apparently been little effort to preserve them. Those which have been saved are copies of the *Memphis Digest* for the years, 1857, 1860, 1863, 1867, 1873, 1876, 1879, 1886, 1892, and 1898. These contain the city's charter, the amendments to it, and local ordinances. Also available are *Municipal Reports* for the years 1872, 1879-1900, *Reports of the Board of Health* for the years 1874, 1879-1900, and the *Manual of the Board of Education,* 1884.

Far more important, however, than the documents of a strictly official nature are the city directories and annual reports of the Chamber of Commerce. Directories exist for the years 1849, 1855, 1856, 1859, 1860, 1865-1900, and they are full of economic and social statistics. The first report of the Chamber of Commerce appeared in the *Appeal,* September 4, 1861, and several excerpts from later reports are given in Keating's *History of Memphis,* Vol. II. The Chamber of Commerce dissolved during the epidemic of 1878, but it was customary, from 1860 on, for the newspapers to give a résumé of trade in Memphis annually, on September 1 or January 1.

Other official and semi-official sources are as follows:

Journal of the Proceedings of the Southern Convention Assembled Oct. 23, 1845. Memphis, 1845.

Memphis Abstract Company, Records.

"Memphis Riots and Massacres," 39 Congress, 1 Session, *House Report,* No. 101.

Meriwether vs. *Garrett.* 102 U. S. 472.

Minutes and Proceedings of the Memphis Convention Assembled Oct. 23, 1849. Memphis, 1850.

"Minutes of the First County Court to 1826," *Old Folks Record,* pp. 372 ff.

National Plan of an Atlantic and Pacific Railroad and the Remarks of Albert Pike Made thereon at Memphis, November, 1849. Little Rock, 1849.

"Original Agreement of the Proprietors of Memphis," *Old Folks Record,* p. 557.

Petition for Relief by the Creditors of Memphis, Memphis, 1878.

Proceedings of the Board of Mayor and Aldermen of Memphis on the Subject of a Western Armory, and a Naval Depot and Dockyard at Memphis. Memphis, 1842.

Proceedings of the Chamber of Commerce of the City of Memphis in Favor of the Repeal of the Cotton Tax, 1867. Memphis, 1867.

Proceedings of the Chamber of Commerce of the City of Memphis: Memorial to Congress, 1871. Memphis, 1871.

Proceedings of the Southern and Western Commercial Convention, 1853. Memphis, 1854.

Register's Office of Shelby and Davidson Counties, Reports.

Report on the Public Water Supply for the City of Memphis. Memphis, 1886.

Official sources of more than a local nature which have been used extensively in this study are the following:

Moore, Frank, comp. *Rebellion Record.* 11 vols. New York, 1861-1868.

United States Census Reports.

War of the Rebellion, The: A Compilation of the Official Records of the Union and Confederate Armies. 130 vols. Washington, 1880-1901.

III. MEMOIRS AND PERSONAL ACCOUNTS

Memoirs of travelers and citizens have been particularly sought for this study, but only the more important will be listed here:

Adair, James. *The History of the American Indians; . . .* London, 1775.

Ashe, Thomas. *Travels in America Performed in 1806. . . .* 3 vols. London, 1808.

Bradbury, John. *Travels in the Interior of America in the Years 1809, 1810, and* 1811. . . . Liverpool, 1817.

Cuming, Fortesque. *Sketches of a Tour to the Western Country, through the states of Ohio and Kentucky; . . .* Pittsburgh, 1810.

Davis, Reuben. *Recollections of Mississippi and Mississippians.* Boston and New York, 1889.

Hallum, John. *Diary of an Old Lawyer.* Nashville, 1895.

Journal of the Chickasaw War, 1739-40, kept by an unknown French soldier. Translated and printed in full in J. F. H. Claiborne, *History of Mississippi,* Jackson, 1880.

Knox, T. W. *Campfire and Cottonfield.* New York, 1865.

McFarland, L. B. *Memoirs and Addresses.* Memphis, 1922.

Official Letterbooks of W. C. C. Claiborne. Ed. Dunbar Rowland. Jackson, 1917.

Olmsted, Frederick Law. *Journey in the Back Country.* 2 vols. New York, 1860.

Rawlings, J. J. *Reminiscenses.* Memphis, 1895.

Schultz, Christian Jun. *Travels on an Inland Voyage through the States of New-York, Pennsylvania, Virginia, Ohio, Kentucky and Tennessee, . . . in the years 1807 and 1808.* 2 vols. in one. New York, 1810.

Sherman, W. T. *Memoirs.* 2nd ed. New York, 1889.

Trollope, Frances. *Domestic Manners of the Americans.* 2 vols. London, 1832.

Vance, C. F. *Past and Future of Memphis.* Memphis, 1892.

Williams, Samuel Cole, ed. *Early Travels in the Tennessee Country, 1540-1800.* Johnson City, 1928.

Williams, J. S. *Old Times in West Tennessee.* Memphis, 1873.

B. Secondary Works

I. GENERAL

Three secondary works must be mentioned specifically in regard to the history of Memphis. J. P. Young's *Standard History of Memphis* (Knoxville, 1912) is typical of the voluminous, prejudiced, and sentimental books that have been written on local history. As to genealogy, it is fair, but it does not deserve to rank as serious history. It shows little evidence of careful research, and much of it is taken outright, and often verbatim, from Keating and Davis. In Young's defense it should be stated that his relation to the work was that of editor, and that most of the actual writing was probably done by a woman secretary. The Judge was too virile a man to have penned such stuff.

Unquestionably the best history of Tennessee is T. P. Abernethy's *From Frontier to Plantation in Tennessee* (Chapel Hill, 1932), but it ends with the year 1860.

One of the few objective studies on early state history, S. C. Williams' *Beginnings of West Tennessee, 1541-1841* (Johnson City, 1930), gives an excellent background for the history of Memphis.

The latest work on Tennessee, covering the entire period, is Philip M. Hamer's *History of Tennessee.* 3 vols. New York, 1933.

Older state histories, on the whole of little value, are the following:

Goodspeed Publishing Company, *History of Tennessee.* Shelby County Edition. Nashville, 1877.

Haywood, John. *The Civil and Political History of the State of Tennessee, from the Earliest Settlement up to the Year 1796;* . . . Knoxville, 1823.

Killebrew, J. B. *Resources of Tennessee.* Nashville, 1874.

Phelan, James. *History of Tennessee: the Making of a State.* Boston, 1888.

Other pertinent secondary works include the following:

Clemens, Samuel (Mark Twain). *Life on the Mississippi.* Boston, 1883.

Coates, Robert. *The Outlaw Years.* New York, 1930. (Exaggerated, but good reading.)

Cole, A. C. *The Whig Party in the South.* Washington, 1913.

Gould, E. W. *Fifty Years on the Mississippi.* St. Louis, 1889. (An excellent history of navigation on the river.)

Lee, G. W. *Beale Street, Where the Blues Began.* New York, 1934. (Definitely spectacular, but written by a Memphis Negro.)

Lewis, Lloyd. *Sherman, Fighting Prophet.* New York, 1932.

Malone, J. H. *The Chickasaw Nation.* Louisville, 1922. (Poor, but the only complete study of the Chickasaws.)

Monette, J. W. *History of the Valley of the Mississippi.* 2 vols. New York, 1846. (Old-fashioned in method, but still useful.)

Phillips, U. B. *American Negro Slavery.* New York, 1918.

———, *Life and Labor in the Old South*. Boston, 1929.

Rowland, Dunbar, ed. *Symposium on the Place of Discovery of the Mississippi River*. Jackson, 1927.

Shea, J. G. *Discovery and Exploration of the Mississippi River*. Redfield, N. Y., 1852.

Sigerist, H. E. *History of American Medicine*. New York, 1934.

South in the Building of the Nation, The. 12 vols. Richmond, 1909. (Vol. VI, *Economic History*, has been used particularly.)

Whitaker, A. P. *The Spanish-American Frontier, 1783-1795*. Boston, 1927.

———, *The Mississippi Question, 1795-1803*. New York and London, 1934.

Winsor, Justin. *The Mississippi Basin. The Struggle in America between England and France, 1697-1763*. Boston, 1895.

II. MONOGRAPHS AND MAGAZINE ARTICLES

Abernethy, T. P. "Origin of the Whig Party in Tennessee," *Miss. Val. Hist. Rev.*, XII, 504-22.

Bancroft, F. *Slave-trading in the Old South*. Baltimore, 1931.

Brooks, A. L. "Early Plans for Railroads in West Tennessee," *Tenn. Hist. Mag.*, Ser. II, Vol. III (Oct., 1932), pp. 25-39.

Carson, W. W. "Transportation and Traffic on the Ohio and the Mississippi before the Steamboat," *Miss. Val. Hist. Rev.*, VII, 26-38.

Cole, A. C. "Nativism in the Lower Mississippi Valley," *Proceedings of the Mississippi Valley Historical Association*, VI, 258-76.

Cotterill, R. S. "Beginnings of Railroads in the Southwest," *Miss. Val. Hist. Rev.*, VIII, 318-27.

———, "Memphis Railroad Convention, 1849," *Tenn. Hist. Mag.*, IV, 83-95.

———, "Southern Railroads and Western Trade, 1840-50," *Miss. Val. Hist. Rev.*, III, 431 ff.

———, "Southern Railroads, 1850-60," *Miss. Val. Hist. Rev.*, X, 396-405.

Coulter, E. M. "Commercial Intercourse with the Confederacy in the Mississippi Valley," *Miss. Val. Hist. Rev.*, V, 377-96.

Dewitt, J. H. "General James Winchester," *Tenn. Hist. Mag.*, I, 79-106, 183-205.

Halley, R. A. "A Rebel Newspaper's War Story," *Tenn. Hist. Mag.*, VIII, 124-53.

James, J. A. "Spanish Influence in the West during the American Revolution," *Miss. Val. Hist. Rev.*, IV, 193-208.

Johnson, R. W. "Geographical Influences in the Location and Growth of Memphis," *Journal of Geography*, XXVII, 85-97.

Lumpkin, J. W. "Memphis and Its Manufacturing Advantages," *DeBow's Review*, X, 525-29.

Patton, J. W. *Unionism and Reconstruction in Tennessee.* Chapel Hill, 1934.

Puckett, E. P. "The Attempt of New Orleans to Meet the Crisis in Her Trade with the West," *Proceedings of the Mississippi Valley Historical Association*, X, 481-95.

Report on the Public School System of Memphis. Department of the Interior, Bureau of Education, Bulletin (1919), Vol. L. (An extensive survey, conducted in 1918, by a commission of experts, which sheds some light on the period of the nineties.)

Robinson, J. H. "A Social History of the Negro in Memphis and Shelby County." Unpublished Yale doctoral dissertation in sociology. 1934. (Poor and rather superficial, but the only scientific study of the Memphis Negro.)

Scroggs, W. O. "Early Trade and Travel in the Lower Mississippi Valley," *Proceedings of the Mississippi Valley Historical Association,* II, 235-56.

Sioussat, S. G. L. "Memphis as a Gateway to the West," *Tenn. Hist. Mag.,* III, 1-27, 77-114.

Waterman, W. W. *Frances Wright.* "Columbia University Studies," Vol. CXV, No. 1. New York, 1924.

Way, R. B. "Commerce of the Lower Mississippi in the Period 1830-1860," *Proceedings of the Mississippi Valley Historical Association,* X, 57-69.

Wilson, M. L. "The Collapse of Steamboat Traffic on the Mississippi," *Proceedings of the Mississippi Valley Historical Association,* IX, 422-40.

Winston, J. E. "Notes on the Economic History of New Orleans," *Miss. Val. Hist. Rev.,* XI, 200-27.

Young, J. P. "Fort Prudhomme," *Tenn. Hist. Mag.,* II. 235-44.

INDEX

MEMPHIS

SATRAPY OF A BENEVOLENT DESPOT

By Dr. Gerald M. Capers

"WE DON'T HAVE politics in Memphis," Edward Crump remarked in New Orleans to a *Times-Picayune* reporter who asked the Memphian to comment on the fight to oust Mayor Maestri, last of Huey Long's lieutenants. In reply to the reporter's query regarding the "rumor" that "he was pretty good friends with the Mayor of Memphis," Crump continued:

"Of course we're friends. We've been friends for years. That's just the point I'm trying to make. We don't need politics in Memphis. It's all a question of brotherly love and affection. And clean government, of course. The same party always wins. I have been elected to various offices twenty-three times. I was Mayor of Memphis four times, among other things. I served in Congress. I have assisted in seventy-nine general elections without defeat, which makes one hundred and two in all."

In this simple fashion "Mister" Crump explained the basis of his rule in Memphis. But the historical development of this "brotherly love" has had its complexities.

The contemporary period of Crump's absolute power, which began with the election of his Overton-Davis ticket in 1927, was the result

GERALD M. CAPERS, educator and writer, was reared in Memphis and is the author of *Biography of a River Town,* the story of Memphis in the nineteenth century. He has taught at Yale and is now Chairman of the History Department at Newcomb College of Tulane University.

of personal ambition and the culmination of a long-range plan executed with a high degree of adroit political opportunism. His present role is that of an omnipotent but extra-legal city manager. The unique methods by which he achieved and has retained his power without organized opposition since 1927 evolved naturally out of two earlier and different periods of less complete control.

In the first period, beginning with his election as a "reform" mayor in 1909, Crump was twice re-elected by large majorities. Apparently well on his way to a coveted absolutism, he was ousted by court action late in 1915 on the "technicality" of his failure to enforce the Tennessee prohibition law. In the second period, despite his ousting, he was elected to the lucrative office of County Trustee, which reputedly paid in fees from thirty-five to fifty thousand dollars a year. After holding this post for eight years, Crump retired in 1924 to give full time to the firm of Crump and Trezevant, a real-estate, mortgage, and insurance business, in which he had previously invested as a "silent" partner.

This apparent retirement from politics ended abruptly three years later with the overwhelming victory of the "Crump" ticket over the incumbent Mayor Rowlett Paine and his commissioners. Thus, in the decade after 1916, Crump consolidated his control of Shelby County, increased his prestige in the state through that control, launched a business enterprise which was to make him a millionaire, and, by patient, persistent tactics of infiltration, regained his dominant position in municipal affairs as an unofficial super-mayor.

The Horatio Alger story of this redheaded country lad from Holly Springs, Mississippi, becomes intelligible only against the larger story of the city of Memphis, where he achieved fame and fortune. Founded in 1819 by a trio of rich Tennessee land speculators, Memphis at the close of the Reconstruction Era had expectations of overtaking New Orleans, Louisville, and St. Louis, the only cities of the middle and lower Mississippi valley which surpassed it in size and wealth. Its population of forty thousand represented a hundred per cent increase during the decade of the Civil War. As a direct result of the war, its economic opportunities were better known throughout the North than those of any other Southern city. Hundreds of enterprising Yankees and natives had made fortunes in the heavy contraband and legitimate trade on which Memphis had thrived during the three years after its capture by the Federals in June, 1862. Not only was it the leading railroad center of an area where the South merged with a rapidly growing Southwest, but it also benefited equally with its river-town rivals from steamboat traffic north and south. Second only to New Orleans as a cotton market and an entrepôt for southern wholesale trade, and conscious of the potentialities of its pristine industries, the Bluff City faced the future confidently.

But in the following decade catastrophe struck. Three devastating epidemics of yellow fever killed eight thousand residents, drove hundreds of businessmen away (notably of the large, enterprising German group), and for half a century branded the city with a reputation for insecurity. Instead of reaching the anticipated eighty thousand in 1880, population declined to thirty-three thousand, plummeting Memphis from thirty-second to fifty-fifth in national rank. Taxes soared to new highs, and the city was compelled to surrender its charter and become a mere taxing district of the state, which selected its officials and controlled its finances for fourteen years. Due to the persistent fear of disease and high taxes, large corporations avoided Memphis until the 1920's, going to other southern cities to invest and to establish branch offices.

Nevertheless, despite these obstacles, a remarkable recovery was made by the turn of the century. No stronger evidence of the superior economic foundation of this river town can be cited than the fact that in the nineties it had become the largest inland cotton and hardwood lumber market in the world, the fifth wholesale grocery market in the U. S. (ahead of St. Louis), and could boast an annual trade of two hundred and seventy-five million dollars.

And the numerous firms profiting from this commerce were in most instances established not by Northerners or pre-fever natives, but by rural newcomers from the surrounding area, like Edward Crump. They were willing to risk the recurrence of fever and all other forms of insecurity in order to participate in the rapid accumulation of what was to them amazing wealth. But few from the North or South cared to make permanent investments in the form of factories. In 1900, the value of local manufactures amounted to only seventeen million dollars, one-fourth the industrial wealth of New Orleans, though by that year Memphis had outstripped its other Southern rivals in population and, with one hundred and two thousand, was second to the Louisiana metropolis.

In the first half of the twentieth century the city experienced a relative decline in its formerly leading role in the cotton, lumber, and wholesale-grocery trade. But in compensation it enjoyed a healthy industrial expansion, indicating the disappearance of the old feeling concerning insecurity of permanent investments.* Because of its economic diversity, its happy balance between commerce and industry, and its interdependence with the fertile, prosperous, agricultural region in Arkansas, Mississippi, and Tennessee of which it has served as a hub, there is no dominant "interest" which today controls the city. Northern capital and national corporations in increasing numbers such as Ford, Fisher Body, Firestone, and Sears-Roebuck, have located there. But local business has been developed in the last half-century and is still owned to a considerable extent by "Bourbon Democrats." There has never been a *white* urban proletariat conscious of itself as a homogeneous, exploited class. On the whole, labor has been generally content and conservative, and as it gradually became organized it attached itself to the A.F.L.

Throughout most of the city's history the vice and gambling common to frontier and river town have been prominent. Until quite recently the forces of "respectability" always had to contend with a powerful underworld supported by as many, and frequently the same, citizens as supported the churches. The thousands of Negroes who, since their emancipation have streamed from country to city, have made Beale Street and the "Memphis Blues" famous the world over. They have also presented Memphis with its major social problem.

In view of the fact that, since the fever decade, from forty to fifty

* The present economic status of Memphis, according to the federal census of 1939, is approximately that of Atlanta, Houston, and Dallas; population 292,000; annual industrial product $134,000,000; annual wholesale trade $433,000,000; annual retail trade $135,000,000.

per cent of the population has been colored, Memphians, like all Southerners, are psychologically conditioned by the potential threat of race conflict. But no more than the South at large can they escape the various consequences of the inferior economic and civil status of the Negro. Upon both these factors, vice and the degradation of the black man, the city attained its unsavory nationwide notoriety in the 1920's as a "murder capital."

Because of these disintegrating social forces, and particularly in view of its hectic and violent career, municipal politics in Memphis has been sordid. The newspapers in 1850, like those in 1916, were full of charges of graft. Prior to the fever epidemics, local officials were crude demagogues who catered to the powerful Irish political machine. The ingenious taxing-district law, passed by the Legislature in 1879, was the work of a Citizens' League of conservative merchants who had long fought in vain against the rule of the small-taxpaying, lower classes with its open municipal corruption. "We hesitate not to affirm," these civic leaders admitted, "that our purpose is to remove our city government and the business interests from the popular elections of the times and from all partisan influences."

The state-controlled taxing-district government in Memphis proved highly efficient. An imperative but expensive public health program was carried out with energy and expedition. The latest methods in urban sanitation, then being popularized by American graduates of European medical schools, were applied. The yellow jack threatened upon occasion but never struck again. Within several years the tremendous indebtedness was funded at various rates of discount. Almost overnight, a new and modern city sprang up on the ruins of the old.

Yet the loss of municipal autonomy rankled, until popular pressure compelled the state in 1893 to restore home rule. The incident which brought about the restoration was typically American. When taxing-district officials announced a realistic policy of toleration but strict control of gambling, the outcry from righteous and God-fearing Memphians was loud and vehement. To quell the uproar which threatened to unhorse them, State legislators hurriedly restored full autonomy to the municipality.

Socially and intellectually, in contrast to most Eastern and Middle Western cities, Memphis is a twentieth-century anachronism.

Here, again, the far-reaching consequences of the fever epidemics are distinctly apparent. Prior to that catastrophe the white population had consisted of a large Irish proletariat and what might be regarded as a mercantile upper and middle class, composed of native Southerners and a sizable minority of Germans who had arrived on the eve of the Civil War. Among the eight thousand victims of the fever were most of the Irish, too poor to flee elsewhere. A majority of the merchants, who survived by flight, left the city the same way. Thus the original, cosmopolitan Memphis was literally annihilated in the seventies. Despite its greater age, the present metropolis on Chickasaw Bluff actually is as young in historical continuity and as new in social composition as those Southern *parvenus,* Birmingham and the Texas cities, which were still "towns" in 1900.

According to a 1918 census of the National Bureau of Education, only two per cent of the white parents in Memphis had been born there. Of the remaining ninety-eight per cent, one-fourth were foreign born or from the North and three-fourths from the rural South, mostly from the surrounding tri-state area. Thus the formative period of modern Memphis was that of the "New" South, not the "Old," from the era between Reconstruction and World War I, when the city was "settled" by an ambitious country folk. As a consequence a rural provincialism, somewhat modified by several decades of urban existence, is still a vital force there today.

New Memphis is Bible Belt. Conspicuous in its ideology is Protestant Fundamentalism, loyalty to a fantastic ideal called the "Old South," and uncompromising insistence upon the preservation of "white supremacy." But, paradoxically intermingled with the natural laissez-faire philosophy of a prosperous business community, is a persistent sub-stratum of nineteenth-century democratic faith, tinged with the Southern populism of Watson and Tillman.

The personal history of Edward Crump, a poor Mississippi farm boy who became a rich Memphis businessman, is typical of many of his fellow citizens.

Between 1893 and 1909, when the commission form of municipal government was inaugurated, the ordinary semicorrupt type of city machine was gradually rebuilt by local officials. To it the average citizen paid little notice, for these were the days of Bryan and the first Roosevelt. Political affairs of the nation and the state occupied whatever time and attention men gave to governmental matters. And it was during those years that Crump was achieving modest success as owner of a harness business, from which he was able to spare enough time to participate actively in local politics as a ward heeler. Pledged to reform, he was elected to the city council in 1905 and after two terms he acquired a sufficiently "progressive" record to win the support of public-spirited citizens. As the "reform" candidate in 1909, he defeated Mayor Williams and his gang by the slender margin of seventy-nine votes.

The contrast between this close race and the large margin by which Crump was re-elected (11,432 to 3,536 in 1911 and 3,572 to 522 * four years later) suggests that the "reformer" lost no time in organizing an efficient machine. Its power at the polls rested basically upon city employees, who, to a man, voted and influenced their friends and kinsmen to vote. It also rested upon the registration of several thousand Negroes, many of them dead or fictitious, whose votes were "cast" by "repeaters" in any quantity desired. This method was not invented by the new Mayor—it was simply appropriated.

It was here at the outset of his career that Crump selected his most trusted and valuable lieutenants, Frank Rice and Will Hale, two henchmen with whom he was never to break.

It was at this time, also, that Crump began to use the influence that his office gave him with the Legislature to extend his control over Shelby County. At one point he sought the Sheriff's office as well as the mayoralty. But this ambitious coup was blocked by a state law which barred double officeholding and by the energetic opposition of C. P. J. Mooney of the *Commercial Appeal,* one of the ablest of the "old-school" Southern editors. Thereupon, Crump se-

* The small size of the 1915 vote is due to the fact that the old "ring" conceded the election to Crump and did not even put up a candidate against him. The 522 votes in opposition, all for the "Socialist" candidate, were protest in nature. In 1911 the terms of mayor and commissioners were extended from two to four years.

lected J. A. Reichman as his candidate. Undaunted by a technicality which prevented Reichman from being placed on the printed ballot, Crump decided to have the voters "write in" Reichman's name. For a week before election, blackboards were set up all along Beale Street, instructing Negroes how to write "Reichman" correctly. This effort was successful, though for some years thereafter "write it Rick" served as the battle-cry for anti-Crump forces.

Operating a successful political machine takes money. Crump saw to it that it was not lacking. The necessary funds were obtained from the vice interests, which received protection, and from liquor dealers who operated openly in violation of a state prohibition law. Perhaps it was this period to which Crump referred when he admitted later, "I don't claim to be as pure as light or as stainless as a star." Vice and liquor were permitted to exist, not merely because they were sources of machine revenue, but, also, because Crump was convinced they were desired by the majority of citizens.

Since Memphis had voted heavily against the dry law in 1909, he regarded his nonenforcement as a realistic recognition of the expressed will of the people.

Crump sought to sell himself, his personality, and his integrity with the instinct of a showman. Improvement in the city streets and fire protection were initiated and loudly touted. As evidence of his "progressivism" Crump constantly reiterated his demand that the local power company be purchased by the city, or, as an alternative, that the municipality construct its own power and light plant. There is no doubt that he won the confidence of a majority of the electorate, despite his use of traditional but politically dishonest methods. Even his enemy, Editor Mooney, admitted that "Crump is no grafter, and no one in truth can accuse him of personal dishonesty."

But Mooney minced no words in his editorials on Crump's "reform" government. The contest in 1911 he bluntly dismissed as a "struggle for office between two contending forces of men, neither of which has any high ideals of government, and all of whom that have held office have administered those offices principally to the end that political combinations could be furthered." Four years later his estimate had not changed. "Commission government conducted along political lines," he commented, "is a legalized boss-controlled machine. From the beginning Crump has been a politician, and in his politics he was not entirely selfish."

This last statement was a reference to the Mayor's practice of scrupulously rewarding his henchmen, and to what had become an accepted axiom among local politicians that the only road to public office in Memphis and Shelby County was under the Crump banner. Such criticism the self-confident Mayor, basking in the sun of public approbation, could well ignore as the inconsequential opinion of an idealistic editor.

But Crump overestimated his power. Mooney and the power company, whose charter would soon require renewal, used the growing indignation of local church folk at the nonobservance of the prohibition law (reminiscent of the popular uprising against gambling in 1893) to attack Crump from an unexpected quarter.

A fearless local attorney, Guston Fitzhugh, introduced an ouster petition against the Mayor under a state law which provided for the removal of local officials failing to enforce the dry law. Since Crump admitted the charge, the lower court ordered his removal from office, and, shortly, the State Supreme Court upheld the decision. The legal implications of the decision were uncertain, however. The courts had ousted him only from his old term of office, not the new term that would begin January 1, 1916, to which he had been re-elected the previous spring.

Fitzhugh announced his intention to reintroduce his suit, supplemented with a new charge of political corruption, as soon as Crump began his new term. Mooney whipped up public opinion against the "most disreputable political machine that has ever cursed this country." After weeks of indecision, Crump chose the lesser evil of avoiding a spectacular investigation, by aroused, organized enemies, which might permanently ruin his reputation. Also, he astutely foresaw the possibilities in the future of parading himself as a martyr to the cause of the people against the evil machinations of the power "trust."

So in the early morning hours of February 22, a holiday on which the courts were not in session, he took the oath of office, collected his back pay, and resigned. At his bidding, his hand-picked Board of

Commissioners selected as his successor Senator Ashcroft, one of the Memphis delegation in the Legislature.

Six months later, Crump received popular exoneration when he was elected County Trustee, after a bitter contest, by a vote of 8,170 to 6,550. This victory, charged the *Commercial Appeal,* was accomplished by fraudulent Negro votes, reckless expenditure of money, the machine's superior political organization, and the support it received from vice. Thus, Trustee Crump replaced Mayor Crump as dictator of the Memphis-Shelby machine.

Yet a serious blow had been dealt to Crump's prestige, a blow which not only profoundly affected his own psychology but one which, also, led to a drastic change in his political methods after 1927. It was a dozen years after his resignation as Mayor before he again enjoyed absolute municipal power, for from his county office he soon found himself unable completely to dominate Ashcroft and the three mayors who followed him in rapid succession. In 1919 the "better" element induced the reluctant Rowlett Paine to run for Mayor against the old "ring" politician Williams. For a time Crump considered entering his own candidate, but instead, the day before election, announced his support of Paine, who received a majority of three thousand votes.

This was a clever move, as it gave the impression that Crump's power was sufficient to swing an election at the last minute. Actually, it was a maneuver to gain the favor of Paine, whom Crump had decided was certain to win. Paine's re-election in 1923 was contested by two tickets, one supported by the Ku Klux Klan, then at the height of its power, and another backed by Frank Rice and the county machine. At the last minute Rice and the "boys" went over to Paine, who defeated the Klan by a small majority. It is still the belief of many Memphians that the machine stole this election, but without the connivance of the Mayor.

Crump, himself, took no public part in this contest, but instead announced that he was physically exhausted by his many battles and planned to retire from politics. His subsequent surrender of the trusteeship and entrance into business lent some credence to his statement. But it may have been a subtle move to throw his opponents off guard. He had the county under his thumb and had formed a mutually advantageous alliance with U. S. Senator Kenneth McKellar.

But Crump was unable, despite his various tactics, to dominate Paine. Whatever Crump's intentions may have been at the time, this much is certain: The politically inept Paine was badly defeated in the next election (19,806 to 7,080) by an opposition led by Watkins Overton and Clifford Davis which proudly presented itself to the electorate as the "Crump" ticket. Since that date no candidate in Memphis or Shelby County, and few in the state of Tennessee, have ever been elected to national, state, or local office without the publicly announced approval of Edward Crump.

This extralegal but highly effective political arrangement, which has existed since 1927, means simply that Crump has been to Memphis what Judge Landis was to organized baseball.

As the "tribune of the people," he is entirely responsible for local government. He selects the public officials and directs and scrutinizes their conduct of office, supposedly with the general welfare of Memphis as the single criterion. To provide a "democratic" sanction for this arrangement, at regular intervals the machine holds plebiscites at which Crump appointees are legally confirmed and in which the electorate expresses its approval of Crump's conduct of his extraordinary "office."

That this system, whatever its critics may say of it, has the general support of Memphians, is clearly evident from the following summary of municipal election returns:

Year	Crump Candidate		Opponent
1931	Overton	23,684	869
1935	Overton	11,086	No opponent
1939	Crump	31,825	No opponent
1943	Chandler	14,431	No opponent

This remarkable success was the result of a radical change from the political methods used by Crump in his earlier career. Certain traditional machine tactics were discarded, because experience proved them defective. To Crump, it became apparent that the use of questionable practices to pile up tremendous majorities aroused public antagonism. So, in line with Lincoln Steffens' thesis that the clever politicians will give the people any type of government for which they create a cogent demand, Crump in 1927 became a benevolent "boss." An ambitious man, he wanted power, not money—power, he would insist, to give Memphis better government than it would obtain under the customary dual party system.

Consequently, by various means, he successfully sought the active support of the vast majority of the populace and of every distinct group within it. Gradually he developed an administration of municipal affairs which Memphians came to regard as spectacularly efficient, economical, and honest. In return they gave him the power he desired or, to be more exact, acquiesced in his assumption of it.

But while this power has been preserved by a *positive* program which conspicuously gives the city more in the way of "services" at less expense than most municipalities offer, the rise of any organized opposition to Crump's personal rule has also been carefully blocked by ingenious *negative* methods.

The most unusual of these is Crump's assiduous rejection of formal office. This self-denial not only increases his prestige, but it enables him, should the necessity arise, to shift responsibility upon some unhappy puppet for the rare measure that meets with unanticipated popular disfavor.

Behind this imposing facade, Frank Rice, trusted lieutenant and leader of the Shelby group in the Legislature, "handled" the finances and attended to all the necessary but sordid details of the machine—a Mr. Hyde to Crump's Dr. Jekyll. The "good" Mr. Crump could not say "no" to his friends. If a request was to be rejected, the petitioner was referred to Rice, who naturally acquired a reputation as a mean, scheming, and merciless "politician." Thus, Crump has craftily utilized public officials as handy buffers against a repetition of the uprising in 1915, which filled him with an abnormal and deep-seated fear. It was imperative political necessity and not desire for office that compelled him to seek two terms as Congressman from

1930 to 1934 and his election, by proxy for Walter Chandler, as Mayor in 1939.

At the same time, Crump derives much of his own popularity from the "voter appeal" of his appointees, who are selected on the basis of their personality, ability, and, particularly, their identity with recognized groups in society. The Overton-Davis combination, in 1927, for example, won the support of the business community and those who considered themselves "socially" superior, because Overton was a member of one of the city's oldest and originally wealthiest families. Clifford Davis, demagogic idol of the masses and churchgoers, who had greatly enhanced his popularity by colorful law enforcement during a three-year term as city judge, attracted the quantitatively more important vote of the "common man."

Similarly, in the next decade, Oscar P. Williams, prominent executive of the local A.F.L. Carpenters' Union, was chosen Commissioner of Public Works. Even the son of Editor Mooney was intrusted with office before his father's death. So also was Frank Gailor, Oxford graduate and son of a distinguished Episcopal Bishop. Although certain individuals have been rewarded with office by reason of long and loyal service, city officials, in general, have been men of some prominence and ability, free from the taint of scandal and any proven dishonesty, and scrupulously obedient to Mr. Crump as guardian of the public weal. They have merely been useful to him, but his favor has been indispensable to them.

The shock troops of the machine, and the core of its voting power, are the thousands of city and county employees who form an hierarchical army organized by ward and precinct. Since Memphis has neither civil service nor voting machines, they and their families vote without exception for Crump candidates as the price of their jobs. They are the field workers who, by house-to-house canvass induce the faithful to register; the agents who report the unfriendly and disaffected; and the "contributors," who are assessed annually a percentage of their salary for campaign funds. Together with numerous nonofficeholding supporters of the machine, they exercise a controlling influence in important social and civic organizations, such as the American Legion, the Parent-Teachers' Association, civic clubs, and churches. Allegedly, Crump keeps in his private office a card-index file on every resident of Shelby County, with a record of his vote and his "loyalty" for the past twenty years.

Crump can win any municipal election, regardless of the opposition, by the votes of city employees alone. But his obvious aim is to dominate the state by casting sixty thousand votes from Shelby in a solid block for his candidates. Because of his fear that the smallest summer cloud of dissent on the horizon may grow into a raging hurricane like that of 1915, he uses every conceivable method to insure the wholehearted support of all citizens. Constantly keeping his finger on the public pulse, he advances as his own idea and effectively carries out any reform measure or civic project for which there is concerted popular demand: parks, new schools, paved streets, traffic-safety devices, fire prevention, T.V.A. power, city-owned power plant, low taxes, low assessments, harbor improvement.

There are no longer any "deadheads" in City Hall, where the latest efficiency methods have been introduced. In recent years petty graft has been largely eliminated from the police force. Vice and gambling, while not abolished, have been restricted sufficiently to prevent an outcry from local ministers and their flocks. In its few strikes, the A.F.L. has been permitted sufficient freedom in picketing to ensure its staunch allegiance to the machine. One of Crump's proudest boasts is that no crook or embezzler has been connected with his organization. Even Editor Edward Meeman of the Scripps-Howard *Press-Scimitar,* who battles singlehanded and in vain against local "fascism," admits that Memphians have few grounds for opposing Crump other than those of principle.

Memphis itself is only dimly aware ot the sturdy skeleton upon which this power rests, so completely is it covered by the flesh of Crump's colorful personality. Intuitive master of mob psychology, he keeps himself in the public eye and permits none of his creatures to share with him the center of the stage. Citizens are constantly presented with concrete evidence of his private benevolence and charity.

At his own expense, he sponsors boat rides on the Mississippi for crippled children and shut-ins, football games at Crump Stadium for the benefit of the blind, and field days at the municipally owned Fair Grounds where children ride free on the various amusement devices.

He knows that bread alone is not enough for a city populace reared on the Southern farms of the 1890's. There must be drama, crisis, and circuses. He speaks their language and voices their prejudice. Governor Browning, for example, he characterized as the "kind of a man who would milk a neighbor's cow through a crack in the fence."

Crump, also, has never wavered in his allegiance to the Democratic Party. He campaigned as energetically for Smith in 1928 and for Roosevelt in all four of his elections as he has for his local candidates. One of the most vitriolic attacks of his stormy career was directed in 1944 against prominent Bob Snowden and a local business group who, denouncing the "dictatorship" of Roosevelt, supported Dewey for president.

If Memphians are to feel keenly the need for the benevolent protection of Mr. Crump, there must be dragons for him to slay. Never a year passes but some "venal politician who has betrayed the people" is excoriated by him in full-page advertisements in the newspapers. As Jonathan Daniels has pointed out, the Memphis Power and Light Company (which was finally forced to sell out to the city in 1939) has served Crump as a whipping post in the same way the Jews served Hitler.

Memphis with its rural heritage is still ideologically in the days of William J. Bryan and Woodrow Wilson, and Crump, without hypocrisy, regards himself as the people's champion. His undiluted populism is evident in his public statements: "I favor submitting anything to the people"; "Robin Hood gathered money from the rich to give to the poor, Gordon Browning does just the reverse"; "Corporation lawyers hung around the Legislature like a bunch of egg-sucking dogs"; "Roosevelt realizes the first law of civilization is to protect the sheep and dull the claws of the wolves."

But this language is mild. A typical example of Crump invective in full withering blast was a recent attack on the editors of the Nashville *Tenneseean,* who insist upon referring to Memphis as "Crumptown." Thundered Crump, "This trio of mangy bubonic rats are conscienceless liars . . . cowards at heart, yellow to the core. . . . There is not one of them who, singly or all together, would meet us on the street . . . and say all the things to our faces that they have said in their scurrilous newspaper behind our backs. The honeymoon of this lying, corroding crowd of murderers of character is over. Their swill barrel is empty."

In the seventeen-hundred-word fusillade, "rat" was used fourteen times and "liar," twenty.

Undisturbed by his populistic utterances, the diversified economic interests of Memphis, both local and Northern, are solidly behind Crump. Their vigorous support is a matter of self-interest. He gives them a low tax dollar, efficient municipal administration, freedom from state sales or income taxes, and the various physical improvements which have attracted outside capital. The contrast between present-day Memphis and that of fifty years ago, with its disease, high taxes, bankruptcy, and lack of autonomy, convinces even those who for less practical reasons might be inclined to independence.

A shrewd and successful business man, Crump runs the city by approved "business" methods. Though his firm gets the bulk of local mortgage and insurance business on real estate, through no coercion on his part but definitely because of the existence of his political power, there is no loud complaint from his competitors who divide among themselves the crumbs that fall from the table. He carefully sees to it that they get enough to keep them quiescent.

The C.I.O.'s first attempt to organize city workers in the Thirties was smashed as "communistic" by physical force by the police, coupled with a warning to union organizers to "get out and stay out." Firestone and other national corporations had probably been promised protection from "radical" unionism. Also, few of Crump's spectacular moves met with more unanimous approval from the mass of the citizenry than this assault on the C.I.O. However, it is noteworthy that since 1940 the C.I.O. has made definite headway—without open interference—in the organization of certain groups, Negroes in particular.

In addition to a municipal government which they regard as beneficial, Crump also gives the people of Memphis complete control of the state of Tennessee. This is not only gratifying to local pride, but it is of inestimable value to local business interests that contribute liberally to machine campaign funds.

More of a Mississippi-Arkansas than a Tennessee town, Memphis could be seriously injured by a Legislature that favored the interests of Nashville, Chattanooga, Knoxville, and their hinterland of middle and east Tennessee. Naturally these interests frequently conflict with those of their larger western rival. Many American cities are suffering at the hands of up-country Legislatures in which they are under-represented and outvoted. But the "corporation" of Tennessee is directed largely by and for the benefit of its minority stockholders in Memphis. The absence of discriminatory taxation is merely one of the numerous instances wherein the Bluff City gains at the expense of the remainder of the state.

The technique of this control is no secret. There is nothing mysterious about it. Since the "official" vote cast in Shelby is usually one-fifth of the state's total, Senator K. D. McKellar, despite the power of his federal patronage, has long realized the necessity of close union with Crump. Much as they dislike it "Kay Dee" and "Ed" are essential to each other and, except for a brief estrangement, have managed to present a united front to their enemies. Whereas the size of the vote in Memphis municipal elections is of little consequence because of the absence of opposition, in state elections it becomes of vital significance.

For this reason the old tactics of fraudulent registration, wholesale Negro "voting," and some tampering with ballot boxes are still used in Shelby in crucial state contests. As elsewhere in the South, these occur in the Democratic primaries, less subject to federal control than the inconsequential, formal elections which follow. Indignation at this political dishonesty has not alienated many Memphians, whose local particularism has been ingeniously cultivated, because in this instance cheating appears to work to their advantage. The official returns from Shelby are not "turned in" until after those from the rest of the state are completely recorded, so that in close contests the extra votes necessary to win can be "cast" at the last minute. It is the belief of Memphis newspapermen that the narrow margin for repeal of prohibition in Tennessee was accomplished in this way.

Sooner or later, Crump has broken with every governor except Prentice Cooper. None has ever survived his disfavor. Gordon Browning, after being badly beaten in 1934 in his race against McKellar, came into the Crump camp and ran for governor in 1936 against Burgin Dossett, who had the nominal backing of McKellar. Shelby gave Browning 59,874 votes to Dossett's 825. In 1938, after he had spent most of his administration fighting Crump and organizing the state for the purpose of ending the "tyranny" of Memphis, Browning received only 9,214 votes in Shelby, as compared with 56,302 for his opponent, Cooper. It has been repeatedly asserted that Browning's vote actually was much less, and that the "official" count was a gift from Crump for the sake of respectability, a gift which he could easily afford, since Browning lost the state outside Shelby by 18,000. The most recent instance of Crump's power was the defeat of E. W. Carmack, who opposed Senator Steward in the 1942 election. Carmack came to Shelby leading by 20,000 votes, but lost when that county went against him, 48,875 to 6,959.

In addition to reducing potential causes for dissent among the populace by incorporating into his program any measure that has appreciable popular support, Crump has taken pains to deprive of leadership the slight opposition that he has been unable to prevent. Capitalizing upon public inertia, Crump, with Hamiltonian cynicism, gives the politically ambitious no alternative but complete acceptance of his patronage. Once he has accepted the "favor" of the machine as the price of office, the public servant becomes enmeshed in an ever growing web of circumstance. At the first indication of independence or of excessive popularity with the citizenry, he suddenly finds himself ruthlessly "purged." In view of the fact that they are all Crump appointees, it is certainly no accident that there has usually been a clash of personalities among the Mayor and his five commissioners.

The careers of Clifford Davis and Watkins Overton illustrate the extreme precautions exercised by Crump to prevent treason on the part of those he puts in office. The single Klan candidate elected in 1923 (supposedly anti-Crump) and the only politician in Memphis ever to enjoy a popularity approaching that of Crump himself, Judge Davis suddenly joined the machine in 1927 and accepted a position on the ticket second to that of Mayor Overton. Twelve years later, Overton apparently acted too independently in the negotiations with the T.V.A. and the Memphis Power and Light, or took too much credit for the project. At any rate, Crump abruptly announced his displeasure. At his order the City Commission voted three to two against the Mayor during the remaining months of his term (Davis voting with the majority), and Overton was dropped in the 1939 election. At the same time, presumably because of his strong popular following, Davis was "banished" to Washington as Congressman, where he would gradually lose his hold upon the local public. Congressman Walter Chandler (formerly campaign manager for Mayor Paine, who, like Davis, had joined the machine) was recalled to Memphis for the mayoralty.

Since he had purged Overton, banished Davis, and at last revenged himself upon the power company, Crump perhaps was hesitant to risk the success of his most important plebiscite by making it dependent upon the uncertain local appeal of Chandler. He therefore kept the latter in Washington upon the pretext that his vote for the pending repeal of the neutrality bill made his presence in the House mandatory. Then Crump announced his own candidacy for Mayor, stating that immediately upon his election he would resign in favor of Chandler, whom the City Commission would select as successor. The thirty-two thousand votes Crump received without opposition, the largest ever cast in municipal history, was convincing proof that his power was still absolute. Furthermore, to the gratification of his own pride, he had cleared his personal record by a unanimous re-election to the office from which he had been ousted twenty-four years before.

It is to some an ugly, but to all an incontrovertible, fact that Crump rules Memphis partly because of a universal sentiment of fear and futility which, to varying degrees, permeates the consciousness of the entire community. This fear deters the politician from treason, the public-spirited citizen from leading a hopeless crusade against what the idealistic few regard as tyranny, and the man in the street from any overt act of opposition to the machine. Crump has deliberately encouraged this fear by certain personal acts.

He has driven into oblivion or scurrilously and publicly attacked the political leader, professional and amateur, who dares to oppose his personal rule or specific policies. He has made spectacular examples of private citizens because of expressions of dissent. For months, Frank Thompson, a local undertaker who openly expressed his criticism, had his hearses and ambulances trailed by squads of motorcycle policemen who gave his drivers summonses for various technical traffic violations. A wealthy wholesale druggist who was "unfriendly" failed to get police protection for his plant during a successful strike of his A.F.L employees. A Negro druggist who would not "take orders" was boycotted by the device of having police search all his customers on the "suspicion" that he was selling narcotics.

Many of the hundreds of similar cases of economic retaliation against private citizens, which are common gossip in Memphis, are probably fictitious. Crump doubtless has selected for conspicuous examples only those individuals for whom he was reasonably certain there would be little or no popular sympathy. The fear of the private citizen, partly irrational but nonetheless potent, arises naturally from the psychology of the human animal and the circumstances of human society. Memphians themselves, far more than Mr. Crump, have forged the chains which bind them. Even the most benevolent authority rests in part on fear; the obvious fact of Crump's invincibility has led to an exaggerated fiction similar to the seventeenth-century obsession with witchcraft.

For Memphis, it is enough that Crump possesses the power and that, upon occasion, he has ruthlessly used it to punish apostasy. Those who in their economic and personal pursuits need the "co-operation" of the municipality, actively support the machine and place their insurance with Crump's firm. Those who are aware of their vulnerability to the numerous forms of discrimination which a city government has at its disposal, simply refrain from open dissent and cease to participate formally in the local body politic. To practical-minded Memphians, dissent is neither intelligent nor "safe," and any of their temperamental fellows who foolishly broadcast their opposition invite a loss of public confidence which tends toward social ostracism.

In addition to the disciplining of officials and his use of fear to keep the populace in line, Crump employs his control of the state as a third negative method. It can be cogently argued that his domination of Tennessee originated as a defensive mechanism for the preservation of his municipal power. Since both county and city are but creations of the state, legislation in Nashville can in endless ways hinder or facilitate his control of Shelby and Memphis. The 1946 defeat of Boss Maestri in New Orleans would have been impossible without the Louisiana laws, passed under Governor Jones five years ago, which enforced voting machines and municipal civil service. By similar devices, which a hostile faction in the Tennessee Legislature will probably introduce if it ever defeats Crump, all of his negative and some of his positive methods might be nullified.

Crump, being what he is, unquestionably has rationalized his own motives and conduct. Convinced of his own personal integrity and held in high esteem by his community, he has so long played the role of "tribune of the people" that he probably has fully persuaded himself that he is. His indignation at any comparison of himself with Hague, Maestri, and Pendergast is sincere, as was his vehement condemnation of Truman's appointment of Pauley.

There is no doubt in Crump's mind that he has a mandate from the people to scourge those whom he regards as their betrayers. But there also can be no question that his purges are motivated primarily by a naïve self-esteem, well illustrated in his attack upon Browning as a "Judas Iscariot." The accumulation of a fortune through his personal firm has never been a conscious motive in his political career. His basic psychological drive, to the critical observer, is derived primarily by a desire for power.

In dealing with present complexities, there is some speculation as to whether Crump, now in his early seventies, will continue to display the undeniable genius by which he has defeated all previous attacks upon his personal rule. It is said that he has become seriously religious, possibly as a result of the tragic death of a son in an airplane crash in 1939. At any rate, his much-publicized campaign in recent years for the protection of our "feathered friends" and his serious proposal of a total war on cats are regarded by many Memphians as a surprising change in character in a formerly ruthless fighter whose chief hobby was football.

Editor Meeman in the *Press-Scimitar* and Tennesseans outside of Shelby incessantly fulminate against Crumpism. But the most forceful attack on "dictatorship" in Memphis was an anonymous criticism which appeared in the London *Economist* in the summer of 1943:

"Memphis is the scene of a defeat—defeat of the cause in which the United Nations fight, the cause of liberty and democracy. For Memphis has a totalitarian government . . . similar in character . . . to that of Mussolini and Hitler, though so far (its people are) not disturbed enough to rebel or even form an underground. . . . An entire generation has grown up in Memphis, and is now fighting on all the battle fronts of the world, which has never taken part in any of the processes of democracy, for these are only nominal in Memphis. 'Ja' elections are held to ratify decisions made by the Leader. . . . The people of Memphis have given up their right to take part in public affairs for light and transient causes. . . . It would have required only ten fairly well-known citizens standing firmly together to have prevented the machine from getting control in the first place and such a group could restore democracy at any time. No ten citizens yet have been willing to get together."

This revolt has not arisen, because Memphians, with the exception of an insignificant minority, have what they regard as a satisfactory answer to these charges, and their defense cannot be dismissed as entirely a rationalization. The municipality, they argue, is not a sovereign government, but, actually, an administrative creature of the nation (state). Instead of the formal city-manager system adopted by other cities, there has evolved in Memphis an arrangement identical in function but technically extralegal. Not for any remuneration, they point out, could the city have hired a "manager" equal to Crump in capability, energy, zeal, and popularity. No "reform" administration under the two-party system would have accomplished the material progress or the administrative efficiency and economy which he has achieved.

Crump has given Memphis a continuity in municipal planning and development directly responsible for much of its current prosperity—a continuity, the proponents assert, which would otherwise have been unattainable. Abler men have been attracted to public service as a career because of their freedom from the fear of an often whimsical electorate. The populace is no longer divided into the bitter factions which political strife normally produces. Considering its former insecurity, its inherent weakness to demagogues, and the political inexperience of its rural-minded citizens in dealing with the many complications of urban existence, the "centralization of power" under Crump in the 1920's was as essential to public welfare as the similar action of the Citizen's League in the fever crisis of the last century. That is the Memphian argument.

That this security and progress has been bought at the expense of loss of liberty, they hotly deny. They contend that what has actually transpired is that for twenty years the majority of citizens have voted for the re-election of Crump, even if his name has not been on the ballot as a candidate for office. The extralegality of this procedure, they insist, has been only a superficial departure from the democratic process. The peculiar political system of Memphis is as much a consequence of precedent and the expression of popular will, they hold, as our national party machinery, for which there is no authority in the Constitution. Crump's extreme sensitivity to public opinion more than offsets the lack of formal party opposition in municipal elections. In practice the current system affords the various minorities more influence on the conduct of public affairs than that enjoyed by recognized political minorities, such as the Republicans in the South.

As for the exaggerated incidents of retaliation against private citizens, it is pointed out that all strong leaders are guilty of occasional temperamental aberrations. Memphians call attention to the fact that at least a hundred of their fellow ciizens, who have consistently fought Crump throughout his long career, have in no way been officially persecuted or denied equal protection of the laws. Citizens of Memphis, they say, consist of two groups: those who enthusiastically support Crump as a "positive good," and those who accept him as the least of evils. Had he seriously abused the power granted him, they add, he would long ago have been repudiated.

Accepting at face value the premises of this defense, there are several consequencs which Memphians clearly have not taken sufficiently into account. Crump completely controls their state and federal representatives no less than he does their municipal. Even if this system be good for Memphis, it subordinates and deprives of their democratic rights the much larger group of Tennesseans who reside outside Shelby county. But, more pertinent from the narrow viewpoint of Memphis, its citizens may discover that the price of present security is, in the long run, excessive.

Memphians have substituted the plebiscite, historically associated with dictatorship, for the traditional American system of elections. Democracy has not and cannot function without the existence of an organized opposition. Such opposition does not exist in Memphis today. Its citizens have abdicated their sovereignty by acquiescence in the dictum that political opposition is both unnecessary and "disloyal."

They forget that the temporary acceptance of despotism because it is benevolent at the moment, frequently leads to a subsequent despotism that is vicious. They would do well to recall that the Louisiana Hayride reached its nadir under Allen, Leche, and Maestri, years after the death of the Kingfish. If a dogfight similar to that in Louisiana occurs among Crump's henchmen upon his death, Memphis will probably find itself badly governed and yet unable for some time to restore the conventional democratic process which it has consciously discarded.

E. H. CRUMP & CO.

INVESTMENT BANKERS

REAL ESTATE LOANS-MORTGAGE BONDS

INSURANCE-REAL ESTATE

NORTH MEMPHIS SAVINGS BANK BLDG

MEMPHIS, TENN.

June 5, 1946

Prof. Gerald Capers,
Tulane University
New Orleans, La.

My dear Professor:-

Understand you are writing another book about Memphis. In fact, I believe you told Auvergne Blaylock that you are getting up data and had gotten a lot of information from Ralph Millett regarding my activities in Memphis, which dates back some forty-four years ago.

If you are writing a book and are going to write anything about me, wouldn't it be the fair thing to talk to me or some neutral person rather than obtain incorrect information from my bitter enemy.

Yours very truly,

EHC:H

My reply to Mr. Crump (abbreviated)

June 8, 1946

Mr. E. H. Crump
North Memphis Savings Bank Bldg.
Memphis, Tennessee

Dear Mr. Crump:

I appreciate the candor of your letter. Had the allegations as stated to you by Auvergne been correct, I agree one hundred per cent that such procedure on my part would have been unfair, and what is worse, damn bad historical method.

As for the facts. I am <u>not</u> writing a book, but I <u>have</u> written an article which was submitted to the publisher on May 1. Back in February I received a letter from Colonel Bob Allen (Drew Pearson's ex-partner) saying that he was editing a book for Vanguard Press on the municipal governments of 20 contemporary American cities and he wanted me to do the chapter on Memphis. At that time I spent several days in Memphis digging up certain facts from sources at the Cossitt Library. At the same time I talked to perhaps a dozen Memphians who were familiar with the various economic and political developments in the city during the past 40 years. The majority of them, I might say, were your hearty supporters. I talked to Mr. Millett as an old newspaper man, not as your enemy, and I discounted what he had to say in the same way as I discounted the statements of the good business men who almost without exception are your enthusiastic backers.

Due to the pressure of my teaching load here and the short time I had to complete the article (27 pages) I was unable to return to Memphis. I did correspond with Albert Johnson at the Cossitt who dug up certain dope for me, and with one young business executive who happens to be my closest friend and one of your staunchest backers. You might be interested in his comment:

"If anything Mr. Crump and his associates have gone to the extreme to invite new businesses to Memphis as well as affording those already here every opportunity to run a successful business. It is my feeling that business men, above all others, appreciate Mr. Crump at his present stage of life. While this may not always have been true I think it is now. In fact I can think of no group that doesn't like Mr. Crump, with the exception of those who go forward with a torch in their hands exemplifying 'democracy'. This group is composed largely of folks who are opposed to everything when seated around the beer-table or those who like to write burning letters to the editor."

I might also point out to you that I lived in Memphis myself for 14 years and have returned there each year for several months. I spent several hours one evening discussing you and your relation to Memphis with your lieutenant, Frank Gailor, and I have had many conversations with your friends and your opponents. I assure you I know enough of the situation from first-hand observation not to be badly misled by what Millett says against or Gailor for you.

I think that, since you are an important American institution as well as a man (and it is the institution rather than the man which I, in all frankness, would oppose were I a Memphis citizen) you owe it to posterity to talk to someone, like Herbert Harper for instance, who might be interested in writing your biography. The thought has always been in the back of my own mind, but I am tied up for the next year and a half with a biography of John C. Calhoun. There will be a lot more written about you when you are gone, and I think it is important to your reputation that you express your justification for your own actions and your views about the fundamentals of democratic government to some critical and disinterested person rather than to a henchman like Will Gerber.

Let me say that in my own mind there is no doubt about your personal honesty, your sincerity, and your desire for and possession of great power, which I admit rests upon the consent of the vast majority of Memphians. Whether or not this is good for Memphis and the future of American democracy is another matter.

I am attaching to this letter the last section of the article to which you will object, but it should satify you that I have considered the arguments of your supporters as well as your opponents.

Sincerely yours,

Gerald M. Capers

Gerald M. Capers

P.S. May I congratulate you on the efficiency of your grapevine. It proves once again that genius is ninety per cent energy and attention to minute details.

G. C.

CPSIA information can be obtained at www.ICGtesting.com
265084BV00001B/19/A

9 780937 130001